Constitutional Law of Papua New Guinea

Constitutional Law of Papua New Guinea

by

ERIC L KWA
Dean, School of Law, University of Papua New Guinea

with a Foreword by

THE HONOURABLE SIR ARNOLD AMET KB, CBE, LLD
Chief Justice of Papua New Guinea

Published by:
UniBOOKS (an imprint of UPNG Press and Bookshop)

ISBN 9980-939-50-8

This is a reprint of the book first published in Sydney by Lawbook Co.

Cover Design: Philemon Yalamu

Typesetting & Layout: Philemon Yalamu

UniBOOKS
P.O.Box 413, University PO,
National Capital District, Papua New Guinea
Phone: 675 + 3267284 Fax: 675 + 3267368

Foreword

This is one of a series prepared under the auspices of the Access to Laws in Papua New Guinea Project funded by the Australian Government through the Australian Agency for International Development (AusAID). The Access to Laws Project comprised three components aimed at improving access to the laws of Papua New Guinea. The Project involved updating and authenticating all the current legislation of this country and the extensive case law developed by the courts. The legislation and judicial decisions have been produced in the modern electronic CD-ROM format. Equally importantly, the Project included the production of a number of legal textbooks to record the distinctive developments in the laws of this country.

The book publishing component of the Access to Laws Project was under the direction of the Publications Committee that I had the pleasure of chairing. The other members of the Publications Committee were, the Commissioning Editor, Professor Don Chalmers, the Chief Magistrate, Mr George Manuhu, the Deputy Chief Magistrate, John Numapo, the Hon the Attorney-General, Mr Francis Damen (previously Mr Sao Gabi, Mr Michael Gene), the Access to Laws Project Manager, Mr Bruce Fulton, the Project Team Leader, Mr Eric Kwa (previously Dr Val Haynes), representatives of AusAID (Mr Stuart Schaefer, Ms Pauline Doonar, Ms Debbie Bowman, Mr John Prescott, Ms Katherine Ruiz-Avila) a representative of the PNG Law Society, Ms Catherine Davani and the Dean of the Law School, Mr Eric Kwa (previously Mr Gerry Linge). The Publications Committee was responsible for choosing authors, settling the contents, assessing the quality and appointing referees for each of the texts. At an early meeting of the Publications Committee it was decided that it was appropriate that Papua New Guinean authors or authors with considerable experience in Papua New Guinea should be chosen.

I am delighted that the Dean of Law, Eric Kwa, has agreed, in spite of his many other duties, to accept the invitation of the Commissioning Editor on behalf of the Publications Committee to write this text. This is the first major consideration of the Constitution of Papua New Guinea since the seminal work of Justice Jack Goldring in *The Constitution of Papua New Guinea: A Study in Legal Nationalism*, which was published by the Law Book Company in 1978. I know that the Dean has acknowledged the scholarly foundations laid by Justice Goldring. On behalf of the Publications Committee I commend the learned author for his work and scholarship. I am confident that this text with the others in this series will be of great value to judges, magistrates, legal practitioners, academics, students and the citizens of Papua New Guinea. If the underlying law is to be developed according to the precepts and principles embodied in our Constitution and *The Underlying Law Act* 2000, it is essential that the Papua New Guinea community has access to texts which can state the

Papua New Guinea law concisely, authoritatively and accurately. On behalf of the Publications Committee I commend the author for his contribution to this important endeavour.

The Hon Sir Arnold Amet, KB, CBE, LLD

Chief Justice of Papua New Guinea,

Chair of the Publications Committee,

Access to Law in Papua New Guinea

Port Moresby, May 2001

Table of Contents

[References are to page numbers]

Table of Cases

[References are to page numbers]

Table of Statutes

[References are to page numbers]

Chapter 1

INTRODUCTION

The *Constitution* of Papua New Guinea (PNG) is a unique and complicated piece of legislation. It is the fundamental law, because it establishes the various institutions of state. It also sets out the parameters in which each of these state organs are to operate. It is also the supreme law of the land.[1] Section 11 of the *Constitution* stipulates that all acts, whether legislative, executive or judicial, that are inconsistent with the *Constitution* or Organic Laws, will be deemed invalid to the extent of the inconsistency.[2]

The judiciary is mandated by the *Constitution* to guard against any abuse or exploitation, especially by those who are in power. The *Constitution* empowers the courts to impose sanctions on violators of the *Constitution*. The judiciary must ensure that the various institutions created by the *Constitution* are restrained from exceeding their powers and operate within their specific boundaries.[3]

The term "constitution" is not defined by the *Constitution* itself. The former premier of New Ireland Province, Mr Robert Setto, exploited this omission. He argued in *SCR No 2 of 1987; Ref by Setto* [1987] PNGLR 31 that the term also extends to provincial constitutions. The Supreme Court dismissed this proposition. Schedule 1.2 of the *Constitution* defines the term "constitutional law". A "constitutional law" means "[in] this *Constitution*, a law altering this *Constitution* or an Organic Law". In the above case, Mr Setto also argued that the Niu Ailan provincial Constitution, being an Organic Law, was covered by the definition under Sch 1.2 of the *Constitution*. Again, the Supreme Court rejected this argument, stating that:

> "the Constitution of a provincial government, whilst attracting the status of an Organic Law under s 13 of the *Organic Law on Provincial Governments* (Ch No 1) is not an Organic Law within s 12 of the *Constitution* and is therefore not a Constitutional Law".

The *Constitution*, being both the fundamental and higher law, is not subject to any ordinary law.[4] It is also quite difficult to change. The Parliament must comply with the strict requirements of ss 14, 15 and 17 to amend the *Constitution*. For a relatively young country like PNG, it might be expected that there would be few amendments to the *Constitution*. However, during its 25 years of independence, the *Constitution* has been amended more than 20 times. Changing economic, social and political factors have necessitated these amendments. For instance, the *Constitutional Amendment No 1*[5] was influenced by the threat of secession by the

1 According to s 11 of the *Constitution*, the *Constitution* and the Organic Laws are the supreme laws of PNG.
2 See, eg, *SCR No 2 of 1982; Re Organic Law* [1982] PNGLR 214; *SCR No 2 of 1984; Re New Ireland Provincial Constitution* [1984] PNGLR 81; *SCR No 5 of 1992* [1992] PNGLR 114.
3 Chapter 11 sets out in detail the extent of this judicial power and its exercise by the judiciary.
4 *Haiveta v Wingti (No 1)* [1994] PNGLR 160 at 228-229 (Jalina J).
5 This amendment ushered in the provincial government system in PNG. The provision of the *Constitution* that was amended was s 187.

people of Bougainville in 1976. Almost 19 years later the Parliament amended the same provision to sweep away the provincial government system and replace it with a "new provincial government system", with the local-level governments at the epicentre of the law. Again, this change was influenced more by political considerations than any other substantial considerations.

Any change to the *Constitution* must follow specific procedures. Amendments can be challenged to ensure that proper procedures have been complied with to bring about the desired result.[6] Persons who are eligible to pursue these challenges are enumerated under s 19 of the *Constitution*. This particular check and balance ensures the viability of the *Constitution*. Fortunately, the constitutional changes that have occurred so far have, on most occasions, been "accepted" calmly by the people of PNG. This general acceptance by the people, the state institutions and judicial officials gives the *Constitution* its validity.

The *Constitution* is a programmatic document, because it prescribes the programs for PNG in great detail. These programs are set out in the Preamble to the *Constitution*. Unlike in most of PNG's neighbouring Pacific Island countries, the Preamble of PNG's *Constitution* is quite lengthy and covers a wide range of issues. Chapter 3 describes the role and functions of the Preamble of the *Constitution*, and especially the National Goals and Directive Principles. The National Goals and Directive Principles are noble in character and reflect the values and aspirations of the people of PNG. They also contain the development programs of PNG. Even after 25 years, they still hold value and are generally accepted as the stepping-stone for PNG's progress.[7]

The *Constitution* can also be described as an exhaustive blueprint, because it is one of the longest constitutions in the world. It contains meticulous descriptions of the state and its instrumentalities, their powers and functions, the responsibilities of the citizens, and the responsibility of the state to its citizens. An example of this is found in Chapter 4, which contains a detailed description of the various categories of the laws prescribed by the *Constitution*. These categories of laws are enumerated by s 9 of the *Constitution*. The details of these laws are, however, spread out across the *Constitution*.

The main organs of the state are also identified and discussed throughout the book. The three main institutions of state – the legislature, the executive and the judiciary – are discussed in Chapters 5, 6 and 7 respectively. The discussions show that, although the separation of powers doctrine is adopted by the *Constitution*, in practical terms some of the powers and functions of these three arms of government sometimes overlap. In certain cases, there have been tensions, if not open confrontation, between these arms.[8]

The *Constitution* has been described as "homegrown", because it was formulated within PNG by the people of PNG. The *Constitution* is the result of a long consultative process undertaken by the Constitutional Planning Committee (CPC) and the people. In SCR No 3 of 1986; *Reference by Simbu Provincial Executive* [1987] PNGLR 151, Barnett J reaffirmed this position. The Supreme Court expressed the

---

6 See *Kaseng v Namaliu* [1995] PNGLR 481 and *SCR No 1 of 1992* [1992] PNGLR 1.

7 Planning the New Century Committee, *Kumul 2020: Preparing Papua New Guinea for Prosperity in the 21st Century* (Planning the New Century Committee, Port Moresby, 1998), p 14. This committee was set up by the former Prime Minister, Sir Julius Chan, to formulate a "vision statement" for PNG. When the report was completed, Sir Julius Chan had lost the government and the elections. His successor, Bill Skate, refused to release the report and, thus, it is still kept in abeyance.

8 A good example is the tussle between the judiciary and the Parliament and the executive in the long-running battle about the "sitting of Parliament": see *SCR No 3 of 1999; Re Calling of Meeting of the Parliament* (1999) SC 628.

same view in *Re Provincial Government Grants* [1990] PNGLR 532. The history of constitutional development in PNG and the excellent work of the CPC are contained in Chapter 2.

In formulating the *Constitution*, the CPC was very mindful of the distribution of power and the exercise of executive power by a select group of elites. The CPC firmly expressed the view that the people of PNG wanted a system of government where the people would be able to participate in the affairs of government. The CPC therefore proposed that a system of provincial government be introduced, whereby government power would be decentralised to the provincial and local levels. This proposal was opposed the government of Chief Minister Somare, and rejected by the House of Assembly. The provincial government system was, however, introduced shortly after independence, after Bougainville threatened to secede from PNG. The provincial government system remained for 19 years until it was revamped in 1995 by *Constitutional Amendment No 16* and the *Organic Law on Provincial Governments and Local-level Governments* (OLPGLLG). The background of the "reformed provincial government system", its structure and its operation are discussed in Chapter 8.

The CPC also proposed a number of intricate mechanisms for controlling the exercise of power by the executive arm of the government. The first of these was the creation of constitutional offices, which would keep an eye on the executive and, of course, the other two arms of government. The CPC was careful to point out that these offices were to be independent and free from any direction and control by any person or authority. It was envisioned that these constitutional offices would play an important role with the government as partners in the development of the country. In the performance of their functions, they are encouraged to work together within their own spheres of operation for the greater good of the country. Chapter 10 reviews the roles and functions of the constitutional offices, and describes the performance of these institutions since independence.[9]

Secondly, the CPC strongly recommended, and it was received overwhelmingly by the House of Assembly, that fundamental rights and freedoms of citizens be contained in the *Constitution*. By entrenching the rights and freedoms of the people in the *Constitution*, the people are certain and know about their rights and freedoms. The availability of these rights in the supreme law of the country acts as a bar against excesses of state power and also against abuse by other citizens.[10] For PNG, the inclusion of the rights and freedoms in the *Constitution* is quite significant, because the power to enforce them is vested in the judiciary.[11] The discussions in Chapter 9 highlight the over-zealousness of the judiciary in protecting and enforcing the rights and freedoms of citizens. The judiciary has performed exceptionally well in this area of the law.

The third clever strategy of the CPC is found in Pt X of the *Constitution*, which provides for the declaration of states of emergency. The CPC understood from the experiences of other countries that, during states of emergency, the rights and freedoms of citizens are extremely vulnerable to abuse by the executive. Not only are the citizens open to abuse by the state through the executive, but the executive

---

9 See generally Regan, Jessep and Kwa (eds), *Twenty Years of the Papua New Guinea Constitution* (Lawbook Co, Sydney, 2001).

10 See Kwa, "Enforcement of Human Rights in Papua New Guinea: Tru O Giaman?" in Kwa, Bhalla, Muroa, Linge, Tennent and Yapao (eds), *Development of Administrative Law in Papua New Guinea* (School of Law and Business Studies, UPNG & UBSPD, New Delhi, 2000), p 179.

11 *Constitution*, s 57.

may use a state of emergency as an opportunity to pursue other political agendas. The CPC proposed that the power to declare a war (s 227) or a state of emergency (s 228) be vested in the executive arm of the government. However, as soon as a state of emergency is declared, the Parliament controls the state of emergency (s 239) and supervises the emergency through the Emergency Committee (s 240) of the Parliament. If the executive declares a state of emergency when the Parliament is not in session, the *Constitution* stipulates, in s 239, that Parliament must be convened to consider the state of emergency or war within 15 days. As soon as the Parliament meets, it can either affirm the state of emergency or war or reject it.[12] The state of emergency is supervised by the Parliamentary Emergency Committee, which is comprised of members of Parliament. The membership of the committee is restricted only to non-Ministers. The underpinning of this arrangement is to ensure that Parliamentarians who are members of the executive do not follow through with their decisions by supervising them. This procedure also ensures that the declaration of a state of emergency is based on genuine grounds. During a state of emergency and war, the fundamental rights and freedoms are not affected by the situation.[13] Only qualified rights, such as freedom of expression, freedom of assembly and association, right to privacy and right to freedom of information, can be altered during a state of emergency by an Emergency Act.[14] Even detainees during a state of emergency are accorded special protection by the *Constitution*.[15]

These mechanisms have been tested and proven worthy over the last 25 years. The executive and its bureaucratic machinery have been restrained. In one case, the army retreated to its quarters through the combined efforts of the civil society, the constitutional institutions and the judiciary.

Although the country has faced, and continues to face, many difficult challenges in the economic, social and political spheres, PNG must be saluted for maintaining a strong and vibrant democracy that derives its strength from the *Constitution*. The rule of law and the doctrine of constitutionalism have survived in PNG for over 25 years. The *Constitution* has weathered time, and it is to the *Constitution* that PNG, a thriving young democracy, and its diverse people and cultures look to find their strength to move into the future.

PNG is truly "one nation, one country, one people and one *Constitution*".

12 Section 229 provides that Parliament must take this decision. The executive is vested with the power to decide whether a state of emergency or war should be terminated after the parliamentary decision. This means that the executive can terminate the situation any time after the Parliament has made the initial decision. Nonetheless, the termination of the situation must still be endorsed by Parliament at a later date.

13 *Constitution*, s 233(3).

14 These rights and freedoms cannot be altered by an Emergency Regulation. An Emergency Regulation must be distinguished from an Emergency Act. The executive makes the regulation, while the Act is a product of the legislature.

15 *Constitution*, ss 244-245.

Chapter 2

CONSTITUTIONAL DEVELOPMENT IN PAPUA NEW GUINEA

2.1 INTRODUCTION

Papua New Guinea (PNG) became an independent state on 16 September 1975. The *Constitution* became operational on Independence Day. As an emerging state, PNG borrowed ideas and practices from other established states to formulate its own constitution. The array of ideas and practices were screened carefully to ensure that those ideas that were adopted were suited to the circumstances of PNG.

The process of distillation began as early as 1965, with the establishment of the Select Committee for Constitutional Development by the House of Assembly. It was, however, only between 1972 and 1974 that the process of constitutional formulation became more apparent and earnest.

This chapter examines the process of constitutional development in PNG before independence. Constitutional development in PNG is usually attributed to the work of the Constitutional Planning Committee (CPC). However, as this chapter will show, the process was initiated well before the inception of the CPC.

2.2 PRE-INDEPENDENCE LEGAL SYSTEM

PNG is a unique country with diverse cultures and people and more than 800 different languages. Papua New Guineans were among the first known agriculturalists. They have been able to live in harmony with their environment over thousands of years. These different groups of people were able to live and manage themselves largely through customary rules and practices. The nature and content of these customary rules and practices varied from one society to another.

Papua New Guineans first sighted Europeans as early as the 17th century. European settlers came and settled in PNG only in the late 19th century, with the arrival of the first Christian missionaries. Formal contact with European governments was initiated in 1884. Britain annexed the southern part of the country (which was later named Papua). The German Imperial Government annexed the eastern part of the country (later called New Guinea) at about the same period.

The establishment of a formal government in Papua and New Guinea led to the introduction of formal laws. From 1884 up to and after the end of World War I, German laws applied in New Guinea by virtue of the *Statute Regarding the Legal Conditions in the German Protectorates*. Certain provisions of this statute were made redundant in New Guinea by the *Imperial Ordinance* of 20 July 1887. This Act also empowered the German New Guinea Company to exercise certain sovereign rights over the territory. The company supplemented the statutes by issuing Directions. The validity of these laws was determined in the case of *Gaya Nomgui v The Administration* [1974] PNGLR 349. In this case, the Supreme Court had to decide whether the land on which the city of Lae is situated was validly purchased by the German administration. The Supreme Court held that the land was validly purchased by the company pursuant to the *Imperial Ordinance* and supported by its Directions issued over the property, and that, through a succession of relevant laws, the administration was the lawful owner of the land. In Papua, *The Courts and Laws Adopting Ordinance* 1888, later amended in 1889, stipulated that British laws as applied in the colony of Queensland were to be applied to the new territory.

When Germany lost in World War I, all rights and titles to overseas territories, including New Guinea, were also lost. Under the terms of the 1919 Treaty of Versailles, the allied and associated powers took possession of these former German territories. By virtue of Art 22 of the Covenant of the League of Nations, New Guinea became a mandated territory of the League of Nations in 1921. It was administered by Australia on behalf of the League of Nations (and later the United Nations).[1] It remained a mandated territory until independence in 1975.

The question of whether Australia had the power to legislate for New Guinea was raised in *Mainka v Custodian of Expropriated Property* (1924) 34 CLR 297, and later in *Jolley v Manika* (1933) 49 CLR 242. It was held that the acceptance of the mandate was authorised by the *Treaty of Peace Act* 1919, an Act passed by the United Kingdom Parliament. The other view was that the Commonwealth Parliament had power to enact laws for New Guinea under s 122 of the Australian *Constitution.*[2]

The Commonwealth Parliament, exercising its plenary powers under s 122 of the Australian *Constitution*, made laws for New Guinea. In 1920, the Commonwealth Parliament passed the *New Guinea Act* 1920. That Act, which came into effect on 9 May 1921, became the *Constitution* of the territory of New Guinea. An important feature of the legislation was s 15, which ensured the protection of indigenous New Guineans and their culture. In 1921, the Commonwealth Parliament passed the *Laws Repeal and Adopting Ordinance* 1921, which came into effect on 9 May 1921. This Act repealed all German laws that were applicable in New Guinea. It also provided for the operation of custom in the territory. By virtue of s 10 of the Act, customary rules and practices were allowed to govern the lives and activities of New Guineans throughout the territory. The coexistence of custom and formal law continues to this day.

The two territories of New Guinea and Papua were administered separately until the outbreak of World War II. In 1949, the two territories were brought under a single administration under the *Papua and New Guinea Act* 1949-1975. This law effectively became the *Constitution* of Papua and New Guinea. The Act provided for the legislature, its composition, and its powers and functions, and the executive, which consisted of the administrator and a number of officials who were replaced by Ministers in the years preceding independence.

There were no significant changes to the *Papua and New Guinea Act* until 1960, when it was amended by the *Papua and New Guinea (No 2) Act* 1960. The most

1 Haynes, *A Short History of the Pre-Independence Legal System of Papua New Guinea* (UPNG Printery, Port Moresby, 1983), p 10.
2 See *Fishwick v Cleland* (1960) 106 CLR 196.

important aspects of the Act related to the composition of the Legislative Council (later called the House of Assembly):

> "They provided that the Council was to consist of the Administrator, 14 official members, 10 persons appointed by the Governor-General on the nomination of the Administrator, and 12 persons elected by the 'electors of the Territory'."[3]

The *Papua and New Guinea Act* was amended several times thereafter, mainly to reflect the changes in the composition of the legislature and the executive.[4] Political pressure for accelerated constitutional change began in 1961, with the establishment of the Select Committee on Constitutional Development by the Legislative Council. This committee recommended a number of sweeping changes relating to the composition of the legislature and the executive, and these were reflected in the *Papua and New Guinea Act* 1961. The visit, in 1962, by the United Nations Visiting Mission, headed by Sir Hugh Foot, also increased the pressure on Australia to facilitate greater constitutional reform in the territory.[5] The colonial administration responded by establishing, through the House of Assembly, two constitutional commissions, one in 1965 and the other in 1969, to recommend ways of formulating proposals for changes to the *Papua and New Guinea Act* (pre-independence *Constitution*).

2.3 FIRST CONSTITUTIONAL COMMISSION

The process of making a constitution for an independent PNG began formally on 19 May 1965, when the House of Assembly appointed the Select Committee on Constitutional Development by a resolution. This committee was specifically mandated "to consider ways and means of preparing and presenting, and to draft for the consideration of the House, a set of constitutional proposals to serve as a guide for future constitutional development in the Territory".[6] This Select Committee can be referred to as the first Constitutional Commission, because it was the first committee that was established by the House of Assembly to consider specific ways of preparing the colony for independence.

The Select Committee presented its first interim report in 1965, highlighting the work of the committee to that date. A second interim report was presented to the House of Assembly on 30 August 1966. This report related mainly to the composition of the House of Assembly, which was to be effected after the 1968 elections. The final report of the Select Committee was presented to the House of Assembly through the administrator in June 1967.

The report of the Select Committee was based largely on the workings of the legislature and the executive arms of the government. The Select Committee's main recommendations were:

---

3 Bayne and Colebatch, *Constitutional Development in Papua New Guinea, 1968-73* (New Guinea Research Bulletin No 51, New Guinea Research Unit, Australian National University, Canberra, 1973), p 11.

4 For instance, see *Papua and New Guinea Act* 1963 (No 27 of 1963), which created the House of Assembly; the *Papua and New Guinea Act* 1966 (No 25 of 1968), which enabled the expansion of the House of Assembly after the 1968 Elections; and the *Papua New Guinea Act* 1971 (No 123 of 1971), which changed the name of the territory from "Papua and New Guinea" to "Papua New Guinea".

5 Bayne and Colebatch, op cit n 3, p 13.

6 Select Committee on Constitutional Development, *Final Report from the Select Committee on Constitutional Development together with Minutes of Proceedings* (Administration of Papua New Guinea, Port Moresby, 1967), p 1.

(a) reduction of administration officials on the Administrator's Executive Council and the increase of elected members on the council; and

(b) the appointment of Ministers and Assistant Ministers. This recommendation "clearly envisaged the development of a parliamentary executive along the lines of the Westminster model".[7]

The recommendations of the Select Committee were effected by the *Papua and New Guinea Act* 1968. In terms of the constitution-making process for the territory, the Select Committee said that "the pace of constitutional change should be dictated by the people of the Territory, and that no change should be proposed without the people's support".[8] In this regard, the Select Committee reported that it had travelled to all the district headquarters and sought views from the people, and the result of their findings were that:

> "One large sector of the community was against any change and wanted the present position continued, at least until 1972. A small group put forward far reaching recommendations amounting to limited self government. The majority maintained an inter-mediate position."[9]

The Select Committee did not make any concrete recommendations on the ways and means of preparing for the consideration of the House a draft set of constitutional proposals to serve as a guide for future constitutional development in the Territory. It concluded that:

> "Constitutional development is a continuing process. The Committee therefore suggests the appointment of a further constitutional committee, which would continue the study of the constitutional advancement of Papua New Guinea including the question of a constitution and system of government best suited to Territory."[10]

2.4 SECOND CONSTITUTIONAL COMMISSION

In line with the Select Committee's recommendations, the House of Assembly established a new Select Committee on Constitutional Development on 24 June 1969. This second Constitutional Commission's terms of reference were the same as its predecessor's. The second Constitutional Commission presented three interim reports on 17 November 1969, 12 March 1970 and 3 September 1970. Its final report, entitled *Final Report from The Select Committee on Constitutional Development together with Minutes of Proceedings*, was presented to the House of Assembly in March 1971.

The scope of the second Select Committee's work was wider than that of the first committee. It had to consider a number of fundamental issues, including internal self-government, system of government, structure of the legislature, structure of the Administrator's Executive Council and national unity. On the first issue, the Select Committee reported that "the majority of the people of Papua and New Guinea expressed opposition to early internal self-government". The committee further reported that:

7 Ibid, p 18.
8 Ibid.
9 Ibid.
10 Ibid, p 10.

> "At the moment the majority of the people of Papua New Guinea feel that internal self-government should come about *no sooner* than during the life of the 1967-1980 House of Assembly."[11]

The committee, however, recommended that "the development of the Territory be geared to preparing the country for internal self-government during the life of the next House of Assembly".[12] The committee was confident that internal self-government was to be achieved in a shorter time than the majority of the people expected. The boldness of the committee in making this recommendation may be attributed to its membership. Unlike the previous committee, the 1969 committee consisted mainly of elected indigenous members who were mostly nationalists. These members included Mr Paulus Arek (Chairman), Mr Donatus Mola, Mr Ebia Olewale, Mr Matthias To Liman, Mr Michael Somare, Mr Sinake Giregire and Mr Oala Oala-Rarua.[13]

Internal self-government was actually achieved in 1973, during the life of the 1972-1977 House of Assembly.

The Select Committee considered the second issue, and recommended that the single central government that was present be maintained. As for the third issue, the committee recommended that one house of Parliament that existed under the current system should be retained. The justification for this proposal, according to the committee, was that it "ensures the best use of the country's manpower and the economic resources".[14] It also recommended increased representation in the 1972-1977 House of Assembly. It recommended that the number of regional electorates should be increased to 18, and open electorates by 13 to bring the total number of open electorates to 81. The committee further recommended that nominated members should be appointed only if it was necessary. If there were to be nominated members, only three were to be appointed, and the nominated person must be a person who had lived in the territory for more than five years.

These recommendations were quite radical at that stage. The committee was clearly signalling to the colonial administration that it wanted a shift in the exercise of power from the executive to the legislature. Nationalist sentiments are reflected in the recommendations relating to the increases in the number of constituencies, the criteria for the selection of appointed members and the reduction in the number of non-elected members on the Administrator's Executive Council.

On its tour, the committee came across differing views on the arrangements for the country. Separatism was being strongly advocated by the Mataungan Association of the Gazelle Peninsula, South Bougainville and Papua. The Mataungan Association wanted an independent Gazelle Peninsula, and the people from South Bougainville wanted to secede from Papua and New Guinea. Many Papuans did not want to integrate with New Guinea to form a single nation. The committee, however, strongly opposed these views. The committee acknowledged that a "unified country and people is of the utmost importance in the move forward to internal self-government and later independence".[15]

The committee also submitted the current national flag and the current coat of arms to the House of Assembly for approval. The committee also recommended

---

11 Select Committee on Constitutional Development, op cit n 6, p 2.

12 Ibid, p 8.

13 The other members of the committee were Mr CG Littler, Mr TJ Leahy, Mr WA Lussick, Mr JM Middleton, Mr Matiabe Yuwi, Mr Tei Abal and Mr Karigl Bonggere.

14 Select Committee on Constitutional Development, op cit n 6, p 4.

15 Ibid, p 7.

that the country be called Niugini, and the people be called Niugians. The House of Assembly rejected this particular recommendation.

Most of the committee's recommendations were incorporated in the *Papua and New Guinea Act* 1971, and the rest were later incorporated in the *Papua New Guinea Act* 1949-1971.

The work of the two Select Constitutional Committees fitted comfortably with the tradition of British dependencies, which was "for the government of the dependency to formulate its independence constitution during a process of gradual constitutional development".[16] The formula was that constitutional development was to be achieved through limited changes to the existing constitution in a timely fashion. The elected representatives of the colony are required to propose changes through the legislature, and the executive concurs or endorses these changes. According to the tradition, the British Government retains formal authority for the constitution and ensures that the changes conform broadly to the principles of constitutional government.

There is no doubt that the Australian Government was following precisely this tradition with the two Constitutional Commissions, and was hoping to repeat the process with the third Constitutional Commission in the form of the Constitutional Planning Committee (CPC). As will be seen below, this tradition was thrown into disarray with the establishment of the CPC and the grant of self-government in April 1973.

2.5 THE CONSTITUTIONAL PLANNING COMMITTEE

In June 1972, the House of Assembly, by a motion of the Chief Minister, Mr Michael Somare, agreed to establish the Constitutional Planning Committee (CPC). The CPC's main term of reference was:

> "To make recommendations for a Constitution for full internal self-government in a united Papua New Guinea with a view to eventual independence. Without limiting the power of the Committee to make any investigation or recommendation which it deems relevant to this objective, matters to be considered by the Committee for possible incorporation into the Constitution or relevant documents ..."[17]

The CPC was also instructed to consider for incorporation in the new *Constitution* matters such as:

- the system of government, executive, legislature and judiciary;
- central-regional-local government relations and district administration;
- relations with Australia;
- defence and external affairs – transitional provisions;
- the machinery of government – control, organisation and structure of the Public Service;
- a Director of Public Prosecutions and Public Solicitor;
- an ombudsman and tribunals of administrative review;
- protection of minority rights;
- a Bill of Rights;

16 Murray, "Constitution-making in Tuvalu and Kiribati" in Sack (ed), *Pacific Constitutions: Proceedings of the Canberra Law Workshop VI* (ANU Printing Services, Canberra, 1982), p 125.

17 Constitutional Planning Committee, *Final Report of the Constitutional Planning Committee 1974 (Part 1)* (Government Printer, Port Moresby, 1974), p iv.

emergency powers;

citizenship;

procedure for amendment of the *Constitution*; and

judicial review – the power of a court to decide whether or not any action by the government or law passed by Parliament is in accordance with the *Constitution*.[18]

The CPC's terms of reference were much wider than those of its predecessors. Unlike the two former Select Committees on Constitutional Development, the CPC was given a definite timeframe within which to complete its work. It was directed to complete its report and submit its recommendations to the House of Assembly by 1974. This timeframe was in line with an agreement signed by the Chief Minister and the Minister for External Territories, Mr WL Morrison, which set the timetable for the full self-government of PNG. Under the terms of the agreement:[19]

formal self-government was to be introduced in Papua and New Guinea by December 1973 by an amendment to the *Papua and New Guinea Act* by the Commonwealth;

by February 1974 the CPC was to table its final report and draft *Constitution* in the House of Assembly;

the House of Assembly was to adopt the *Constitution* by April 1974; and

full self-government was to be attained by mid-1974.

This time frame was accepted by the Australians, because their original intention was:

> "that following the granting of Internal Self-Government by the *Papua New Guinea Act (No 2)* 1973 of Australia, a 'self-government' constitution would be prepared by, and enacted in, Papua New Guinea in about February 1974, which was then to be made law in one form or another by or by virtue of an Australian Act, and was to be followed, after a working-in-period by an Independence Constitution".[20]

This lengthy process and the non-committal attitude of Australia towards PNG were viewed by the CPC with contempt. To the CPC, the timeframe was unrealistic, as it wanted immediate independence. As it turned out, the CPC completed its work and submitted its final report on 13 August 1974. The Parliament then took a year to finally adopt the draft *Constitution* for PNG, and by 16 September 1975 PNG was an independent nation.

Fr John Momis, who was really the Deputy Chairman and a member of the Pangu Party, chaired the CPC. Michael Somare was the ex officio chairman of the CPC and leader of the Pangu Party. The CPC was a bipartisan committee, and its members represented the various parties in Parliament at that time and broadly represented the four main regions of the country. It was decided at the time that the CPC should consist only of indigenous parliamentarians.[21] The other members of the CPC were:

---

18 Ibid.

19 The agreement was entitled "Joint Communique on Agreement for Two Stage Self-Government" and signed by the two men representing their respective governments on 22 May 1974.

20 Lynch, "Current Developments in the Pacific: The Achievement of Independence in Papua New Guinea – The Legal Aspect" (1980) Vol XV *Journal of Pacific History* (No 3) 175.

21 Narokobi, *My Helping Finger in the Making of Papua New Guinea's 1975 Constitution* (Paper presented at the "Twenty Years of the Constitution Conference", Port Moresby, March 1996), p 4.

- Mr Tei Abel (Leader of the Opposition and Leader of the United Party);
- Mr Paulus Arek (Pangu Party), who died in November 1973;
- Mr Angmai Bilas (United Party);
- Mr Mackenzi Daugi (United Party);
- Mr Sinake Giregire (United Party);
- Dr John Guise (Independent), who was the Deputy Chief Minister;
- Mr Toni Ila (Pangu Party);
- Mr John Kaputin (Mataungan Association);
- Mr Pikah Kasau (Pangu Party);
- Mr John Kaupa (National Party);
- Mr Paul Langro (United Party), who was the Deputy Leader of the Opposition;
- Mr Anton Parao (United Party);
- Mr Stanis Toliman (People's Progress Party); and
- Mr Matiabe Yuwi (United Party).

Of these 16 members, six (Mr Somare, Mr Arek, Mr Parao, Mr Yuwi, Mr Giregire and Mr Abel) were members of the second Constitutional Commission of 1969-1971.[22] Although these men were laymen and were being advised by Western experts using Western legal language, Barnett J acknowledged in *The State v NTN Pty Ltd* [1992] PNGLR 1 at 13 that, "the members of the Constitutional Planning Committee made a determined effort to try to express in layman's language the principles and spirit which were intended to enlighten the legal prose".

The CPC was made up of both conservative and radical members. The conservatives were led by Tei Abel, who was opposed to early independence, while the radicals were led by John Momis, who wanted immediate independence. Describing the commonality of the members, Narokobi said, they "were excited, tickled, motivated and inspired."[23] The CPC wanted see "an egalitarian society with justice, equality, fair play and opportunity for all". It "believed deeply in human dignity, equal worth and social obligations".[24] The CPC toured the country widely, visiting many districts, towns and villages to ascertain the people's views on its visions. The CPC consulted the people by speaking to them and listening to many thousands of them. The people consulted by the CPC ranged from village men and women to private enterprise people and public servants. The CPC formulated six discussion papers which were distributed to discussion groups and interested individuals. In response, the CPC received well over 2000 written submissions on these papers and held talks with the people through various discussion groups and public meetings.

The work of the CPC was given wide coverage by the local media. As a result, large numbers of people attended the public meetings and participated in the discussion groups. The various CPC consultants also provided discussion papers on the various topics that were relevant to the work of the CPC. Barnett J correctly pointed out in *The State v NTN Pty Ltd*:

> "The legal language too is familiar. Perhaps this is not surprising as the Deputy Chairman of the Constitutional Planning Committee was a Roman

22 The CPC was assisted by an administrative staff and a group of permanent consultants such as Edward Wolfers, Dr David Stone, Mr Benard Narokobi and visiting specialist consultants from overseas.

23 Narokobi, op cit n 21, p 7.

24 Ibid.

Catholic priest and its advisers were Western-trained lawyers and social scientists."

When the final report of the CPC was submitted to the Chief Minister in August 1974, the CPC had taken 22 months to complete its task. The CPC explained that it had taken a longer period to do its work because of the "need for extensive consultation with the people",[25] and that it had to formulate a truly "home-grown" *Constitution*. In *SCR No 3 of 1986; Reference by Simbu Provincial Executive* [1987] PNGLR 151 at 173, Barnett J explained that the prolonged process of community consultation was to enable the CPC to tap the will and spirit of the people. The CPC initially pushed for immediate independence. Somare, and most of his members who pressured firmly for early independence, quickly embraced the idea. The CPC was aware that independence was imminent, and therefore concluded "our recommendations are now based on the assumption that the *Constitution* will be one for an independent Papua New Guinea".[26]

2.6 CONCLUSION

The constitution-making process was completed by 15 August 1975, when the House of Assembly, sitting as the Constituent Assembly, adopted the *Constitution* by a resolution moved by Michael Somare. The *Constitution*, which is mostly based on the CPC's final report, was debated at intervals from 16 August 1974 to 11 March 1975. The first draft of the *Constitution* was prepared by the First Legislative Counsel on the general basis of the CPC's final report. The fourth draft of the *Constitution* was completed and circulated to members on 19 May 1975. The fifth and final draft of the *Constitution* was adopted on 15 August 1975.

The move for greater autonomy and, later, full independence, became more apparent after the 1968 election. The results of the election were encouraging for Papua New Guineans, because it was at this election that a large number of indigenous Papua New Guineans were elected to the legislature for the first time. Many of these indigenous Papua New Guineans pushed strongly for greater autonomy from Australia. Their views were firmly rooted in the radical recommendations of the second Constitutional Commission.

By the time the CPC was instituted, the scene had been set for the final countdown for independence. The desire for independence was very loud and clear. The House of Assembly did not only want a constitution, but "a Constitution for full internal self-government in a united Papua New Guinea with a view to eventual independence". Independence was achieved by PNG on 16 September 1975. The new *Constitution* came into operation smoothly on Independence Day.

25 Constitutional Planning Committee, op cit n 17, pp 1-2.
26 Ibid.

Chapter 3

THE NATIONAL GOALS AND DIRECTIVE PRINCIPLES

3.1 INTRODUCTION

When Papua New Guinea (PNG) became an independent state on 16 September 1975, PNG was, by world standards, a young nation.[1] As an emerging state, PNG needed guidelines to help achieve a certain level of change that would bring happiness and prosperity to the people of PNG. These guidelines find form in the National Goals and Directive Principles (the NGDPs). The NGDPs are also referred to as goals that the people of PNG aspire to achieve as an independent state.

The NGDPs set out broad principles for the development of PNG as a country. The inclusion of the NGDPs in the *Constitution* is to ensure that every one is involved in the implementation of government policies "in the light of a basic indication of the direction of national policy".[2]

This chapter looks at the origin, aims, implementation and enforcement of the NGDPs. The issues associated with the interplay of the NGDPs and state actions will also be discussed.

3.2 THE NATIONAL GOALS AND DIRECTIVE PRINCIPLES

The idea of inserting general guidelines in the *Constitution* is not peculiar to PNG. Other countries, such as India, Pakistan, Nigeria and Uganda, also have similar guidelines in their constitutions.[3] In the Pacific, these guidelines are sometimes referred to as the "Pacific Way" or, in Melanesia, the "Melanesian Way".[4] In PNG, these guidelines were promulgated as the NGDPs. There are five NGDPs, and they are located in the Preamble of the *Constitution*.

- Goal 1 promotes the integral human development of every Papua New Guinean.
- Goal 2 encourages equality and participation in the development of PNG.

---

1 PNG emerged as an independent state at a time when many former colonies of the Western powers in Africa, Asia and the Pacific had rejected, or were rejecting, colonialism and embracing independence: see Herlihy, "Rituals, Rhetoric and Reality: Decolonisation and Associated Phenomena" in Sack (ed), *Pacific Constitutions: Proceedings of the Canberra Law Workshop VI* (ANU Printing Services, Canberra, 1982), pp 37-49.

2 Goldring, *The Constitution of Papua New Guinea* (Law Book Co Ltd, Sydney, 1978), p 32.

3 *Constitution of the Republic of India*, Pt IV (Directive Principles of State Policy); *Constitution of the Republic of Nigeria*, Ch 11 (Fundamental Objectives and Directive Principles of State Policy); *Constitution of the Islamic Republic of Pakistan*, Ch 2 (Principles of Policy); *Constitution of the Republic of Uganda*, Ch 3 (National Objectives and Directive Principles of State policy).

4 Herlihy, op cit, p 46.

- Goal 3 strengthens national sovereignty and calls on Papua New Guineans to be self-reliant.
- Goal 4 reminds Papua New Guineans about the importance of their natural resources and their environment.
- Goal 5 calls on Papua New Guineans to promote and utilise Papua New Guinean ways in their dealings with each other, the state and foreigners.

The most important of these goals is Goal 1, which declares that:

> "We declare our first goal to be for every person to be dynamically involved in the process of freeing himself or herself from every form of domination or oppression so that each man or woman will have the opportunity to develop as a whole person in relationship to others."

This goal takes a holistic view of development. The emphasis of this goal is on social, political and spiritual development. The other four goals are geared towards the achievement of this primary goal. Barnett J said, in *The State v NTN Pty Ltd* [1992] PNGLR 1 at 17, that "under the banner of 'Integral Human Development', the call is for such activities" to promote and encourage the achievement of the full development of Papua New Guineans. The call is directed more strongly at the "National executive Council, the National Parliament and the Supreme Court".

Goal 2 is quite significant, as it encourages gender, colour and ethnic equality. It encourages all citizens to have an equal opportunity to participate in, and benefit from, the development of the country. The principles of equality under this goal must be seen in the context of s 55 of the *Constitution*. This provision declares that all citizens are equal, regardless of their race, political affiliation, tribe, place of origin, colour, creed, religion or sex. Of course, the courts have been the main protectors of this goal. The courts have, on various occasions, come to the aid of victims of inequality. Thus, in *The State v Robinson* [1992] PNGLR 205 at 208 (Los J), a case involving the offence of bigamy under the *Criminal Code*, the court held that the combined effect of Goal 2 and s 55(1) was that the wife had the same rights as the husband in a marriage. In *Public Curator of Papua New Guinea v Public Trustee of New Zealand* [1976] PNGLR 427, the National Court ruled that where there was limited access to legal processes and services necessary to execute a valid will, a defect, informality or statutory non-compliance in the last will and testament of a testator will not, by these reasons alone, cause the will to be declared invalid.

It is, however, generally accepted that not all opportunities are available to every citizen of the country. Considerations such as location, educational standards and access to government services and infrastructure can become important factors in determining the issue of equality. These factors were considered in *Public Curator of Papua New Guinea v Public Trustee of New Zealand* and, in *Rakatani Peter v South Pacific Brewery* [1976] PNGLR 537 (at 556), Prentice DCJ considered these factors and said that to require the appearance of the defendant in court regularly, only to get adjournments, would be cumbersome and expensive for defendants living in remote parts of the country. He therefore ruled that to achieve the NGDPs, a defendant's trial could proceed in his or her absence with his or her consent. Consequently, s 131 of the *District Courts Act* 1961 was not inconsistent with s 37(5) of the *Constitution* in regards to simple offences.

In an apparent move to expand the meaning of the NGDPs, Kapi DCJ held, in *Haivetta v Wingti (No 3)* [1994] PNGLR 197 (at 221), that equality and participation under Goal 2 also means that Members of Parliament must be given an opportunity to participate fairly in the election of the Prime Minister. Similar sentiments were raised by Barnett J in *SCR No 3 of 1986; Reference by Simbu Provincial Executive* [1987] PNGLR 151 at 174, where his Honour noted that the provincial government system provided under the *Organic Law on Provincial Governments* was intended to enable the people to equally and actively participate in the governmental process.

Goal 3, in pursuance of Goal 1, is for the country to be politically and economically independent and self-reliant. Principle 1 of this goal declares that:

> "Our leaders are to be committed to these National Goals and Directive Principles, to ensure that their freedom to make decisions is not restricted by obligations to or relationship with others, and to make all of their decisions in the national interest."

The achievement of the NGDPs at the political level was, according to the Constitutional Planning Committee (CPC), firmly in the hands of the leaders of PNG. Our leaders are given a special mandate under the *Constitution* to ensure that their dealings with each other and with others are in the national interest, so that the aims and aspirations of the people, as enshrined in the NGDPs, are fulfilled.

The enormity of this responsibility was stressed by Amet CJ in *Haivetta v Wigti (No 3)* [1994] PNGLR 197 at 207. The Chief Justice pointed out that the election of a new Prime Minister is a matter of national interest as exhorted by Goal 3(1) and, as such, elected leaders are required to be more responsible when making their decisions on this matter. In the national interest, leaders are required to abstain from activities that will demean their offices. This was implicit in *SCR No 2 of 1992* [1992] PNGLR 336 at 346.

Goal 4 incorporates the concept of "wise use", which was later coined (by the Bruntland Commission in 1987) as "sustainable development".[5] The goal acknowledges that PNG as a nation has to advance, but cautions the government and people of PNG to wisely use their natural resources and the environment in the pursuit of Goal 1.

The goal encourages the use of both Papua New Guinean ways and established international rules and principles of using the environment and natural resources, to achieve development. International laws relating to the environment that are in conformity with Goal 4 can be adopted and applied in PNG, as was declared in *Chern Jin Fa v Naniura* [1990] PNGLR 506.

Goal 5 departs from the other goals in the scheme of the Preamble, and is quite unique. This goal upholds Papua New Guinean ways, and specifically calls on the people of PNG to "foster the use of Papuan New Guinean forms of social, political and economic organisations as the tools for achieving the social, political and economic development of Papua New Guinea".[6] On a definition of this expression "Papua New Guinean ways", the *Constitution* is silent. Some commentators have suggested that it refers to the customs of Papua New Guineans that guide their interactions with each other within the political, social and economic spheres within their own given environments.[7] The courts have not had much

5 See generally the report of the World Commission on Environment and Development (Bruntland Commission): World Commission on Environment and Development, *Our Common Future* (Oxford University Press, Oxford, 1987).

6 Gawi, Ghai and Paliwala, "National Goals and Law Reform: A Report on the Goroka Seminar" (1976) 4(2) Mel LJ 259 at 261.

7 The most ardent supporter of this concept is Bernard Narokobi. His strongest views are published in his book, *The Melanesian Way* (Institute of PNG Studies, 1983). See also Ntumy, "The Dream of a Melanesian Jurisprudence: The Purpose and Limits of Law Reform" in Aleck and Rannells (eds), *Custom at the Crossroads* (UPNG Law Faculty, Port Moresby, 1995), p 7.

opportunity to give a definitive meaning to the expression. In *SCR No 2 of 1992* [1992] PNGLR 336 (at 360), Kapi DCJ (see also *Re Raka Ruk* [1991] PNGLR 105 at 106-107) mentioned Goal 5, but went on to discuss the application of custom.

These five NGDPs represent signposts for the evolution of PNG as a nation state. The NGDPs "set the agenda for all aspects of government in Papua New Guinea, and represent a clear break with the colonial past. They seek control over foreign investment, and the protection of the environment and the Papua New Guinean way of life".[8]

Origins

The NGDPs were the product of the work of the Constitutional Planning Committee (CPC). The CPC took 22 months to complete its report after wide consultation with the people. In formulating the NGDPs, the CPC expanded upon the Eight Point Plan, which was adopted by the House of Assembly in 1973.[9] The Eight Point Plan represented the first statement of the fundamental guidelines for the development of PNG. The CPC said:

> "There are several basic principles which lie behind these aims. These have been summed up in the ideas of Equality, Self-Reliance and Rural Development. In evolving the National Goals and Directive Principles of Policy which we propose should be incorporated in the *Constitution*, we have taken full account of the Eight Aims. The Goals and Directive Principles we recommend are broader and more comprehensive than the Aims, in that, they provide for the full development of our people, whereas the Aims emphasise the economic aspects of our society."[10]

The NGDPs were carefully and critically analysed by the CPC before being recommended to the Constituent Assembly. In the words of the CPC:

> "We did not determine these national goals in a matter of days or weeks. We have distilled them after a great deal of thought and discussion over the twenty-two months during which our Committee has been at work."[11]

The NGDPs are, therefore, a coherent woven development policy reflecting the aims and aspirations of the leaders at that time and the ordinary people whose views were readily accepted by the CPC. According to Bredmeyer J in *SCR No 1 of 1984; Re Minimum Penalties Legislation* [1984] PNGLR 314 at 334-335, the NGDPs reflect a great idealism of the people of PNG. The NGDPs, in their totality, form PNG's ideology.[12]

Aims and implementation

The NGDPs, as envisioned by the CPC, were to act as the catalyst for restructuring PNG's society. This was to be attained through the:

---

8 Brunton, *Constitutionality and Resource Development in Papua New Guinea* (National Research Institute Discussion Paper Number 77) (National Research Institute, Port Moresby, 1994), p 3.

9 See the discussion of the implementation of the eight aims by Utula Samana, "The Eight Aims, Development and Decentralisation: The Morobe Experience" in King, Lee and Warakai (eds), *Papua New Guinea's Eight Point Plan and National Goals after a Decade: From Rhetoric to Reality (Papers from the Fifteenth Waigani Seminar)* (UPNG Press, Port Moresby, 1985), pp 209-222.

10 Constitutional Planning Committee, *Final Report of the Constitutional Planning Committee 1974 (Part1)* (Government Printing Office, Port Moresby, 1974), p 2/2, paras 8-9.

11 Narakobi, *The Melanesian Way* (Institute of PNG Studies, 1983), p 10.

12 Ghai, "Constitution Making and Decolonisation" in Ghai (ed), *Law, Politics and Government in the Pacific Island States* (Institute of Pacific Studies, University of the South Pacific, Suva, 1988), p 49.

> "[f]undamental re-orientation of our attitudes and the institutions of government, commerce, education and religion towards Papua New Guinea forms of participation, consultation, and consensus, and a continuous renewal of the responsiveness of these institutions to the needs and attitudes of the People (No 5(1))."[13]

Regan has argued that the NGDPs are aimed at striking a balance between the civil and political rights of individuals on the one hand, and social and economic rights on the other hand.[14] By contrast, Barnett J said, in *The State v NTN Pty Ltd* [1992] PNGLR 1 at 17, that the NGDPs are aimed at promoting "national identity, integrity and self respect". The NGDPs, therefore, according to Barnett J (at 13), "embody the principles and spirit which is intended to enlighten the legal prose". Generally, it is agreed that the NGDPs are to be the "guiding lamp" for the working of the government[15] and its instrumentalities.

The CPC was mindful of the difficulty of implementing the NGDPs. The CPC said:

> "We are well aware that it is one thing to establish inspiring goals for the nation, and sound principles to guide the government and our people in seeking to achieve these goals, yet quite another for effective steps to be taken which are directed towards achieving these goals."[16]

The CPC therefore recommended that all activities of the state and its institutions should be based on the *Directive Principles* and directed towards achieving the *National Goals*. It was envisaged that, by taking this approach, it would help to reorient the thinking and attitudes of everyone who is a member of an elected body or who works in a government department, institution or authority, and to redirect the policies of those bodies towards the goals.[17]

These recommendations found form under s 25(2) of the *Constitution*. Section 25(2) states that:

> "Nevertheless, it is the duty of all governmental bodies to apply and give effect to them as far as lies within their respective powers."

The *Constitution* encourages collaboration by all governmental bodies in the implementation of the NGDPs. The Ombudsman Commission is, however, given the specific duty to take the NGDPs into full account in the performance of its functions.[18]

The government implements the NGDPs mainly through the introduction and adoption of government policies. The various national policies that are introduced and adopted by the government spell out specifically that the policies are aimed at implementing either one or some of the NGDPs. For instance, the Environment Policy of 1976, the National Forest Policy of 1990 and the Fisheries Policy of 1993 implement Goal 4, and the National Information Policy implements Goals 1, 2, 3 and 5. Laws that give effect to these and other policies therefore implement the NGDPs. This relationship was exposed in *Chern Jin Fa v Naniura* [1990] PNGLR 506.

---

13 Weisbrot, "The Impact of the Papua New Guinea Constitution on the Recognition and Application of Customary Law" in Sack (ed), *Pacific Constitutions: Proceedings of the Canberra Law Workshop VI* (ANU Printing Services, Canberra, 1982), p 273.

14 Regan, "Constitutionalism, Legitimacy and the Judiciary" in James and Fraser (eds), *Legal Issues in a Developing Society* (UPNG, Faculty of Law, Port Moresby, 1992), p 26.

15 Weisbrot, Paliwala and Sawyerr (eds), *Law and Social Change in Papua New Guinea* (Butterworths, Sydney, 1982), p 7. See also *The State v NTN Pty Ltd* [1992] PNGLR 1 at 17.

16 Constitutional Planning Committee, op cit n 10, p 2/15.

17 Ibid.

18 *Constitution*, s 25(4).

In this case, the appellant was charged with fishing illegally in Papua New Guinean waters, and was convicted by the District Court. On appeal to the National Court, Los J considered the relationship between Goal 4 and the *Fisheries Act* (Ch 214), and held (at 511) that:

> "[t]he *Constitution* of Papua New Guinea through the Fourth Goal calls for wise use of the natural resources on the land, air and in the sea ... Those calls have been translated into regulatory form and they appear for example in the *Fisheries Act* (Ch No 214), the *Tuna Resources Management Act* (Ch No 224) and the *Continental Shelf (Living Natural Resources Act* (Ch No 210)".

Enforcement

The NGDPs are non-justiciable[19] or, in other words, they are generally not enforceable. Section 25(1) of the *Constitution* expressly states that "except to the extent provided in Subsection (3) and (4), the National Goals and Directive Principles are non-justiciable". This proviso allows for a partial enforcement of the NGDPs.[20] Subsections (3) and (4) are in the following terms:

> "(3) Where any law, or any power conferred by any law (whether the power be of a legislative, judicial, executive, administrative or other kind), can reasonably be understood, applied, exercised or enforced, without failing to give effect to the intention of the Parliament or to this *Constitution*, in such a way as to give effect to the National Goals and Directive Principles, or at least not to derogate them, it is to be understood, applied or exercised, and shall be enforced, in that way.
>
> (4) Subsection (1) does not apply to the jurisdiction of the Ombudsman Commission or of any other body prescribed for the purposes of Division III.2 (leadership code)[21], which shall take the National Goals and Directive Principles fully into account in all cases as appropriate."

The CPC was aware of the limited enforceability of the NGDPs. The CPC, therefore, recommended that the courts and other tribunals, "like other institutions of government, be guided in carrying out their functions by the National Goals and Directive Principles".[22] By this, the CPC meant that:

> "... the courts and other tribunals should, in interpreting the law, the procedures they adopt for the hearing of cases, and in other aspects of their work, try to give effect to the goals and principles. Where the meaning of a particular law or rule of law is unclear or ambiguous, the courts should give an interpretation which is consistent with the goals and principles and not contrary to them."[23]

The power of the courts under s 25 and other provisions of the *Constitution*, including ss 22, 39, 60 and Sch 2.3, is very wide. According to Prentice DCJ in *Peter*

---

19 Schedule 1.7 of the *Constitution* states that "Where a Constitutional Law declares a question to be non-justiciable, the question may not be heard or determined by any court or tribunal, but nothing in this section limits the jurisdiction of the Ombudsman Commission or of any other tribunal established for the purposes of Division III.2 (*leadership code*)." The issue of non-justiciability was discussed by the Supreme Court a year after independence in *The State v The Independent Tribunal; Ex parte Sasakila* [1976] PNGLR 491 at 499-500 (Frost CJ).

20 Regan, "Constitutionalism, Legitimacy and the Judiciary" in James and Fraser (eds), *Legal Issues in a Developing Society* (UPNG, Faculty of Law, Port Moresby, 1992).

21 The Supreme Court has ruled that this body is the Leadership Tribunal: see *SCR No 2 of 1992* [1992] PNGLR 336 at 346.

22 Constitutional Planning Committee, op cit n 10, p 2/16, para 126.

23 Ibid.

v South Pacific Brewery [1976] PNGLR 537 at 555, the vesting of these wide powers in the courts is "frightening". Prentice DCJ also said (at 555) that this power enables the courts:

> "to select, discard, interpret, modify and apply the law. There is even power given to the Supreme Court to dispense with the application of a valid law in a particular case by declaring an Act done thereunder unlawful if harsh and oppressive".

This is one of a list of authorities that show that the judiciary has been vigilant in its efforts to implement the NGDPs through the exercise of its powers under s 25.

In a short study on how the Supreme Court had handled the NGDPs in the period from 1975 to 1980, Peter Bayne reviewed eight cases, and concluded that "the courts have occasionally relied on the provisions which permit reference to the Preamble, the National Goals and the Basic Social Obligation".[24] According to Bayne, the courts were cautious and reluctant to take on the challenge placed on them by the CPC during this early period. For example, he found that in *Rakatani Peter v South Pacific Brewery* only Prentice DCJ made reference to Goal 2(4) of the NGDPs, while the other two judges (Frost CJ and Kearney J) declined to rely on the NGDPs. Also, in *Constitutional Reference No 1 of 1978* [1978] PNGLR 460 (*Re Leo Morgan*), the Supreme Court did not rely on Goal 3(1) to support its views.[25] In *The State v The Independent Tribunal; Ex parte Sasakila* [1976] PNGLR 491, the court was faced with the task of quashing or confirming a decision of the Leadership Tribunal to dismiss Mr Sasakila as a Minister and a Member of Parliament. In reaching its decision on this crucial issue, the Supreme Court refused to seek any guidance from the NGDPs.

Apart from the case of *Rakatani Peter v South Pacific Brewery*, most Supreme Court judges after 1980 have responded positively to the challenge espoused by the CPC. Examples include *SCR No 3 of 1986; Reference by Simbu Provincial Executive, Re Raka Ruk* [1991] PNGLR 105, *The State v NTN Pty Ltd* [1992] PNGLR 1 and *Haiveta v Wingti (No 3)* [1994] PNGLR 197. These cases reflect the desire of the courts to ensure that the visions and aspirations of the people, as contained in the NGDPs, are implemented and alive.

The change in the attitude of the courts after 1980 may be attributed to the events that proceeded from the famous "Rooney Affair". The history of the affair is recorded in *Public Prosecutor v Rooney (No 1)* [1979] PNGLR 403 and *Public Prosecutor v Rooney (No 2)* [1979] PNGLR 448. As a result of this controversy, the expatriates who dominated the bench resigned or retired. For the first time, a Papua New Guinean was appointed Chief Justice, along with other nationals as judges of the National and Supreme Courts. They, with their non-indigenous colleagues, have readily sought (and continue to seek) guidance from the NGDPs in resolving difficult constitutional issues. However, as Regan correctly pointed out:

> "while the courts were to have an important role [enforcement of NGDPs] it is also clear this was not to be an initiating one – that was to be left to the legislature and the executive".[26]

The legislature's response to the NGDPs has mainly been in the form of legislation. The approach by the legislature is to declare in the statute that the legislation

24 Bayne, "The Constitution in the Courts 1975-1980" in Weisbrot, Paliwala and Sawyerr (eds), op cit n 15, pp 227-228.

25 Ibid.

26 Regan, op cit n 20.

either gives effect to, or is in compliance with, a particular NGDP or a number of NGDPs. Various pieces of legislation bear this declaration in their preambles. Examples include the *Environmental Planning Act* 1978,[27] the *Fisheries Act* 1994, the *Forestry Act* 1991 and the *Organic Law on Provincial Governments and Local-Level Governments* 1995.

The enforcement, by the executive, the state instrumentalities and the courts, of legislation effecting the NGDPs, plays an important part in the enforcement of the NGDPs.

3.3 CONCLUSION

The partial implementation of the NGDPs has been a cause for concern amongst a number of individuals and institutions.

In its analysis of the implementation of the NGDPs from 1975 to 1982, the General Constitutional Commission concluded that there was a failure at every level of government in implementing the NGDPs.[28] In 1994, a similar observation was made by Brian Brunton.[29] Both recommended that the NGDPs be made enforceable. The legal implications of this proposition have not been fully analysed. Colquhoun-Kerr, commenting on this proposal, said:

> "Presumably, it [General Constitutional Commission] intends that the National Goals and Directive Principles be re-drafted in the form of self-executing laws and that section 25(1), (2) and (4) of the *Constitution* be repealed."[30]

The consequence of such a move would be that:

> "The National Goals and Directive Principles would then operate both so as to impose mandatory duties upon the various arms of government and so as to invalidate, to the extent of the inconsistency, all acts (whether legislative, executive or judicial) that were inconsistent with them."[31]

The General Constitutional Commission also proposed that the "non-compliance with the National Goals and Directive Principles should be a ground for the dismissal of the government or the holder of any leadership office".[32] These reform proposals did not find favour with the Parliament at that time. The General Constitutional Commission's final report was never debated by Parliament. Consequently, its recommendations remain dormant.

The non-justiciability of the NGDPs has not been a hindrance to their evolution and application in the country. There is ample evidence that the legislature, the judiciary and the government have played a major role in the elevation, protection and expansion of the NGDPs. As the Supreme Court noted in *The State v NTN Pty Ltd* [1992] PNGLR 1, the spirit of the people who had given themselves the *Constitution*, which is illuminated in the NGDPs as a glowing light, must be

---

27 Revised Laws, Ch No 370.

28 General Constitutional Commission, *General Constitutional Commission Final Report* (Government Printer, Port Moresby, 1983), pp 19-20.

29 Brunton, op cit n 8.

30 Colquhoun-Kerr, "Sources of Political Legitimacy in Conflict and Naturalised Foreigners: Some Comments on the General constitutional Commission's Final Report, 1983" in De Vere, Colquhoun-Kerr and Kaburise (eds), *Essays on the Constitution of Papua New Guinea* (Government Printing Office, Port Moresby, 1985), p 116.

31 Ibid.

32 Ibid.

given effect wherever it is fairly possible to do so. To this end, the Planning the New Century Committee declared in its 1998 report that:

> "Kumul 2020 accepts the Five National Goals and Directive Principles as the broad goals set out by the *Constitution*. It adopts, reasserts, and builds on these broad aims as the foundation directives upon which Kumul 2020 stands."[33]

The Parliament, courts and the government have not shied away from their role under s 25 of the *Constitution*. They have played, and continue to play, a very pro-active role in moving the country in the direction envisaged by the NGDPs.

33 This committee (also known as the "Baloiloi Committee") was set up in 1996 by the Chan Government to develop and formulate a vision statement for the development of PNG over the next 25 years. The committee completed its task in 1998, and came up with a very comprehensive report on a vision statement, entitled *Kumul 2020 – Preparing Papua New Guinea for Prosperity in the 21st Century*. The committee had hoped to present its report to the Skate Government in that year, but due to political differences, the Skate Government refused to accept the report. The report has not become an official document of the government.

Chapter 4

HIERARCHY OF LAWS OF PAPUA NEW GUINEA

4.1 INTRODUCTION

The *Constitution* of Papua New Guinea (PNG) is a very complex and difficult document, especially in the area of hierarchy of laws. The *Constitution* itself provides for various categories of laws that are not clear to the ordinary Papua New Guinean. Most of these laws are listed in s 9 of the *Constitution*. Other sections of the *Constitution* and the *Organic Law on Provincial Governments and Local-level Governments* (OLPGLLG) spell out the ways that laws in the different categories relate to one another.

This chapter highlights and outlines the factors that make each category of law distinctive, and the way that laws in these different categories relate to one another.

4.2 CHARACTERISTICS OF THE CATEGORIES OF LAWS

The categories of laws are set out in s 9 of the *Constitution* in the following terms:

> "The laws of Papua New Guinea consists of:
>
> (a) this *Constitution*; and
>
> (b) the Organic Laws; and
>
> (c) the Acts of the Parliament; and
>
> (d) Emergency Regulations; and
>
> (da) the provincial laws; and
>
> (e) laws made under or adopted by or under this *Constitution* or any of those laws including subordinate legislative enactments made under this *Constitution* or any of those laws; and
>
> (f) the underlying law
>
> and none other."

This provision enumerates the sources of laws of PNG. It is clearly an exclusionary clause and prohibits the creation and recognition of any other sources of law outside its ambit. Section 9 also plays another pivotal role; it provides the hierarchy of laws in PNG. To identify the characteristics of each category of law, and to understand how each of these laws operates, reference will be made to:

the relevant background issues (origins, purpose etc), any necessary definitions or special considerations;

the body or bodies that can make the laws;

what the constitutional laws say about the manner in which laws of the category are to be made;

what the constitutional laws say about altering or repealing laws in the category (if the provisions concerning alteration are different from those concerning the making of laws in the category);

the subject matter with which laws in the category can deal; and

the relationship of laws in the category with other categories of laws.

4.2.1 The Constitution: s 9(a)

The *Constitution* was enacted by the Constituent Assembly in August 1975, and was brought into effect on 16 September 1975. It has been amended 22 times since its enactment. The first amendment ushered in the provincial government system in 1976, and the latest amendment was in relation to the integrity of political parties.

The term "constitution" is not specifically defined by the *Constitution*. However, Sch 1.2 of the *Constitution* defines "constitutional law" as "this *Constitution*, a law altering this *Constitution* or an Organic Law". According to s 11 of the *Constitution*, the *Constitution* and the Organic Laws are the supreme laws of PNG.[1] Reading these two provisions, it may appear that the Organic Laws are of the same stature as the *Constitution*. However, s 9 clearly states that the *Constitution* is superior to an Organic Law.

The *Constitution* can be amended by following the procedures set out in ss 13-17 of the *Constitution*. Only the Parliament has the power to alter the *Constitution*. Section 13 stipulates that the *Constitution* cannot be amended by the Parliament unless the amending law is expressed to be a law to alter the *Constitution*. The specific procedure for altering the *Constitution* is set out in s 14. This section contains two sets of procedures. The first set of procedures must be followed before the proposed law is introduced in Parliament. The second set of procedures applies when the proposed law is introduced into Parliament. The requirements of the first set of procedures have been summarised by Amet CJ in *Kaseng v Namaliu* [1995] PNGLR 481. The Chief Justice said that there are four main requirements of this section.[2]

The nature of the requirements under s 14 became one of the central issues in *Kaseng v Namaliu*. In that case, the applicant, who was the Premier for Western Province, sought orders from the Supreme Court to declare that *Constitutional Amendment No 16* 1995 and the *Organic Law on Provincial Governments and Local-level Governments* 1995 (OLPGLLG), which ushered in the "reformed" provincial government system, were null and void as they contravened ss 12, 13 and 14 of the *Constitution*.

---

1 A similar provision is found in the constitutions of a number of the Pacific Island states, eg, Cook Islands' *Constitution*, Art 39; Fiji's *Constitution* 1990, s 2; Marshall Islands' *Constitution*, Art 1(1); Solomon Islands' *Constitution*, s 2; Vanuatu's *Constitution*, s 2.

2 It is submitted that his Honour was referring to the four main requirements of the first procedure, namely, that the proposed law must be: (a) published by the Speaker in full in the *National Gazette*; (b) circulated, in accordance with the *Standing Orders of the Parliament*; (c) to all members of Parliament; (d) not less than one month before it is formally introduced into the Parliament.

On 27 June 1995, the Parliament simultaneously passed *Constitutional Amendment No 16* and the OLPGLLG. Both laws came into operation on 19 July 1995. *Constitutional Amendment No 16,* which was entitled *Constitutional Amendment (Provincial Governments and Local-level Governments),* repealed and replaced s 187 of the *Constitution.* This section established the provincial government system that was introduced in 1976. The OLPGLLG repealed and replaced the *Organic Law on Provincial Governments* that was enacted and came into operation in 1977. The enactment of these two laws resulted in the applicant and all the provincial politicians losing their jobs.

The applicant argued that the Parliament had not complied with the one-month notice period under s 14. There was no dispute that the notice was circulated 21 days prior to it being tabled in Parliament. The Supreme Court unanimously held that the requirements of s 14 were mandatory and, by a majority, further held that, in the absence of any provision in the Standing Orders specifying the manner of circulation, the requirement for one month's circulation was directory and not mandatory at this stage.

The requirements of the second set of procedures under s 14 (that is, after the proposed law has been introduced into Parliament) are that the proposed law must be:

- debated during different meetings separated by two months;
- supported by the prescribed majority under s 17; and
- passed after opportunity for debate.

These requirements were first tested by the Supreme Court in *SCR No 3 of 1984; Re Constitutional Alterations* [1984] PNGLR 375. The Supreme Court was not given the opportunity to determine the first limb of s 14. It was more concerned with the requirements of the second set of procedures. The Supreme Court concluded that the requirements of s 14 were mandatory.

In *Kaseng v Namaliu* [1995] PNGLR 481, the Supreme Court considered the issue of "opportunity for debate". The majority took the view that, because no Member of Parliament complained about this issue, it was imperative that there was compliance. Kapi DCJ, in a strong dissenting judgment, reviewed the proceedings of Parliament and found that only eight Members of Parliament spoke on the proposed law, and the procedures of Parliament relating to review by Permanent Parliamentary Committees were breached.[3] Following the decision in *SCR No 3 of 1984; Re Constitutional Alterations,* his Honour held that there was no adequate and meaningful opportunity for debate.

The *Constitution* is a broad legal document and covers a wide range of subject matters. The *Constitution* is not limited in any manner, except by s 100(3). This provision prohibits the Parliament from permanently transferring its law-making power to any other authority or person through a constitutional law.

In terms of its relationship to other laws, the *Constitution* is the supreme law. All other laws must comply with it. Where a law is inconsistent with the *Constitution,* it will be declared null and void. This is shown in the cases of *SCR No 2 of 1984; Re New Ireland Constitution* [1984] PNGLR 81; *SCR No 2 of 1982; Re Organic Law* [1982] PNGLR 214; and *The State v NTN Ltd* [1992] PNGLR 1.

3 In this case, the Permanent Parliamentary Referral Committee on Justice.

4.2.2 The Organic Laws: s 9(b)

Organic Laws are part of the *Constitution*. Together with the *Constitution* they are the supreme laws of the country. Organic Laws are really the creatures of the *Constitution*, as they derive their existence from the *Constitution*. The draftsman of the *Constitution* explained that "there is no especial magic in the word 'Organic' and that it has no great technical meaning".[4] The idea of making Organic Laws part of the *Constitution* was really a compromise between the Constitutional Planning Committee's report, which contained more than 550 recommendations, and the government's wish to have a relatively short and simple constitution. Lynch points out that "a concept of subsidiary constitutional laws borrowed from the Israeli *Constitution* and certain European constitutions"[5] were developed further to become the Organic Laws. The result was that Organic Laws were introduced to cover in detail certain aspects of the *Constitution* and, consequently, the *Constitution* was made shorter.

Section 12 of the *Constitution* provides for the creation of Organic Laws. It states:

> "(1) For the purposes of this *Constitution*, an Organic Law is a law made by the Parliament that is:
>
> (a) for or in respect of a matter provision for which by way of an Organic Law is expressly authorised by this *Constitution*; and
>
> (b) expressed to be an Organic Law.
>
> (2) An Organic Law may be altered only by another Organic Law, or by an alteration to this *Constitution*."

This provision first came before the Supreme Court for determination in 1976 in the case of *The State v The Independent Tribunal; Ex Parte Sasakila* [1976] PNGLR 491. In this case, the court was asked to decide whether or not Mr Sasakila was validly dismissed as a Member of Parliament by a Leadership Tribunal established under s 27(5) of the *Organic Law on the Duties and Responsibilities of Leadership*. Frost CJ (at 494-495), commenting on the relationship between the Organic Law and s 12(1) of the *Constitution*, said that "an Organic Law is a law made by Parliament in respect of a matter provision for which by way of an Organic Law is expressly authorised by the Constitution". The other two members of the court did not avert to this section.

The question of what is meant by the phrase "expressly authorised by the *Constitution*" became a crucial issue in the case of *Kaseng v Namaliu* [1995] PNGLR 481. The applicant argued that as *Constitutional Amendment No 16* and the OLPGLLG were enacted at the same time and came into operation simultaneously, the OLPGLLG was not expressly authorised by s 12(1)(a), and was therefore null and void. The majority (Amet CJ and Hinchliff and Andrew JJ) held that the OLPGLLG was validly enacted by Parliament. Kapi DCJ and Los J set out strong reasons for their dissent. Both firmly held that the OLPGLLG could not have been authorised by the *Constitution*, because *Constitutional Amendment No 16*, which authorised the OPLGLLG, was not enacted first in time and space. Their view was that because the OLPGLLG was enacted at the same time and brought into force at the same instance with *Constitutional Amendment No 16*, it was not expressly authorised.

---

4 Lynch, "The Achievement of Independence in Papua New Guinea: The Legal Aspect" (1980) 3 *Journal of Pacific History* 175 at 191.

5 Ibid.

This decision may be compared with a number of Organic Laws that were enacted before the *Constitution* came into operation. These laws were called "provisional Organic Laws", and were passed by the National Constituent Assembly prior to independence. Some of these Organic Laws include the:

(a) *Organic Law on the National Elections* (which was repealed in 1996 and replaced by the *Organic Law on National and Local-level Government Elections*);

(b) *Organic Law on the Ombudsman Commission;*

(c) *Organic Law on the Duties and Responsibilities of Leadership*; and the

(d) *Organic Law on Provincial Boundaries.*

Provisional Organic Laws

The courts have discussed these provisional Organic Laws at length at various stages. For instance, the history and purpose of the *Leadership Code* has been discussed by *The State v The Independent Tribunal; Ex Parte Sasakila* [1976] PNGLR 491. The powers and functions of the Ombudsman Commission under the *Organic Law on the Ombudsman Commission* were considered in *Ombudsman Commission of Papua New Guinea v Donohoe* [1988] PNGLR 348. The origin and aims of the *Organic Law on the National Elections* have been dealt with in the case of *In Re Moresby North East Election Petition* [1977] PNGLR 424.

Could it be argued that these Organic Laws were not expressly authorised by the *Constitution*? Lynch gives the reason why these provisional Organic Laws were enacted before independence. He states that:

> "It will be seen that the adoption of the 'Organic Law' concept meant that unless at Independence at least some of the Organic Laws had been approved in some form or other, the Independent State of Papua New Guinea could come into existence without a complete constitution – which was not what was wanted and would have been contrary to undertakings given by the Papua New Guinea Government to various groups in the country."[6]

He states further that:

> "The National Constituent Assembly, however, was a 'home-grown' institution and did not owe anything to any other country, and so it was decided that, if the Constituent Assembly made documents (which would not at that stage be 'laws') that it declared to be 'provisional' Organic Laws or 'provisional' Acts of the Parliament, the *Constitution* itself would give them force of law when it came into operation on Independence Day; they would then become the first Organic Laws or the first Acts Parliament, as the case may be."[7]

The fundamental difference between the situation in *Kaseng v Namaliu* [1995] PNGLR 481 and the provisional Organic Laws is that, in the latter case, the Organic Laws were enacted and came into operation together with the *Constitution* pursuant to ss 266 and 267 of the *Constitution*. In *Kaseng v Namaliu*, the OLPGLLG had to meet a pre-condition that *it had to be expressly authorised*. Being enacted simultaneously with the authorising law and coming into force together with that same law, did not give the OLPGLLG its validity. As Los J correctly pointed out:

6 See Lynch, op cit n 4 at 192-193.
7 Ibid.

"It is fundamentally wrong, in my view, to proceed on the basis that an authorising bill may be passed together with an authorised bill. It may be possible, though I think offensive, to enact certain rules and regulations simultaneously with an Act that is supposed to authorise these rules, but the importance of an Organic Law is such that it has to go through the ss 12 and 14 requirements separately."[8]

Making, altering and repealing Organic Laws

The procedures for making, altering and repealing Organic Laws are the same as those for altering and repealing provisions of the *Constitution*. The only exception is a law envisaged by s 12(3) of the *Constitution*. The operation of s 12(3) was explained by the Supreme Court in *SCR No 2 of 1982; Re Organic Law* [1982] PNGLR 214. In 1981, the Parliament increased the nomination fees for national elections from K100 to K1,000 by amending s 86(c) of the *Organic Law on National Elections*. The Parliament complied with the provisions of ss 14 and 17 of the *Constitution*. The Ombudsman Commission sought the Supreme Court's opinion on three issues. The relevant issue was whether s 86(c) may be altered by a simple majority or only by a special majority. It was not disputed that the alteration to the Organic Law was dealt with as an ordinary Act of Parliament and was passed on the voices. It was also agreed that s 86(c) was one of the provisions enumerated under s 1 of the *Organic Law on National Elections*[9] that came under the ambit of s 12(3) of the *Constitution*. The Ombudsman Commission argued that the Parliament did not comply with the requirements of ss 14 and 17 of the *Constitution*, because the amendment was not published in the National Gazette by the Speaker of Parliament, circulated to all the members of Parliament one month in advance, and debated on two occasions supported by a division.

The Supreme Court held that s 12(3) of the *Constitution* only deals with the size of the majority of votes, and does not affect the procedural requirements of the *Constitution* relating to an Organic Law. It went on to say that, being a part of the Organic Law, the alteration of s 86(c) should have complied with the procedural requirements of s 14 of the *Constitution*.

Interestingly, similar grounds and arguments were raised by the Ombudsman Commission in 1992 in *SCR No 1 of 1992* [1992] PNGLR 77. In this instance, the Parliament complied with all the rules set out in *SCR No 2 of 1982* and raised the nomination fee from K100 to K1,000. When the Ombudsman Commission referred the matter to the Supreme Court under s 19 of the *Constitution*, the court ruled that the amendment to the *Organic Law on National Elections* was validly made and that it did not prohibit the citizens from exercising their right to stand for elections under s 50 of the *Constitution*.

Organic Laws may only cover those subject matters that they are explicitly required to provide for under the *Constitution*. Unless laws are expressly stated, they cannot be Organic Laws.

The relationship of Organic Laws to other laws is similar to the *Constitution*'s relationship to other laws. The only law to which the Organic Laws are subject is the *Constitution*. In *SCR No 5 of 1992* [1992] PNGLR 114, the Supreme Court was asked to decide whether amendments to the *Organic Law on National Elections*, requiring voters to be photographed for purposes of identification before voting, were contrary to s 49 of the *Constitution*. The Supreme Court ruled that the amendment to the Organic Law was a violation of a citizen's right to privacy under

---

8 *Kaseng v Namaliu* [1995] PNGLR 481 at 507.

9 The only other law that has a similar provision is the *Organic Law on the Ombudsman Commission*.

s 49 of the *Constitution*. An Act of Parliament, or a provision of an Act of Parliament, that is inconsistent with an Organic Law, will be declared invalid. In *Re Sigulogo* [1988-1989] PNGLR 384, the Supreme Court held that s 13 of the *Commissions of Inquiry Act* (Ch 31), which prevented the use of evidence adduced in a Commission of Inquiry in a Leadership Tribunal, was inconsistent with s 27(4) of the *Organic Law on the Duties and Responsibilities of Leadership* and was, therefore, invalid and of no effect.

4.2.3 Acts of the Parliament: s 9(c)

Schedule 1.2 of the *Constitution* stipulates that "an Act of Parliament means a law (other than a Constitutional Law) made by the Parliament, and includes a subordinate legislative enactment made under any such law". The Constitutional Planning Committee (CPC) had seriously considered the role of the Parliament and concluded that:

> "The primary powers of the National Parliament under our proposal will be to make laws for the peace, progress and welfare of Papua New Guinea."[10]

The power of the Parliament to enact these types of laws is vested by s 100 of the *Constitution*. The recommendation of the CPC finds form in s 109. This provision grants plenary powers to the Parliament to make laws "having effect within and outside the country, for the peace, order and good government of Papua New Guinea and the welfare of the people". Section 109(3) clearly expresses that the question of whether an Act of Parliament has been made for the peace, order and good government of PNG is not open to challenge in any court.[11] The Parliament is also permitted, under ss 109(1), 109(3)(b) and 110(2), to enact laws that can have an extra-territorial or retrospective effect.

The power of the Parliament to enact a law having a retrospective effect was tested in 1986 in *NTN Pty Ltd v The State* [1986] PNGLR 167. In 1985, the state and the applicant entered into an agreement whereby the applicant was permitted to broadcast television in the country beginning in 1986. In pursuance of that agreement, the applicant went about setting up a television station in the country. There was a change in government in 1986. The new government, through the Parliament, exercised its legislative powers under s 109(3)(b) and enacted the *Radiocommunications (Television) Regulation* 1986, which prohibited the broadcast of television until 31 January 1988. This Regulation purported to retrospectively limit the operation of the contract entered into between the state and the applicant in 1985. The National Court ruled that the Regulation was invalid as it was prohibitory. To avoid the effect of the National Court ruling, the Parliament again exercised its powers under the same section and enacted the *Television (Prohibition and Control) Act* 1986. This Act again prohibited television broadcast until 31 January 1988. This Act also purported to retrospectively prohibit NTN Pty Ltd from broadcasting television in PNG. NTN applied to the National Court pursuant to s 57 of the *Constitution*, seeking enforcement of its right to the freedom of information under s 46 of the *Constitution*. The matter eventually went on appeal to the Supreme Court in *The State v NTN Pty Ltd* [1992] PNGLR 1. The Supreme Court held that the Act was unconstitutional, as it did not comply with

---

10 Constitutional Planning Committee, *Final Report of the Constitutional Planning Committee 1974 (Part 1)* (Government Printer, Port Moresby, 1974), pp 6/7 and 6/24.

11 However, see how the court was drawn into deliberating this issue in an Australia court in *Building Construction Employees and Builders' Labourers Federation (NSW) v Minister for Industrial Relations* (1986) 7 NSWLR 372 at 382-385 and 421-422.

s 38 and it also violated the applicant's right to publish and broadcast information under s 46 of the *Constitution*.

The wide-ranging legislative power of the Parliament is, however, limited by the *Constitution* itself, as was highlighted by Kapi J in *Minister for Lands v Frame* [1980] PNGLR 433. In that case, the state compulsorily acquired the respondent's land and paid him compensation for the acquisition pursuant to the *Lands Acquisition Act* 1974. The question of the amount of compensation went on appeal to the Supreme Court. In considering the validity of the Act against s 53 of the *Constitution* regarding compensation, his Honour said (at 470-471):

> "The legislative power is vested in the National Parliament (s 100 of the *Constitution*). This power, however, is made subject to the other provisions of the *Constitution*. Where restrictions or limitations are placed by the *Constitution*, the Parliament may only legislate within these bounds; or where the *Constitution* provides for something, no Act of Parliament may be passed so as to be inconsistent with that provision."

An example of a provision of the *Constitution* that limits the legislative power of the Parliament under this provision is s 37(7), which prohibits the Parliament from enacting a law that retrospectively makes an act illegal. A number of other provisions of the *Constitution* have also been relied on to cut down pieces of legislation. Examples of such cases include *Constitutional Reference No 3 of 1978; Re Inter-Group Fighting Act 1977* [1982] PNGLR 421; *SCR No 1A of 1981; Re Motor Traffic Act* [1982] PNGLR 122; *SCR No 3 of 1993; Re Internal Security Act* [1994] PNGLR 341; and *The State v NTN Pty Ltd* [1992] PNGLR 1.

The procedure for making an Act of Parliament is quite simple. PNG's system of government is basically a Westminster export model. Therefore, the ordinary parliamentary processes of enacting an Act in the United Kingdom and Australia apply to PNG. The procedure for making an ordinary law by Parliament is set out both in the *Constitution* (particularly ss 110, 111, 114 and 210) and the Standing Orders[12] of Parliament. According to these provisions, the procedure for enacting a law is:

- introduction of the bill by any Member of Parliament and First Reading;
- Second Reading and debate;
- Third Reading and passage by a simple majority of those Members present and voting;
- law certified by Speaker; and
- law brought into force.

A number of mechanisms may come into play at various stages of the passage of the law. The procedure for amending or repealing an Act is similar to the procedure for making it.

Apart from the various statutes that have been enacted by Parliament since independence in 1975, a number of pre-independence statutes were also adopted as part of the laws of PNG at independence. These pre-independence statutes were adopted as Acts of Parliament by virtue of Sch 2.6(2) of the *Constitution*. Some of these statutes include the:

- *Criminal Code Act* (Ch 262);
- *Land Act* (Ch 185), repealed and replaced by the *Land Act* 1996;
- *Evidence Act* (Ch 48);

---

12 See Standing Orders, ss 191-220.

- *District Courts Act* (Ch 40);
- *Mining Act* (Ch 195), repealed and replaced by the *Mining Act* 1992; and
- *Forestry Act* (Ch 216), repealed and replaced by the *Forestry Act* 1991.
- *Evidence Act* (Ch 48).

The position of these laws is that they are deemed to have been made by the Parliament. Their status is the same as those laws enacted by Parliament after independence. Acts of Parliament are lower in status to the *Constitution*, Organic Laws and Emergency Regulations.

4.2.4 Emergency Regulations: s 9(d)

PNG emerged from its colonial period without any violence or major upheaval. However, it became an independent state at a time when many other emerging states were experiencing difficult social and political turmoils. The CPC was aware that:

> "... there are times of great national crisis or emergency due to war, very serious civil disturbances such as organised attacks on many government officers, or natural disasters such as famine, an earthquake or a fire. The first and third of these situations are all too familiar to many of us, who remember the Pacific War and natural disasters such as the Mount Lamington eruption in 1951 and the Highlands' famine in 1972."[13]

The CPC's major concern was the exercise of power in times of national crisis or emergency. The CPC was mindful of the temptation of the executive arm of government to abuse power during times of emergency. The CPC said:

> "Too often, in other countries, the wide powers which governments are able to exercise in public emergency situations are used arbitrarily, without regard to the fundamental rights and freedoms of the people."[14]

The CPC wanted very much to strike a balance between the exercise of power by the executive to promptly and effectively engage in times of emergencies and the protection of fundamental rights and freedoms of the citizens during the period of emergencies. It said:

> "We have given very careful thought to the question of what powers should be exercised by the executive government in public emergency situations, as we fully appreciate the need to ensure that, on the one hand, the executive is able to cope with crisis situations promptly and effectively, whilst on the other hand, the rights of individuals should not be disregarded."[15]

To prevent any abuse by the executive government in times of national emergencies, the CPC suggested that "the introduction and continuation of emergency powers should be subject to effective and regular parliamentary control". The government and the National Constituent Assembly agreed that the Parliament should ensure strict control of the exercise of emergency powers by the executive arm of government.[16]

---

13 Constitutional Planning Committee, op cit n 10, p 5/2/1.
14 Ibid.
15 Ibid.
16 See Goldring, *The Constitution of Papua New Guinea* (Law Book Co Ltd, Sydney, 1978), p 248.

Emergency laws

Part X of the *Constitution* (ss 226-246) deals with states of emergency. Section 226 contains a list of definitions of specific words and terms used in this part of the *Constitution*. For our present purposes, the relevant terms we need to consider are "emergency regulation" and "emergency law". According to s 226, an "emergency regulation" means a law that is made in accordance with s 231. Section 231 provides for emergency regulations that can be made by the National Executive Council (NEC). These laws are to cater for the emergency until the Parliament meets. An emergency regulation expires after 28 days, or 14 days after the Parliament meets, whichever is the earliest. The Parliament can, however, extend an emergency regulation for a longer period.

The definition of the phrase "emergency law" means:

(a) an Emergency Act; or

(b) an Emergency Regulation.

Together, these species of law are called emergency laws. Emergency Acts are made pursuant to s 230 of the *Constitution*. An Emergency Act can be made before or during a period of national emergency. A number of permanent Emergency Acts have been made by Parliament pursuant to this section. These include the:

- *Emergency Committees Act* (Ch 33A);
- *Emergency (Custody of Members of Parliament) Act* (Ch 33B);
- *Emergency (General Powers) Act*;
- *Curfew Act* 1987; and
- *Emergency (Defence Force) Act* 1994.

The Emergency Committee first mooted the *Curfew Act* in 1979 to cater for non-emergency situations. The Act became a reality after the experiences of the 1985 National Capital District (NCD) Curfew.[17] The Act was made pursuant to s 38 of the *Constitution* and "provides for curfew which is initiated by a proclamation by the Head of State, acting on advice of the NEC".[18] Under the Act the Prime Minister must report to Parliament at its first meeting after the proclamation of a curfew. There is little parliamentary control under the Act.

During a state of emergency the Parliament may enact specific pieces of legislation that cater only for that specific state of emergency. Examples include:

(a) the *Emergency (National Capital District) (Curfew) Act* 1985 (Ch 408) and the *Emergency (National Capital District) (Defence Force) Act* 1985 (Ch 409), which catered for the curfew in the nation's capital in that year;

(b) the *Emergency (Bougainville) (General Powers) Act* 1989, which was enacted to deal with the rebel uprising on Bougainville; and

(c) the *Emergency (General Powers) Act* 1994, which was enacted to accommodate the Rabaul volcanic eruptions in that year.

These statutes ceased to operate after the end of the curfew and emergencies respectively.

Emergency Regulations

Emergency Regulations may restrict the freedom from forced labour (*Constitution*, s 43), freedom from arbitrary search and entry (s 44) and the freedom of

17 Fraser, *Part X of the Constitution: Emergency Powers* (Paper presented at the "Twenty Years of the Constitution Conference", Port Moresby, March 1996), p 9.

18 Ibid.

movement (s 52). As an example, under s 5 of the *Emergency (General Powers) Regulation* 1994, the Controller of the Rabaul State of Emergency was empowered to restrict the movement of the people, authorise persons to enter and search premises and authorise persons to perform labour as he thought fit.[19]

An Emergency Regulation cannot, however, restrict certain rights specified under s 233(4) of the *Constitution*. These are:

(a) freedom of expression;

(b) freedom of assembly and association;

(c) the right to privacy; and

(d) the right to freedom of information.

On the other hand, an Emergency Act can restrict the rights stipulated under s 233(4), but it cannot alter the rights and freedoms set out in s 233(3). A person's right to life (s 35), freedom from inhuman treatment (s 36), freedom of conscience, thought and religion (s 45), right to vote and stand for public office (s 50), and, if he or she is a citizen, his or her other rights under ss 55 and 56, cannot be altered in a state of emergency. The protection of these rights and freedoms during a state of emergency reflects the recommendations of the CPC.

In 1993 the Supreme Court was asked by the Ombudsman Commission, in *Re Internal Security Act* [1994] PNGLR 341, to declare that the controversial *Internal Security Act* 1993 was unconstitutional as it was not enacted in accordance with the provisions of Pt X of the *Constitution*. The Parliament had enacted the *Internal Security Act* 1993 which was aimed at maintaining the internal security of PNG through the provision of measures directed at combating terrorism and terrorist activities. The Act restricted and regulated the rights and freedoms under ss 44, 45, 46, 47, 48, 49, 51 and 52 of the *Constitution*. Section 1 of the Act stated that it "is made for the purpose of giving effect to the public interest in public safety and public order and public welfare". Essentially, the Ombudsman Commission submitted that because there was no declared state of emergency pursuant to s 228 of the *Constitution* that would enable the Parliament to enact a law restricting the rights of individuals under s 234(3), the Act was inconsistent with Pt X and ss 32(2), 36(1), 37(2), 37(3), 37(4)(a), 37(7), 37(11), 37(15), 42, 44, 49, 52 and 53 of the *Constitution*.

The Supreme Court, however, ruled that only certain portions of the Act were invalid as they infringed some of the human rights in the *Constitution*. The Act as a whole was itself valid.

Emergency Orders

A lesser law allowed to operate during a state of emergency is an Emergency Order. These Orders are allowed under s 232 of the *Constitution*. An Emergency Order can only be made under an Emergency Act by a person authorised by the Act to issue those Orders. In a state of emergency it is usually the Controller of the State of Emergency that is empowered to issue such orders. For instance, in 1985 during the curfew in the National Capital District, the Controller of the Curfew issued a number of Orders for the proper management of the curfew. These included the

19 The Rabaul State of Emergency was declared on 19 September 1994. On the same day, the Governor-General, acting on the advice of the NEC, issued the *Emergency (General Powers) Regulation*. This Regulation was consequently repealed by the *Emergency (General Powers) Act* 1994 on 27 October 1994.

prohibition of demonstrations and protests in the NCD,[20] the prohibition of alcoholic beverages after 9 pm[21] and the prohibition of street markets[22] during the curfew period.

To be valid, an Emergency Order must be in writing and forwarded immediately to the Emergency Committee and the Speaker of Parliament for presentation to Parliament. Any matters that could otherwise be provided by an Emergency Act cannot be issued as Emergency Orders. This requirement is vague and open to contention.

It is possible to argue that what the *Constitution* is really saying is that where the Act is silent on certain matters, the Controller of the State of Emergency can issue Emergency Orders to fill those gaps. By its nature, an Emergency Act is broad, and therefore Emergency Orders are issued to cater for very specific situations not covered by the Act. This would be the correct approach, because an Emergency Order can only be made after an Emergency Act is in place. Thus, an Emergency Order cannot possibly cater for matters that are already covered by the Emergency Act.

Alteration

Section 236 of the *Constitution* provides that an Emergency Act may be altered by an Act of the Parliament and, in very exceptional circumstances, by an Emergency Regulation. An Emergency Regulation, on the other hand, may be altered any time by the Head of State acting on advice, or by an Emergency Act or by a decision of Parliament. According to s 237, an emergency law ceases to have effect after the end of the day on which the period of declared national emergency ends. Any laws that were dormant during the period of national emergency will revive at the cessation of the emergency law. Under s 238, an Emergency Act may be extended by Parliament after the end of a national emergency. However, the extension can only be valid if it is approved by an absolute majority vote and it is necessary to deal with the aftermath of the national emergency.

In a period of national emergency, emergency laws take precedence over ordinary statutes. According to s 233(2), an emergency law may alter, wholly or partly, and absolutely or subject to conditions, the basic rights and any Organic Law made for that purpose. The restrictions of basic rights have been discussed above.

4.2.5 Provincial laws: s 9(da)

General

Schedule 1.2(1) of the *Constitution* defines "provincial law" as "a law made or adopted by a provincial legislature, and includes a subordinate legislative enactment made under any such law". Provincial laws are, therefore, enacted by provincial governments and are expressly recognised by the *Constitution* as part of the laws of PNG. The *Constitution* and the OLPGLLG provide rules on how provincial laws are made, the subject matter of those laws and how they relate to the other categories of laws. The provisions are detailed and complex, and will be

20 Order No 002 issued by the Controller Mr David Tasion on 15 June 1985.
21 Order No 003 issued by the Controller Mr David Tasion on 15 June 1985.
22 Order No 009 issued on 15 June 1985. For the curfew period, Mr Tasion issued 14 orders for the efficient management of the curfew.

examined more closely in Chapter 10. At this stage we will make a brief examination of the provisions.[23]

Section 187B of the *Constitution* (as amended by *Constitutional Amendment No 16* 1995) established the provincial and local-level government system in PNG in 1995. Under s 187C (as amended) provision is made for an Organic Law that would spell out the composition, powers, functions and other related matters of the provincial governments and local-level governments. The pertinent Organic Law is the *Organic Law on Provincial Governments and Local-level Governments* 1995 (OPLGLLG). The OLPGLLG sets out in some detail the procedures for the establishment of provincial and local-level governments, their composition and their administrative, legislative and financial powers. For our present purposes we will consider only the legislative functions.[24]

Establishment of provincial and local-level governments

Section 10 of the OLPGLLG provides for the establishment of provincial governments and provincial legislatures in the 19 provinces of the country. Local-level governments are established under s 27. The law-making powers of the provincial and local-level governments are located in ss 42 and 44 respectively. By virtue of s 42, provincial legislatures are allowed to enact laws on 27 subjects. Local-level governments, on the other hand, are permitted to make laws on 31 subject matters. These subjects include:

- cemeteries;
- provision of water supply;
- improvement of villages;
- dispute settlement;
- bride and groom wealth;
- housing;
- protection of tradition sites;
- local trading; and
- hygiene and sanitation.

The law-making powers of these two levels of government are limited in three main ways. First, their powers of law-making are restrained by ss 42 and 44 of the OLPGLLG respectively. Secondly, the sphere of their powers to enact laws is vague under the Organic Law. Thirdly, their powers are severely restricted by the operation of other sections of the OLPGLLG. The first two points are discussed together, and the latter is discussed separately below.

Limitations on the legislative powers of provincial and local-level governments

Sections 42(1) and 44(1) of the OLPGLLG begin by stating that "[S]ubject to the *Constitution* and this Organic Law (and a Provincial Government law), a provincial legislature (local-level Government) may make laws on the following matters". These particular provisos clearly signal that the exercise of the law-making power of the provincial legislatures and the local-level governments must comply with the *Constitution* and the Organic Law. Kapi J, in *Michael Ayakamp v Guringng* [1981]

23 Those interested to make a more detailed examination at this point should see Ghai and Regan, *The Law, Politics and Administration of Decentralisation in Papua New Guinea* (National Research Institute, Port Moresby, Monograph 30, 1992), Ch 5.

24 See Chapter 10 for a detailed discussion of the OLPGLLG.

PNGLR 531, considered a number of authorities on the meaning and effect of the phrase "subject to", and accepted the meaning given in those authorities. The phrase subject to "is a simple provision which merely subjects the provisions of the subject subsections to the provisions of the master subsection." Put another way, it "is an expression used to avoid conflict between one part of the enactment and another." These meanings were accepted by the Supreme Court in *SCR No 1 of 1982; Re Bouraga* [1982] PNGLR 178 at 199 and *SCR No 2 of 1982; Re Organic Law* [1982] PNGLR 214 at 220.

It follows that where the *Constitution* or the Organic Law (and provincial law) have made a provision or authorised a certain Act to cover any of the matters covered under ss 42(1) and 44(1), then a provincial legislature (and a local-level government) is restrained from enacting a law on the same subject matter. For instance, s 42(3) of the OLPGLLG states that:

> "A law made under Subsection (1) shall have effect so far as it is not inconsistent with an Act of the Parliament made:
>
> (a) before the coming into operation of this Organic Law; or
>
> (b) in accordance with Section 41."[25]

Section 41 of the OLPGLLG combines ss 28-31 of the *Organic Law on Provincial Governments*. It is a general provision that seeks to retain the general law-making power of the Parliament under s 109 of the *Constitution*. Section 41(1), (2) and (3) of the OLPGLLG are in the following form:

> "41. *Law-making Powers of the National Parliament, Etc*
>
> (1) A law-making power that is not specified in Section 42 or 44 remains with the National Parliament.
>
> (2) Subject to this section, the National Parliament may make an Act of the Parliament on a matter specified in Section 42 or 44 only where the matter is of national interest.
>
> (3) Subject to Subsection (4),[26] the National Parliament shall not make an Act to which Subsection (2) applies unless there has been consultation between the Minister responsible for provincial governments and local-level government matters, and the Provincial Government or Local-level Government concerned."

It appears that the exercise of the power by Parliament under s 41(2) to make laws relating to matters under s 42 (and s 44) is limited by s 41(3). This limitation is, however, affected by s 41(6) of the OLPGLLG, which reads:

> "An Act of the Parliament on a matter specified in Section 42 or 44 shall prevail over any law made under Section 42 or 44, whether such law is made before or after the date of the making of the Act of the Parliament, to the extent of any inconsistency with the Act of Parliament."

It may be argued that s 41(6) relates to the question of inconsistency, and not to the intent and context of the provincial law or a local-level government law. If this argument is accepted, then s 41(6) cannot affect the operation of s 41(3). It is, however, suggested that the phrase "whether such law is made *before or after* the date of the making of the Act of the Parliament" in s 41(6) reaffirms the stipulation

25 Section 44(3) of the OLPGLLG is in the same language as this provision.

26 Section 41(4) of the OLPGLLG relates to times of national emergencies and urgency.

in s 41(2), establishing the position of Acts of Parliament over provincial and local-level government laws. Moreover, s 187D(2) (as amended) unequivocally states that "the application by its own force of an Act of the Parliament is not affected by a provincial law or a local-level law".

It is also suggested that s 41(3) of the OLPGLLG has a very limited application, as it relates only to specific circumstances within a particular province or a local-level government area. This is explained by the phrase "*consultation* between the Minister responsible for provincial government and local-level government matters, and the Provincial Government or Local-level Government *concerned*". This proviso was probably inserted to cater for situations falling outside of an emergency provided for in Pt X of the *Constitution*. In these special situations, s 41(3) of the OLPGLLG requires the Minister for Provincial and Local-level Governments Affairs to consult the appropriate provincial government or local-level governments. Section 41(3) is, therefore, not of a general application.

Section 41(3) of the OLPGLLG is, however, affected in two ways. The first way it is affected is by the application of s 139, which expressly states that the failure to consult a provincial government or a local-level government under the OLPGLLG does not invalidate an Act of Parliament. Secondly, it would appear that s 41(3) is contrary to s 100(3) of the *Constitution*, as it attempts to permanently exclude the power of the Parliament to make laws. Section 100(1) of the *Constitution* stipulates that:

> "Nothing in any Constitutional Law enables or may enable the Parliament to transfer permanently, or divest itself of, legislative power."

Section 41(3) of the OLPGLLG, which originates from s 29 of the old Organic Law, was described by Goldring as offending s 100(3) of the *Constitution*.[27] According to Goldring, s 29 (now s 41(3)) attempted to limit the power of the Parliament to legislate on matters enumerated in ss 42 and 44, and was, therefore, of no effect whatsoever. Regan and Ghai rejected this view.[28] According to Regan and Ghai, s 187D(1) merely provides for questions on inconsistency, and the Organic Law does not involve the permanent transfer of power. Contrary to the views held by Regan and Ghai, Goldring's view was accepted by the Supreme Court in *SCR No 7 of 1992; Re Forestry Act 1991* [1992] PNGLR 514. The Supreme Court (at 521) rejected the submission by the East New Britain Provincial Government that s 29 of the Organic Law (now s 41(3)) limited the legislative power of the Parliament to enact laws on matters listed under s 27 (now s 42) and therefore, the Parliament could not legislate on those subjects.

Seen in this light, s 41(3) of the OLPGLLG does not stand in the way of the Parliament's power to make laws on the subjects listed under s 42(1). This position is strengthened by the decision in *SCR No 7 of 1992; Re Forestry Act 1991*. In that case, the East New Britain Provincial Government sought the opinion of the Supreme Court on the validity of its provincial law on forestry made pursuant to s 27 of the old *Organic Law on Provincial Governments*. Section 27 of the *Organic Law on Provincial Governments* is the predecessor of s 42 of the OLPGLLG. The Supreme Court reviewed the provincial law against the *Forestry Act* 1991, and ruled that even though provincial governments had legislative powers to make such a law under s 27, the national forestry law prevailed, because forestry is a subject matter

27 Goldring, *The Constitution of Papua New Guinea* (Law Book Co Ltd, Sydney, 1978), p 84. Goldring based his arguments on the decision of the Privy Council in *In Re the Initiative and Referendum Act* [1919] AC 935, where the Privy Council had to determine the validity of a provincial legislation of a Canadian provincial legislature.

28 Ghai and Regan, op cit n 23, pp 144-145.

of "national interest". The provincial forestry law was therefore declared null and void.

This decision must be seen in the light of the legislative arrangements under the old Organic Law. Under the old Organic Law, provincial legislatures had three different sets of legislative powers: "exclusive provincial subjects", "primary provincial subjects", and "concurrent subjects". Exclusive provincial subjects related to:

> "two narrow but important areas of legislative subject matters reserved to the provinces – exclusive provincial taxes and those aspects of provincial institutions and administration that can be provided for in provincial constitution".[29]

This power was given to the provincial governments to enable them to maintain a certain degree of financial autonomy. The national government was prohibited from fettering this power. The provinces were able to exercise this power to raise their own revenues within the province to supplement funds they received from the national government.

The primary provincial subjects were matters over which the provincial governments had powers to legislate. The primary provincial matters were listed under s 24 of the Organic Law. These included:

- licensing of mobile traders;
- primary schools and primary education;
- sale and distribution of alcohol;
- housing; and
- sporting activities.

In the third legislative regime (concurrent subjects), the provincial government shared this power with the national government. In a sense, the provincial legislatures had to coordinate this legislative power with the Parliament. The matters for which these two levels of government shared legislative responsibility were listed under s 27 of the Organic Law. These included:

- tourism;
- town planning;
- land and land development;
- forestry;
- wildlife;
- parks and reserves; and
- renewal and non-renewal natural resources.

Unlike the old Organic Law, the OLPGLLG does not differentiate the legislative powers of the provincial legislatures. Section 42 of the OLPGLLG is an expansion of s 27 of the old Organic Law. There were 25 matters listed under s 27 of the old Organic Law, while s 42 of the OLPGLLG lists 27 matters. The subject matters enumerated under s 42 are concurrent matters. A simple reading of s 42 indicates that provincial legislatures have the power to enact laws relating to those matters enumerated. However, if the decision in *SCR No 7 of 1992; Re Forestry Act 1991* is adopted, provincial legislatures are *severely* restrained from exercising this power. This restraint does not mean that the provincial governments are prevented permanently from legislating on these subjects. It is suggested that provincial

29 Ibid, p 161.

governments can legislate on s 42 matters, but only insofar as the national legislation expressly empowers them to do so, or where the national law does not adequately cover the field. This view can be presented in tabular form.[30]

TABLE 1

Matters under s 42 (OLPGLLG)	**Existing Acts of Parliament**	**Provincial legislature's power to enact law (SCR No 7 of 1992)**
Tourism	*National Tourism Authority Act*	Limited
Forestry	*Forestry Act* 1991	Limited
Town planning	*Physical Planning Act* 1989	Limited
Renewal and non-renewal natural resources	*Mining Act* 1992 *Fisheries Act* 1998 *Petroleum Act* 1998 *Forestry Act* 1991	Limited
Land and land development	*Land Act* 1996	Limited
Parks and reserves	*National Parks Act* (Ch 157) *Conservation Areas Act* 1978 *Fauna (Protection and Control) Act* (Ch 154)	Limited
Family law, marriage, adoption and maintenance	*Child Welfare Act* (Ch 276) *Deserted Wives and Children Act* (Ch 277) *Marriage Act* (Ch 280) *Infants Act* (Ch 278) *Matrimonial Causes Act* (Ch 282)	Limited
Registration of vehicles	*Motor Vehicle (Third Party) Insurance Act*	Limited
Commissions of inquiry	*Commissions of Inquiry Act* (Ch 31)	Limited
Village and urban or community courts	*Village Courts Act* (Ch 44)	Limited

30 This table does not include the 27 matters listed under s 42 of the OLPGLLG. It is only indicative of the points raised.

To a certain extent the same argument applies to local-level government laws. Local-level government laws are subject to the *Constitution*, the OLPGLLG and the relevant provincial laws. National laws cover some of the subjects over which a local-level government has power to legislate, and therefore local-level governments have little room for legislative enactments. Table 2 illustrates this.

TABLE 2

Matters under s 44 (OLPGLLG)	**Existing Acts of Parliament**	**Local-level government's power to enact law**
Labour and employment	*Industrial Relations Act* *Employment Act*	Very limited
Cemeteries	*Cemeteries Act*	Very limited
Water supply	*Environment Act* 2000	Very limited
Electricity	*Electricity Act*	Very limited
Domestic animals, flora and fauna	*Animals Act* *Fauna (Protection and Control) Act* (Ch 154) *International Trade (Fauna and Flora) Act* (Ch 391)	Very limited
Local environment	*Environmental Planning Act*	Very limited
Traditional sacred sites	*Cultural Property Act*	Very limited

Provincial legislatures may also enact laws that may cover the same fields and, consequently, local-level government laws can either be ousted or cut down by the operation of those provincial laws. There are, however, certain matters under s 44(1) of the OLPGLLG that seem to be in the exclusive jurisdiction of the local-level governments. These matters include:

- improvement of villages and communities;
- cottage industries;
- community sport;
- bride and groom wealth;
- human settlement;
- census and village records;
- community day work or service;
- village communities;
- traditional barter system; and
- traditional and customary copyrights.

Apart from their legislative powers over the matters listed under ss 42 and 44 of the OLPGLLG, provincial and local-level governments can exercise legislative powers over other matters delegated to them by the Parliament under s 50. Certain legislative powers of the Parliament can be transferred to a provincial or a local-level government under s 50 as required by the provincial or local-level government.[31] Those responsibilities must, however, be set out clearly by an Act of the Parliament.[32] Provincial and local-level governments can, conversely, delegate their powers to the Parliament (and, in the case of local-level governments, to the provincial legislatures).

This provision is, however, unclear. It does not clarify whether the process of delegation is to be initiated by the national government or the provincial and local-level governments. It also does not specify whether the initiative is to be started by *request*. It is not even clear whether this section is reminiscence of s 114 of the old Organic Law. Section 114 set out a formula whereby national laws on "concurrent subjects" would cease to apply in a particular province at the insistence of the provincial government. Under s 114, provincial governments would request the national government to repeal certain national laws relating to concurrent subjects, and the national government would revoke the application of them.[33]

It is suggested that s 50 of the OLPGLLG entrenches the principles of the old s 114, even though they are not verbatim. It follows that provincial and local-level governments can request the national government through Parliament to repeal laws on the concurrent subjects under ss 42 and 44, to enable their provincial laws or local-level laws to apply in their provinces or local-level government areas. On the same premise, local-level governments can request their provincial governments to repeal provincial laws relating to matters listed under s 44.

Provincial and local-level governments cannot pass laws on a number of important matters, because specific provisions of the OLPGLLG require an Act of Parliament to bring them into effect. Many of these provisions have been inoperative for almost four years, because the relevant Acts of Parliament have not been enacted. Some of the provisions which are of importance to provincial and local-level governments include ss 98(3) and (6) (natural resources), 105(2) (financial autonomy), 106(4) (data collection and planning), 116(1) (natural resources) and 118(3) (mediation and arbitration).

These provisions have a direct bearing on ss 42 and 44. The lack of national legislation on these relevant matters has delayed the provincial and local-level governments in their legislative programs and, in most cases, this is to the detriment of these two institutions.

Inconsistency

Provincial laws are subject to the *Constitution*, Organic Laws, emergency laws, and Acts of Parliament. Local-level government laws are subject to all of these laws. Goldring correctly points out that:

> "Questions of whether a provincial law is or is not consistent with a Constitutional law are justiciable at the suit of any person with sufficient standing by s 187D(2) of the *Constitution*, but a question of inconsistency between a provincial [and local-level] law and an Act of the National Parliament is justiciable only at the instance of the National Government or of a provincial government[34] [or a local-level government[35]]."[36]

31 This provision also allows the provincial legislatures to delegate some of their legislative powers to the local-level governments where appropriate.

32 No such legislation is yet in place.

33 According to Ghai and Regan, by mid-1990 there was no significant sharing of responsibilities initiated under this provision: Ghai and Regan, op cit n 23, p 178.

34 See OLPGLLG, s 42(4).

35 See OLPGLLG, s 44(4).

36 Goldring, op cit n 27, p 85.

Making, altering and repealing provincial and local-level laws

Provincial laws are made by provincial legislatures established by s 187C(2)(a) of the *Constitution* and ss 10(2) and 29(1) of the OLPGLLG. Provincial and local-level laws are passed in the same manner as ordinary Acts of Parliament. Alteration and repeal follows a process similar to that applied in the national Parliament.

A proposed provincial or local-level law or a proposed amendment may be presented to the Minister for Provincial and Local-level Government Affairs for comments before its enactment by the provincial legislature or the local-level government by virtue of s 140. Failure to comply with this requirement, however, does not invalidate a provincial or local-level law.

A provincial or local-level law can only commence if it complies with s 141 of the OLPGLLG. Three different people are required to endorse provincial and local-level laws before they come into force. Under s 141(3)(c)(ii), all provincial and local-level government budget appropriations are to be approved by the Minister for Finance before they become law. Under s 141(4), all other laws are to be approved by the Minister for Provincial and Local-level Government Affairs.

To avoid abuse and undue delay by the national government or the relevant Minister who may be a political opponent of a provincial governor or a local-level government president, s 141(5) provides that where the relevant Minister has not made any decision on the provincial or local-level law within 60 days after its service on the relevant Minister and the Attorney-General, the provincial or local-level law will be deemed to have been accepted and the law will come into force.

4.2.6 Subordinate legislative enactments and other laws made under or adopted by or under other laws: s 9(e)

Introduction

The kinds of laws in this category are numerous, and may give rise to some complex legal problems. The main point to note is that there are numerous kinds of "regulations" and other minor laws, which are nevertheless laws of the country. The role of "regulations", in particular, is important, as much modern law is contained in them. The main reason for their extensive use is flexibility – they are generally simpler to make and to alter than Acts of Parliament and other "higher" forms of law. They are also a form of "delegated legislation".[37]

Definition

"Subordinate legislative enactment" is defined under Sch 1.2(1) of the *Constitution* as a regulation or any other instrument (whether of a legislative nature or not) made under statute. This definition is broad, and encompasses various kinds of laws. The definition deals only with regulations and "any other instrument (whether of a legislative nature or not)" made under a "statute". From this definition, two points follow. First, by including "instruments", a wide range of documents created by or under laws is given the force of law.[38] Secondly, the definition of "statute" (in the same schedule) includes Acts of Parliament, Emergency Regulations, provincial laws and local-level laws, but does not include constitutional laws. Subordinate legislative enactments made under the

37 Discussed in Chapter 5.

38 The *Osborne's Concise Law Dictionary* (8th ed) defines "instrument" as meaning "a formal legal document in writing".

Constitution and the Organic Laws are included in the laws of PNG by virtue of the wording of s 9(e) of the *Constitution.*

The expression used in s 9(e) is wide and includes a wide category of laws made under or adopted by or under other laws. Other kinds of laws may therefore be included in the definition. In particular, laws made by bodies exercising delegated legislative powers seem to be envisaged. Examples include the *Code of Military Discipline* made under the *Defence Force Act* (Ch 74) and *Defence (Period of Service) Regulation,*[39] the *Papua New Guinea Fire Service Standing Orders* made pursuant to s 35 of the *Fire Service Act,* and Disciplinary Rules issued by educational institutions such as high schools, National High Schools and universities.

The definition becomes more complicated if the meaning of the phrase is extended to include orders and directions issued under a subordinate legislation. For instance, s 51(1) of the OLPGLLG empowers the NEC to direct a provincial or local-level government to take certain measures to rectify certain anomalies in the government. Are these orders and directions "laws"? In a very shallow decision, Woods J held in *Peter Rose v Yamu Samuel* [1987] PNGLR 1 at 3-4 that "notices made under an Act are not laws made by the Parliament or the Assembly, they are proclamations or notices made under law and they must be proved in evidence". His Honour reached the conclusion that notices and proclamations made under a law are not laws: at 3-4. His Honour arrived at this conclusion without averting to s 9(e) of the *Constitution.* It is suggested that this decision is contrary to principle. An order or proclamation made under a subordinate legislation is for all purposes legal and valid. To say that an order or a declaration made under a subordinate legislation is not law because it is not made by a legislature, is fallacious. Putting this point aside, the case highlights the difficulty in ascertaining or establishing (even by the courts) the demarcation between law and simple and ordinary orders and directives issued by relevant authorities for the day-to-day management of their institutions.

Delegation of legislative powers is envisaged by s 100(2) of the *Constitution.* The power of the Head of State to make regulations on advice is a form of delegated legislative power, but there are others. Examples include the laws made under s 50 and directions issued under s 137 of the OLPGLLG.

Nature of subordinate legislative enactments

As s 9(e) of the *Constitution* includes both subordinate legislative enactments made under the constitutional laws as well as those made under other laws, it must include at least the following:

- regulations and instruments made under statutes;
- regulations made under the *Constitution* or an Organic Law as provided for under s 258;
- other forms of subordinate legislative enactments made under the *Constitution,* such as the rules of court which are made by the Supreme Court and National Court pursuant to s 184;
- the Standing Orders of the Parliament[40] made under s 133; and
- Emergency Orders issued under s 232.

39 In *Nuia v Benias Sabumei* [1992] PNGLR 90, Los J was able to use the Code of Military Discipline to find that the applicant was wrongfully dismissed from the Defence Force.

40 In *Kaguel Koroka v Kapal* [1985] PNGLR 117, Woods J refused to consider whether or not the Western Highlands Provincial Assembly followed its Standing Orders, because he was of the view that the judiciary should not interfere in the affairs of the legislature: see Chapter 5. The judiciary seems to have deviated from this view.

Subordinate legislative enactments are made by the authorities empowered to make the delegated legislation under the various statutes. Constitutional Regulations under s 258 are made by the Head of State upon advice. Regulations made under the Organic Laws, such as s 41 of the *Organic Law on the Duties and Responsibilities of Leadership*, are made by the Head of State acting on advice. There are numerous examples of subordinate legislative enactments made under statutes. Examples include the *National Parks Regulation* made pursuant to the *National Parks Act*, *Public Service General Orders* made under the *Public Service (Management) Act* 1995, the *National Court Rules* made under the *National Courts Act* and the *Supreme Court Rules* made under the *Supreme Court Act*.

A subordinate legislative enactment is subject to the enabling law. Where subordinate legislation is inconsistent with the enabling law, that subordinate legislation will be invalid. The subject matters to be covered by a subordinate law vary from one category of law to another. In general, subordinate laws can only deal with matters authorised by (and to the extent authorised by) the provisions enabling them to be made. In *Mairi v Alkan Tololo (No 2)* [1976] PNGLR 125 and *James Saleng Mileng v Alkan Tololo* [1976] PNGLR 447, the Supreme Court held that the imposition of extra fees on parents by the school Board of Management on the orders of the National Education Board, purporting to exercise its power to issue directives under the *Education Act* 1970, was unconstitutional, as the subordinate law (directive) was not authorised by the Act. In *SCR No 5 of 1987; Re Central Bank Reg* [1987] PNGLR 433, the Supreme Court held that the *Central Banking (Foreign Exchange and Gold) Regulation*, and especially s 33 made pursuant to ss 61 and 70 of the *Central Banking Act* (Ch 138), was perfectly valid, as it was in conformity with the basic legislation. A subordinate legislative enactment can be used to give meaning to another subordinate legislative enactment, as used in the case of *Central Pomio Logging Corp Pty Ltd v The State* [1992] PNGLR 20, where the Supreme Court relied on the *Forestry Regulations* to hold that the Collector of Customs properly exercised his powers under the *Customs (Prohibited Export) Regulations* and the *Customs Tariff (Amendment) Act* 1990. Subordinate laws can be struck down by the courts if they go further than authorised, as was the case in *Acting Public Solicitor v Uname Aumane* [1980] PNGLR 510, where the Supreme Court said that s 32 of the *Supreme Court Rules* was inconsistent with s 23 of the *Supreme Court Act* 1975. In *Curtain Bros (Qld) Pty Ltd v PNG* [1993] PNGLR 285 at 290-291, the Supreme Court warned that the courts must, however, exercise caution when considering the appropriateness or otherwise of a regulation. The court said that the court must not confuse its *legislative powers* under the *National Court Rules* with its *judicial review power* in the performance of their functions.

Section 116 of the *Constitution* provides that subordinate legislative enactment must be presented to Parliament for endorsement. Under ss 116, 258 and 184 the Parliament can disallow subordinate legislative enactments. Failure to table a subordinate legislation in Parliament, however, does not invalidate the law: s 116(3).

4.2.7 Underlying law: s 9(f)

The concept of the underlying law can be difficult. It is, however, an important part of the law in PNG. Essentially, it performs the same role as the common law in England. It is the law that applies when there is no clear written law on a subject. Its development and application is perhaps more complex in PNG than is the case with the common law in Australia or the United Kingdom. This is because of constitutional requirements and particularly because at present either the common law or custom may apply to a particular case.

The *Constitution* does not define the term "underlying law". The definition offered by the draftsman of the *Constitution* is "it means the same in essence as 'the common law' (including the rules of equity). It means the 'unwritten' law, the rules of which have not only to be applied, but also enunciated and developed, by the courts".[41] The nature and content of the underlying law was initially set out in Sch 2 of the *Constitution*. This schedule envisaged the enactment of specific legislation, and this is now provided for in the *Underlying Law Act* 2000.[42] The source of the underlying law, and its application, are dealt with in ss 3 and 4 as follows:

> "3. (1)The sources of the underlying law shall be:
>
> (a) the customary law; and
>
> (b) the common law in force in England immediately before the 16th September, 1975.
>
> (2) The principles and rules of customary law shall be applied with the qualifications and subject to the conditions as set out in this Act.
>
> (3) The principles and rules of common law shall be applied:
>
> (a) with the qualifications and subject to the conditions as set out in this Act; and
>
> (b) notwithstanding their modification through an amendment, repeal or alteration by a statute of England unless the modifying statute has been adopted in Papua New Guinea.
>
> 4. (1)Subject to Subsection (2) or (3):
>
> (a) the customary law; and
>
> (b) the common law,
>
> shall be adopted and applied as part of the underlying law.
>
> (2) The customary law shall apply unless:
>
> (a) it is inconsistent with a written law; or
>
> (b) its application and enforcement would be contrary to the National Goals and Directive Principles and the Basic Social Obligations established by the *Constitution*; or
>
> (c) its application and enforcement would be contrary to the basic rights guaranteed by Division III.3 (*Basic Rights*) of the *Constitution*.
>
> (3) The common law shall not be applied unless:
>
> (a) it is consistent with a written law; or
>
> (b) it is applicable and appropriate to the circumstance of the country; or
>
> (c) it is consistent with the customary law as applied under Subsection (2); or
>
> (d) its application and enforcement would not be contrary to the National Goals and Directive Principles and Basic Social Obligations established by the *Constitution*; or

---

41 Lynch, "The Adoption of an Underlying Law by the Constitution of Papua New Guinea" (1976) 4(1) MLJ 37 at 38. Lynch sets out in detail the intricacies of the issues involved in the formulation of Sch 2 and ss 20 and 21 of the *Constitution*.

42 *Underlying Law Act* 2000 (No 13 of 2000).

(e) its application and enforcement would not be contrary to the basic rights guaranteed by Division III.3 (*Basic Rights*) of the *Constitution.*

(4) A court which:

(a) refuses to apply a principle or rule of customary law, shall give reasons for its refusal in terms of Subsection (2)(a), (b) or (c); or

(b) applies a principle or rule of common law, shall give its reasons for the application in terms of Subsection (3)(a), (b), (c), (d) or (e).

(5) A principle or rule of customary law or common law applied under Subsection (2) or (3) shall become part of the underlying law."

The underlying law under s 3 of the *Underlying Law Act* 2000[43] (and see Sch 2.1(c)) consists of customary law and common law and equity as applied in England immediately before independence. A custom cannot form part of the underlying law if it is inconsistent with a constitutional law or a statute, or is repugnant to the principles of humanity. Similarly, a common law or principle of equity cannot form part of the underlying law if it is inconsistent with a constitutional law or a statute, or if it is inapplicable and inappropriate to the circumstances of PNG.

The national judicial system and the underlying law

The National Judicial System, especially the National Court and the Supreme Court, are also vested with the responsibility of developing the underlying law in the country. Section 5 of the *Underlying Law Act* 2000 provides that:

> "The Courts, especially the Supreme Court and the National Court, shall ensure that, with due regard to the need for consistency, the underlying law develops as a coherent system in a manner that is appropriate to the circumstances of the country."

The judiciary's first and foremost duty is to *develop*[44] the underlying law of PNG. In addition, the judiciary is directed by s 60 of the *Constitution* to take into account the development of a system of principles of natural justice and administrative law when it is formulating the underlying law. The judiciary is required, under Sch 2.5, to report annually to Parliament on the state of the underlying law and also recommend for improvements where appropriate.

The development of the underlying law began[45] as early as October 1975 in the case of *Johns v Thomas* [1976] PNGLR 15. In this case, Frost CJ considered whether

43 The Law Reform Commission had been mandated, by Sch 2.14 of the *Constitution*, with the special responsibility of investigating and reporting to Parliament and the National Executive on the development and adaptation of the underlying law, and on the appropriateness of the rules and principles of the underlying law, to the circumstances of the country from time to time. In pursuit of this objective, the Law Reform Commission attempted to implement s 20 by presenting the Underlying Law Bill 1977 to Parliament: Law Reform Commission, *The Role of Customary Law in the Legal System (Report No 7)* (Law Reform Commission, Port Moresby, 1977). The aim of the Bill was to elevate custom and codify the principles of underlying law as adopted under Sch 2, and to provide a mechanism for the future development of the underlying law (that is, an indigenous jurisprudence). The Bill was rejected by Parliament. Since then, the *Underlying Law Act* 2000 has been introduced.

44 This concept is distinct from the term "adopt". The courts are required to develop the underlying law, rather than adopt a foreign law and apply it to the circumstances of PNG. The role of the courts in this area has been criticised by Nonggorr in "The Development of an 'Indigenous Jurisprudence' in Papua New Guinea: The Past Record and Future Prospects" in Aleck and Rannells (eds), *Custom at the Crossroads* (UPNG, Faculty of Law, Port Moresby, 1995), p 68

45 According to the findings of Srivastava, "The Underlying Law and its Development by the Courts" in Aleck and Rannells, op cit n 44. See Ntumy "The Dream of a Melanesian Jurisprudence: The Purpose and Limits of Law Reform" in Aleck and Rannells, op cit n 44, p 7; Narokobi, *The Melanesian Way* (Institute of PNG Studies, Goroka, 1983).

or not the common law doctrine of ratification[46] was appropriate to the circumstances of PNG. His Honour accepted that the doctrine was appropriate to the circumstances of PNG, without consideration of the relevant customary rules applying to the circumstances of the case. The following year, in *The State v Kewa Kai* [1976] PNGLR 481, Prentice DCJ considered the applicability of the common law rules relating to the corroboration of a prosecutrix's evidence. He held that the rule was applicable to the circumstances of the country.

The judiciary has been consistent in its use of its powers under the former Sch 2.3-4 of the *Constitution.* This power has been used sparingly in appropriate cases ranging from simple contract cases such as *Arinako v Minipe* [1994] PNGLR 450 at 452-454, to complex civil cases such as the *Federal Huron v Ok Tedi Ltd* [1986] PNGLR 5 and *Wallbank v PNG* [1994] PNGLR 78. In the latter case, the Supreme Court refused to consider the appropriateness of the common law in PNG, because the common law rule that was being considered was not appropriate to the applicant, who was an expatriate woman living in Australia. The National and Supreme Courts have also invoked this power to venture into other areas of the law such as family law, criminal law, customary law and even constitutional law. In *Ubuk v Darius* [1994] PNGLR 279 the applicant relied on custom to seek custody of a child of a de facto relationship with the respondent. The court ruled that the custom was repugnant to the principles of humanity, and awarded custody to the woman.[47]

A long list of criminal cases demonstrates the readiness of the courts to invoke their power (under the former Sch 2.3-4). However, only three cases need be discussed to highlight the significance of our discussion. In *The State v Goli Golu* [1979] PNGLR 11, the National Court ruled that "Judges Rules" were of the underlying law. In *The State v Amoko-Amoko* [1981] PNGLR 373, the court held that the common law rules of "accessory after the fact", and not the Australian rules, should be accepted as part of the underlying law. The Supreme Court, however, relying on its power under Sch 2.4, had to depend largely on Australian precedents in *PLAR No 1 of 1980* [1980] PNGLR 326 to conclude that provocation was available as a complete defence to an accused charged for manslaughter under s 307 of the *Criminal Code.*

The formation and development of the underlying law

Part III of the *Underlying Law Act* deals with the manner in which the underlying law is to be developed. The principal duty for formation and development falls on the judiciary: s 5. The relevant sections are as follows:

> "6. *Order of application of law.*
>
> Subject to this Act, in dealing with the subject matter of a proceeding, the court shall apply the laws in the following order:
>
> (a) written law; and
>
> (b) the underlying law; and

46 According to *Halsbury's Laws of England* (4th ed), Vol 1, the doctrine of ratification is: "under certain conditions an act which, at the time it was entered into or done by an agent, lacked the authority, express or implied, of a principal, may by the subsequent conduct of the principal become ratified by him and made as effectively his own as if he had previously authorised it".

47 See also *Tom v Kayiak* [1992] PNGLR 172 at 174, where Los J held that the custom as applied in towns is different from the same custom as applied in the villages. On this ground, he awarded custody to the husband who had paid bride price under custom. See also *Kere v Bessi Timon and Family* (1990) N 807.

(c) the customary law; and

(d) the common law.

7. *Formulation of law.*

(1) Where the written law does not apply to the subject matter of a proceeding, the court shall apply the underlying law.

(2) If the underlying law does not apply to the subject matter of a proceeding, the court shall apply the customary law unless:

(a) subject to Subsection (6), the court is satisfied that the parties intended that the customary law shall not apply to the subject matter of the proceeding; or

(b) the subject matter of the proceedings is unknown to the customary law and cannot be resolved by analogy to a rule of customary law without causing injustice to one or more parties.

(3) If:

(a) the underlying law; and

(b) the customary law,

do not apply to the subject matter of a proceeding, the court shall consider applying the common law under the conditions set out in Section 4(3).

(4) Subject to Subsection (5), if:

(a) the underlying law; and

(b) the customary law; and

(c) the common law,

do not apply to the subject matter of a proceeding, the court shall formulate a rule, appropriate to the circumstances of the country, as part of the underlying law.

(5) The court in formulating a rule under Subsection (4) shall have regard to:

(a) the National Goals and Directive Principles and Basic Social Obligation established by the *Constitution*; and

(b) the basic rights guaranteed by Division III.3 (*Basic Rights*) of the *Constitution*; and

(c) analogies drawn from the relevant written law and customary law; and

(d) the laws of a foreign country relevant to the subject matter of a proceeding.

(6) The court may apply the customary law, if it is satisfied that a party to the subject matter of a proceeding under Subsection (2)(a) intended to avoid, for an unjust purpose, the consequences of the customary law.

9. *Inappropriate underlying law.*

In a proceeding, if the Supreme Court or the National Court considers that a rule of the underlying law is no longer appropriate to the circumstance of the country, it may formulate a new rule, appropriate to the circumstances of the country, as part of the underlying law, having regard to:

(a) the National Goals and Directive Principles and Basic Social Obligations established by the *Constitution*; and

(b) the basic rights guaranteed by Division III.3 (*Basic Rights*) of the *Constitution*; and

(c) analogies drawn from the relevant written law and customary law; and

(d) the laws of a foreign country relevant to the subject matter of a proceeding."

The Act gives flexibility on granting remedies as well as developing the law. When the remedy sought is based on the underlying law, the court may grant any remedies that are available under a source of the underlying law or a formulated rule of the underlying law: s 10. In addition, the parties[48] to a proceeding shall bring evidence or information to assist the court in deciding whether to apply a principle or rule of customary law, to apply a principle or rule of common law, or to formulate a rule of the underlying law, to resolve the subject matter of a proceeding: s 11(1). It is for the court, upon receiving the evidence or information, to make a decision: s 11(2).

Custom and common law

The issue of whether custom is higher in status than the common law was settled in *Madaha Resena v PNG* [1991] PNGLR 171. In that case, the Supreme Court held that, in the development of the underlying law, custom is to be given preference over common law. The elevation of custom has been maintained consistently since,[49] and has been confirmed by s 6 of the *Underlying Law Act* 2000. Lawyers and litigants who intend to rely on custom have a duty under the Act to present evidence of custom: s 15. In *Piel v Ranpi* [1996] PNGLR 396 at 400, Injia J made it clear that if custom is to be pleaded, it must be in clear, precise and adequate terms, to enable the court to ascertain whether it is inconsistent with the constitutional law, a statute, or principles of humanity. The courts are also mindful of the dangers of extending the excesses of custom to, for example, permit a payback killing (as was argued by the accused in *Public Prosecutor v Apava Keru and Aia Moroi* [1985] PNGLR 78), temporarily release a prisoner to perform customary duties upon the death of his father (as was argued in *Wambun v The State* [1992] PNGLR 488), or replace the concept of "master/servant relationship" (as was put forward in *National Airline Employees' Association v Air Niugini* [1992] PNGLR 287).

The judiciary is very much aware that it has a duty under s 5 of the Act (former Sch 2.3) to create rules to fill the gaps in the law. This was highlighted in *SCR No 4 of 1980; Re Petition of Somare (No 1)* [1981] PNGLR 265, where the Supreme Court had to formulate a new rule to extend the list under s 19(3) to include the Leader of the Opposition, because of lack of custom and the inappropriateness of the common law on standing in constitutional matters. In a strong judgment in *SCR No 4 of 1990* [1994] PNGLR 141 at 156, Kapi DCJ said *where it was urgent* the Supreme Court could formulate a rule to fill the gap in the law. The courts' role in this field is precarious. As Andrew J pointed out in *The State v Misimb Kais* [1978] PNGLR 241, and Kapi DCJ said in *The State v Kor* [1983] PNGLR 24 and again in *SCR No 4 of 1990*, it is more appropriate for Parliament to fill the gap in the law

48 This essentially means the lawyer representing the party. See also s 15 of the *Underlying Law Act*, which places a duty on counsel to present evidence to the court in relation to customary law.

49 *Tom v Kayiak* [1992] PNGLR 171; *The State v Mek* [1993] PNGLR 330; *Kombea v Peke* [1994] PNGLR 572 at 573.

than the judiciary. In this regard, the Supreme Court, realising that there was a gap in the *Leadership Code*, refrained from filling the gap in *SCR No 5 of 1980; Re Joseph Auna* [1980] PNGLR 500.[50] The judiciary has shown a willingness to initiate the procedure under Sch 2.3-4, even when it is not argued[51] or raised.[52]

Review of the Underlying Law Act

The judiciary's development over the years of the underlying law has been promising, and has been clarified by the *Underlying Law Act* 2000. The process is continuing and must be kept under review. This is recognised in the following sections of the *Underlying Law Act* 2000:

> "8. *Submission of decision to Chief Justice, etc.*
>
> (1) Where a court, other than the Supreme Court or the National Court, makes a decision under Section 7, it shall, forthwith, send a copy of the decision to:
>
> (a) the Chief Justice; and
>
> (b) the Chairman of the Law Reform Commission.
>
> (2) A decision under this Section may be dealt with under Section 12 or 13.
>
> 12. *Review instituted by Chief Justice.*
>
> (1) Subject to Section 14, the Chief Justice, upon the receipt of a decision under Section 8, shall consider that decision and if he is of the opinion that the decision should be reviewed, he may:
>
> (a) within 40 days of receiving the decision, refer it to the National Court for review; and
>
> (b) call upon the parties to the proceedings and such other persons as he considers appropriate to present arguments as to the appropriateness of the decision.
>
> (2) If the National Court varies the decision in question, it shall state what it considers to be the appropriate rule of the underlying law to dispose of the case.
>
> (3) Where a person is aggrieved by a decision of the National Court made under Subsection (2), he may appeal to the Supreme Court within 40 days after the decision in question was made or within such further period as is allowed by a judge upon application made to him within that period of 40 days.
>
> (4) An appeal under Subsection (3) shall be heard and conducted as if it was an appeal under the *Supreme Court Act* 1975.
>
> 13. *Review instituted by Law Reform Commission.*
>
> (1) Subject to Section 14, the Chairman of the Law Reform Commission, upon the receipt of a decision under Section 8, shall consider the decision and if he is of the opinion, after consultation with the other members of the Law Reform Commission, that the decision is

50 However, consider the ruling in *SCR No 2 of 1992* [1992] PNGLR 336, which reviewed this decision.

51 This was the case in *Johns v Thomas* [1976] PNGLR 15.

52 In *Ubuk v Darius* [1994] PNGLR 279, Sevua J proceeded to consider Sch 2.3, even though both parties did not raise this issue.

inconsistent with the proper development of the underlying law, he may:

(a) within 40 days of receiving the decision, refer it to the National Court for review; and

(b) call upon the parties to the proceedings to present arguments as to the appropriateness of the decision.

(2) The Chairman of the Law Reform Commission shall appear or be represented at a review instituted by him under Subsection (1) and with the leave of the court, may call upon other persons to make submissions to the court in relation to the decision.

(3) If the National Court varies the decision in question, it shall state what it considers to be the appropriate rule of the underlying law to dispose of the case.

(4) A person aggrieved by the decision of the National Court made under Subsection (3), may appeal to the Supreme Court within 40 days after the decision in question is made or within such further period as is allowed by a judge upon application made to him within that period of 40 days.

(5) An appeal under Subsection (4) shall be heard and conducted as if it was an appeal under the *Supreme Court Act* 1975."

Melanesian jurisprudence

It is envisaged that the development of the underlying law will result in the evolution of an indigenous jurisprudence.[53] Section 21 of the *Constitution* implores the judiciary and the Law Reform Commission to hasten the evolution of an indigenous jurisprudence through the development of the underlying law and the Act declaring the underlying law. This has been done by the passage of the *Underlying Law Act* 2000, particularly s 20. Section 20 provides two mechanisms: one permanent and the other temporary.[54] Section 20(1) provides the permanent mechanism. The Parliament has now declared the underlying law through the *Underlying Law Act* 2000. This Act will then provide the basis for the future development of the underlying law. Section 20(1) envisages the continued development of an indigenous jurisprudence, taking the *Underlying Law Act* 2000[55] as its starting point.

---

53 Before the *Underlying Law Act* 2000, the scheme of ss 21 and 20 and Sch 2 of the *Constitution* was that:
(1) The Law Reform Commission and the judiciary were required to collaborate on the development of the underlying law.
(2) The judiciary was given more prominence in this task because of its special role as an adjudicator of disputes.
(3) It was envisioned that by annual reporting to Parliament of the progress of the underlying law, the judiciary could inform the Parliament of the state of the underlying law.
(4) Based on this report and any appropriate reports by the Law Reform Commission, the Parliament could, with the assistance of the Law Reform Commission, formulate and enact legislation to declare the underlying law.
Based on this Act, the judiciary can then more confidently systematically develop an indigenous jurisprudence.

54 The temporary mechanism is provided for under s 20(2) of the *Underlying Law Act* 2000, and is really the alternative to s 20(1). The formula is that in the absence of an Act declaring the underlying law, the underlying law will be that which is set out in Sch 2 until the *Underlying Law Act* is passed.

55 The assumption here is that with the declaration of the underlying law, the provisions of Sch 2 will be rendered obsolete.

Over the years, the judiciary and the Parliament have been accused of doing very little in this area of the law.[56] In this vacuum, a number of Papua New Guinean and expatriate commentators[57] have interpreted the concept of underlying law to mean the supremacy of custom over the common law, and elevation of a "Melanesian jurisprudence". It is suggested that a truly Melanesian jurisprudence cannot be developed without the declaration of the underlying law. The *Constitution* and the judicial precedents are very clear. It calls for the integration of common law with custom (not the other way round), which are *together* the underlying law. The judicial precedents developed under Sch 2 over the years since independence cannot be the *truly* Melanesian jurisprudence. That remains to be achieved under the *Underlying Law Act* 2000.

4.3 CONCLUSION

It is important to determine the constitutional rules and their respective categories. The applicable category is critical, because the category of law that prevails in cases of inconsistency may be regarded as a superior category. This hierarchy determines invalidity. In general, the category of law that prevails over another category of law in a case of inconsistency can be said to be higher in the hierarchy.

The *Constitution* is at the apex of the hierarchy in PNG. Section 10 of the *Constitution* provides that all other laws are to be "read and construed subject to this *Constitution*".

In descending order of importance, the hierarchy is as follows:

1. The *Constitution*
2. Organic Laws
3. Emergency Regulations
4. Ordinary Acts of Parliament
5. Provincial laws
6. Local-level laws
7. Subordinate legislative enactments
8. The underlying law.

56 William Kaputin places the blame squarely on the judiciary and the legislature for their apathy in the development of the underlying law: Kaputin, "Western Law and Melanesian Consciousness" in Thirlwall and Hughes (eds), *The Ethics of Development: In Search of Justice* (Papers from the 17th Waigani Seminar, UPNG Press, Port Moresby, 1989), p 38.

57 See Ntumy, "The Dream of a Melanesian Jurisprudence: The Purpose and Limits of Law Reform" in Aleck and Rannells (eds), op cit n 44, p 7; Narokobi, op cit n 45.

Chapter 5

THE LEGISLATURE

5.1 INTRODUCTION

Section 99(1) of the *Constitution* declares that the power, authority and jurisdiction of the people of Papua New Guinea (PNG) shall be exercised by the national government. The section further declares that the national government consists of three principal arms. The first is the National Parliament, which is the legislature, the second is the national executive, and the third is the national judicial system comprising the National Court and the Supreme Court. In principle, the exercise of the powers and functions of these principal arms shall be kept separate.

The powers and functions of the National Parliament are specifically set out in the *Constitution* and other legislation such as the *Parliamentary Powers and Privileges Act* 1996, the *Parliamentary Service Act*, the *Permanent Parliamentary Committees Act* 1994 and the *Organic Law on National and Local-level Elections* 1996.

Historically, the legislature was regarded as a body made up of individuals representing their constituencies. The legislature, as a body, had various powers and functions, including:

- constituent power;
- legislative power;
- control of government expenditure and revenue-raising; and
- ensuring accountability of the executive.

The legislature as an institution was a place where grievances were redressed and, in England, it also performed a judicial function (House of Lords).

Many of these powers and functions are mirrored in the *Constitution*. These powers and functions have, in some cases, been given constitutional character, and others have been clearly defined by the judiciary. The nature and content of these powers and functions differ markedly from those found in the Parliaments of the United Kingdom, Australia, New Zealand, Canada or in other countries which have adopted the Westminster system of government.

5.2 THE CPC VISION OF THE PARLIAMENT

The Constitutional Planning Committee (CPC) envisaged the National Parliament playing a key role in its complex constitutional scheme. The CPC was concerned that dominance of the executive could reduce the effectiveness of the Parliament. This concern was not only a response to the experiences of the colonial system, where the legislature had been subservient to the executive, but also assumed development of a strong political party system which could lead to executive dominance of a different kind. Hence, the CPC sought ways of ensuring that, as the people's representatives, the Parliament would not be a "mere rubber stamp" for the executive.[1] Rather, the CPC's recommendations were directed towards it ensuring the overall effectiveness of government by keeping the executive accountable to the people.

The CPC recommended a system of government that was, in some ways, based on the Westminster system and, in other ways, quite distinct from it. The main ways in which their recommendations derived from the Westminster system concerned the executive being responsible to the legislature. Major differences included their rejection of a ceremonial head of state – a recommendation that was, in turn, rejected by the government, which persuaded the House of Assembly and the National Constituent Assembly of the benefits of monarchy, Governors-General and knighthoods.

In accepting the Westminster model for the relationship of the executive government and the legislature, the CPC was concerned that the National Parliament should be a far more effective body. Not only should the CPC and the National Parliament be more effective than had been the case with their House of Assembly, but also than was the case in other countries with similar systems. As members of the House of Assembly, many members of the CPC had considerable reservations about the effectiveness of the House. Indeed, it cannot be said that the CPC opted for a variant of the Westminster system because that is what they were used to, for the fact is that, for most of the colonial period, the system of government in PNG did not satisfy the essential requirements of the Westminster system. In particular, until the election of the Somare government in 1972, the Administrator of the territory of Papua and New Guinea expressed reservations on a motion passed by the newly elected House of Assembly requesting recognition of a position of Leader of the Opposition in the House. The move was "consolidating what is growing into a Westminster system of Government before the country itself has really made a decision that this is the sort of government that it does want".[2]

The experience of the CPC members was of a system where the executive arm, under the control of the colonial regime, clearly dominated the legislature. The moves towards "responsible government", where the executive was drawn from and answerable to the legislature, had been made largely according to the program of the colonial regime. It was, in part, in response to this experience that the CPC and other members of the House of Assembly were so committed to a new constitution and political system based on the authority of the people. That authority would be manifested by a much more active role than in the past for the institution most representative of the people.

The CPC members were also clearly aware of the problem inherent in most modern systems of government, and in particular the Westminster system, where political parties dominate. In a two party system, it can be argued that the major question determined at the ballot box is that of which political party hierarchy controls the Parliament. Concerns of this kind underlay the CPC's desire to ensure that the decline of Parliament frequently criticised in other countries, not least in the new states, should not occur here.[3] The CPC sought to avoid the Parliament

---

1 Constitutional Planning Committee, *Final Report of the Constitutional Planning Committee 1974 (Part 1)* (Government Printer, Port Moresby, 1974) (CPC, *Final Report*), Ch 6, p 6/1.

2 Cited in Bayne and Colebatch "Constitutional Development in Papua New Guinea, 1968-73: The Transfer of Executive Power" (1973) 51 *New Guinea Research Bulletin* 126.

3 CPC, *Final Report*, Ch 1, p 1/4.

becoming a "mere rubber stamp" for the executive, as they apparently regarded the position of the legislature in many modern states. Their optimistic vision for an expansive role for the legislature can be seen in the following passage:

> "If government is to be truly responsive to the people, it is vital that those whom the people elect to represent them should be able to contribute actively and effectively to the government of the nation. The legislature should not be seen as a rival to the executive arm, but rather as a full and constructive partner. It can then help to ensure the overall effectiveness of government by keeping the executive accountable to the people."[4]

Reflecting the wishes of the people, the CPC sought a system of government based on popular participation "with maximum emphasis on consultation and consensus", and, hence, the national legislature had to have a central role. A strong legislature with an active role in government is perhaps more consistent with a parliamentary executive system than is a presidential system, and helps to explain why the CPC recommended the former rather than the latter.

However, when it came to giving the Parliament significant new powers, the CPC found that it had limited room to move. While it made detailed recommendations about numerous aspects of the composition, meetings, powers, procedures, privileges and resources of the Parliament, its major distinct proposed initiative was to create a system of committees "intended to bring about continuing participation in government by the non-ministerial elected representatives".[5]

5.3 ROLES AND FUNCTIONS OF THE LEGISLATURE IN PNG

As is normally the case with the various models of the Westminster system, general perceptions tend to focus on the legislative role of the National Parliament. This is, however, only one of the many roles normally exercised by legislatures in the Westminster system. Most of the roles and functions noted above apply to the PNG Parliament.[6]

There is, of course, considerable overlap between these roles. For example, constituent power is exercised through passing laws (albeit using special procedures). Further, as the CPC noted in Ch 9 of its final report, control of raising the expenditure of finance is normally achieved through the exercise of legislative powers. However, the powers in relation to finance can also be regarded as a special category of the powers to supervise and control the executive, and so on.

Representation

Representation of the people is, perhaps, the most fundamental of the roles of a national legislature. This role is best understood by reference to the discussion of the provisions of the *Constitution* on the composition of the Parliament. The representatives provide the links between the people and the Parliament. It is then the manner in which it carries out its other roles and functions that determines how effectively a legislature represents the interests of the people.

---

4 CPC, *Final Report*, Ch 6, p 6/1.
5 CPC, *Final Report*, Ch 1, p 1/4.
6 Chalmers and Paliwala, *An Introduction to the Law in Papua New Guinea* (Law Book Co Ltd, Sydney, 1982), p 111.

Parliament's role as a representative of the people was eloquently expressed by Kapi DCJ in *SCR No 3 of 1999; Re Calling of Meeting of the Parliament* (unreported, 1999). Commenting on the importance of this role, His Honour said:

> "Every member of the Parliament represents the interests of the common people including the unemployed person living in the squatter settlements in Port Moresby to the ordinary subsistence farmer living in a remote village in the outback. The Parliament is there to serve the interests of the people."

It is, therefore, imperative that changes to the *Constitution* and all statutes are made in the interests of the people represented by the Parliament. The role of supervision and control of the executive should also be carried out in the interests of the people.

Constituent power

The power of a legislature to change the *Constitution* involves the changing of the fundamental law creating the state and its institutions. It is, therefore, not a matter of the exercise of normal legislative power. The special nature of what is involved is sometimes referred to as *constituent power*. The special majorities and procedures that apply to the exercise of constituent power highlight the distinction between such power and the exercise of normal legislative power.

In PNG, the Parliament alone has power to amend the constitutional laws (that is, exercise constituent power). The main provisions governing its exercise are ss 12-17 of the *Constitution*. The procedural steps required and the majorities involved are, to some extent, complex. This is highlighted in *SCR No 2 of 1982; Re Organic Law* [1982] PNGLR 214. In that case, the Parliament, following the procedures set out ss 12 and 14 of the *Constitution*, proceeded to amend certain provisions of the *Organic Law on National Elections*. On a reference to the Supreme Court by the Ombudsman Commission, the court was asked to declare that the amendments to s 86(c) of the Organic Law was null and void, as it was one of the provisions of the Organic Law which only required a simple majority for its passage, and not a special majority, as set out by s 17.

The exercise of the constituent power of the Parliament must, however, not be taken lightly, as exemplified by *Kaseng v Namaliu* [1995] PNGLR 481 and *Christian v Namaliu and The State* (unreported, 1996). These two cases clearly illustrate the unwillingness of the judiciary to fetter this special power of the Parliament.

Supervision and control of the executive

Due to the concerns raised by the CPC that Parliament should be more than "a mere rubber stamp" for the executive, the constitutional provisions place considerable emphasis on the role of Parliament in the "supervision and control" of the executive.[7]

The executive has responsibility for the day-to-day conduct of government activities, and, in so doing, has a wide range of roles and functions, and relatively vast financial and personnel resources at its disposal. The executive is, in general, responsible to the legislature. Generally, the executive derives its functions from the legislature, in that it implements the laws made by Parliament and exercises a wide (and ever growing) range of delegated legislative powers. The notion here is one of accountability. The doctrine of accountability, or "ministerial

7 See CPC, *Final Report*, Ch 1, p 1/2; Ch 6, pp 6/7-6/12; Ch 7, p 7/1; Ch 9, p 9/1.

responsibility", involves two propositions. First, Ministers are individually responsible to the Parliament for the affairs of their departments. Secondly, Cabinet is collectively responsible to the Parliament and electorate for the conduct of government.[8]

The *Constitution* aims to make the national executive responsible to the Parliament in a range of ways.

Executive responsible to the Parliament

In the Westminster system, the executive is drawn from, and is responsible to, the legislature. In theory, the executive can be removed from office by the legislature if the legislature loses confidence in the executive. In practice, votes of no confidence tend to depend far more on party numbers in the legislature than on the "confidence" the legislature has in the capacity of the Prime Minister and the Ministers to carry out the tasks of the executive.

In PNG, the basic features of responsible government are spelt out in the *Constitution*. Goldring described this relationship as follows:

> "The *Constitution* establishes a system of government in which the executive branch of the government, in theory, is controlled by, and is responsible and accountable to the National Parliament."[9]

Section 141 of the *Constitution* spells out that all members of the executive (other than the Head of State and her representative in PNG) must be Members of Parliament. The head of the executive, who is the Prime Minister, is a Member of, and effectively elected by, the Parliament. By its nature, s 141 makes the National Executive Council (NEC) responsible "in the sense of being answerable and accountable – to the people's representatives in the Parliament".[10]

The Prime Minister can be removed by the Parliament through a motion of no confidence, as can the entire ministry or individual Ministers. The procedure for their removal must, however, comply strictly with ss 142(5)(a), 144(4)(a) and 145 of the *Constitution*. Since independence, the Parliament has successfully invoked this mechanism five times to remove and replace five Prime Ministers. Even the representative of the Head of State (the Governor-General) is effectively appointed under s 88, and is subject to removal by the Parliament through the procedure set out by s 93.

The theory of the executive being responsible to the Parliament was an important influence on the decision of the Supreme Court in *Haiveta v Wingti (No 3)* [1994] PNGLR 197. The court was considering a challenge to a vote by the Parliament on 24 September 1993, whereby it elected Mr Paias Wingti as Prime Minister after he had resigned on the evening of the previous day (23 September 1993). The whole case hinged on the definition of the phrase "next sitting day" as used in s 142(3) of the *Constitution*. The court took the view that the phrase "next sitting day" meant the next sitting day after the Parliament had been notified of the fact of the vacancy, and not the next sitting day after the resignation. An important factor in the Supreme Court's reasoning was that it is the Parliament that appoints the

8 Emy, *The Politics of Australian Democracy: Fundamentals in Dispute* (2nd ed, Macmillan, Melbourne, 1978), p 246.

9 Goldring, "The Executive Government: Power, Politics and Responsibility" in DeVere, Colquhoun-Kerr and Kaburise, *Essays on the Constitution of Papua New Guinea* (Government Printing Office, Port Moresby, 1985), p 69.

10 Ibid, p 71.

Prime Minister, and it therefore needs time to consider who it will appoint, and it should not be caught by surprise.

Committees of the Parliament

The CPC intended that committees of the Parliament would play a major role in ensuring that Parliament should be a "truly effective body".[11] It recommended detailed provisions for six main "permanent" committees. For the CPC, the name "permanent" was intended to indicate that they were appointed for the full term of a Parliament.

Three of these committees (the First, Second and Third Parliamentary Committees) were to have responsibility for specified groups of subjects related to the major areas of government activity. In addition, there were to be a Public Accounts Committee, a General Parliamentary Committee and a Private Business Committee. Details of their proposed functions can be found in the narrative text and the recommendations in Ch 6 of the CPC's final report. In addition to the "permanent" committees, the CPC envisaged "select" committees being set up from time to time to inquire into particular matters.

In the interests of ensuring flexibility, the *Constitution* does not include the detail about the specific committees suggested by the CPC. However, in many other respects, the provisions on committees reflect the CPC's proposal. It is worth noting the functions of committees as envisaged by the CPC. The most basic functions involve, first, ensuring the satisfactory consideration of proposed legislation coming before the Parliament (increasing volume and complexity meant it could not be considered adequately by the Parliament as a whole), and secondly, probing and checking of government activity.[12]

In relation to legislation, the CPC envisaged that each Bill going before Parliament would have to be referred to the appropriate committee for consideration and report, unless the Parliament agreed by absolute majority not to do so. Committees were expected to work with government in preparation of legislation, thereby facilitating participation of backbench members in government, and removing "artificial barriers between Ministers and other members, and between legislators and bureaucrats".[13]

An additional function relating to the probing and checking of government activity involved consideration by committees of reports and papers tabled in the Parliament. Committees were also to have power to carry out inquiries into matters of national importance, either on referral from Parliament or on their own initiative.

A final vital function was for the main subject committees to act, in their own spheres of responsibility, as consultative bodies in the appointment of persons to a number of statutory positions provided for by the *Constitution*. Although ultimate appointment powers would remain with the executive, the aim was to "open up the selection process in a number of constitutional and statutory offices, where it is imperative that the holders should enjoy widespread confidence of the community".[14]

11 CPC, *Final Report*, Ch 6, pp 6/9-6/10.
12 Ibid, p 6/10.
13 Ibid, p 6/11.
14 Ibid.

The introductory words of s 118(1) of the *Constitution* set out the aims of the system of Permanent Parliamentary Committees in terms similar to the CPC's. It states:

> "In order to achieve full and active participation by backbenchers in the work of the Parliament and of government, there shall be the following Permanent Parliamentary Committees, which in principle, should cover all major fields of the activities of the National Government."

The committees established by s 118 are the Public Accounts Committee (the powers and functions of which are set out by ss 215 and 216) and such other committees of the Parliament. One other such committee created by the *Constitution* is the Emergency Committee.[15] This committee is established by s 240, and its functions are specified under s 242. The composition, powers and functions of the committee are provided for under the *Emergency Committees Act* (Ch 33A). Another permanent committee that was established under the *Organic Law on Provincial Governments* was the Permanent Parliamentary Committee on Provincial Government Suspensions. This committee was abolished with the repeal of the *Organic Law on Provincial Governments* in 1995.

Under s 118(2) of the *Constitution,* provision for particular subject matter committees (as well as composition, powers etc of committees) can be made by the Parliament in almost any way it wishes - by an Organic Law, an Act of the Parliament or the Standing Orders. In 1994, the Parliament enacted the *Permanent Parliamentary Committees Act* 1994 to give effect to the provision. The Act does not establish the committees envisaged by s 118, but makes detailed provisions on the procedures, composition, powers and functions of committees established by the Parliament. The Act is clearly intended to give greater status and powers to the committees.

The positions of Chairperson and Deputy Chairperson, and their powers and functions, are set out in ss 119 and 120 respectively. Apart from the Permanent Parliamentary Committees, a "Sessional or Select Committee or other committees for any purpose" may be created under s 121 of the *Constitution*. Moreover, s 121 also empowers the Parliament to sit as a "Committee of the Whole".

According to s 118(3) of the *Constitution,* membership of Permanent Parliamentary Committees is restricted only to backbench members. To ensure fairness, s 118(4) requires that members should be spread "as widely as practicable" among backbenchers. Moreover, to create balance, s 119(2) requires that the Chairperson of each committee should be from the government side of the Parliament, while the Deputy Chairperson should be from the Opposition.

The CPC's idea that the members of the "permanent" committees would be appointed for the whole of the term of the Parliament is not spelt out in the *Constitution* or the parliamentary Standing Orders. Section 5(2) of the *Permanent Parliamentary Committees Act* 1994 attempts to fill this gap in the law by stipulating that the members hold office at the pleasure of the Parliament. Presumably, the aim of s 5(2) is to ensure flexibility, because membership needs to change as governments change, etc.

15 The provisions create "Emergency Committees" rather than "an Emergency Committee". The reason for this is that only one Emergency Committee is established for a specific national emergency. After the cessation of that particular national emergency, the Emergency Committee also ceases. When another national emergency arises, another Emergency Committee is set up to deal with that national emergency.

The names of the Permanent Parliamentary Committees are provided for by the Standing Orders of the Parliament, as varied from time to time. The Standing Orders as of 1988 provided for Permanent Parliamentary Committees on the following subjects:

- Standing Orders;
- privileges;
- National Parliament (its buildings, services and facilities);
- private business (determining priorities, etc, of private motions);
- subordinate legislation;
- parliamentary legislation;
- appointments;
- constitutional laws and Acts;
- economic affairs;
- foreign affairs and defence; and
- law and order.

The precise functions of each committee were determined by the Standing Orders.

Consistent with the general ideas of the CPC, the *Constitution* suggests that particular committees may be allocated responsibilities relating to particular aspects of the government's functions. This is evident in s 120(1) of the *Constitution*, which suggests that the Chairperson and Deputy Chairperson of each committee have full access to each Minister having responsibilities relevant to the jurisdiction and functions of his or her committee. Moreover, through the Minister, they are to have access to the head of the Minister's Department, and are "entitled to be briefed and consulted on major policy issues".

There is recognition, in a number of the provisions of the *Constitution*, Organic Laws and Acts of Parliament, that various subject matters will be the subject of report or recommendation by whatever parliamentary committee is the most appropriate.[16] The role of reporting on proposed appointments to constitutional offices, as recommended by the CPC, is provided for in the *Constitution*[17] *and other laws.*[18]

The *Permanent Parliamentary Committees Act* 1994 provides a new title for committees with jurisdiction and functions relevant to a Minister or group of Ministers, as envisaged by s 120(1) of the *Constitution*. Under s 3(2) of the *Permanent Parliamentary Committees Act*, they are now to be called Permanent Parliamentary Referral Committees.

Two particularly important provisions of the *Permanent Parliamentary Committees Act* 1994 are the provisions on referral of matters to committees under s 15, and the limits under s 20 on the powers of the Parliament to consider any matters referred to a committee until a committee has made a report on the matter and the Parliament has made a resolution on the report. Section 20 could fetter the power of the Parliament to exercise its legislative powers. If a Bill for a proposed law is referred to a Permanent Parliamentary Committee under the Standing Orders or by motion of a Member of Parliament, the question of passing the Bill cannot be dealt with until after a resolution has been made on the committee's report. The only exception is where the referral is made under the Standing Orders,

16 See, for instance, *Constitution*, s 217(2)(d).
17 For example, *Constitution*, ss 190(2), 209(3) and 260(2)(a).
18 For instance, the *Citizenship Act* (Ch 12) envisages a Permanent Parliamentary Committee with special functions in relation to citizenship matters.

in which case the Parliament can vote to suspend the Standing Orders.[19] The use of this provision was raised in *Kaseng v Namaliu* [1995] PNGLR 481 by Mr Kaseng. Mr Kaseng argued that the Parliament abused the process when it voted to by-pass the requirements of s 20(1) of the 1994 Act and passed the *Organic Law on Provincial Governments and Local-level Governments* 1995. Kapi DCJ, who was the only judge who considered this issue, held that the Parliament correctly invoked s 20(2), but that the eventual outcome of the suspension of the Standing Orders resulted in a breach.

These provisions are similar to those suggested by the CPC in respect of referral of proposed laws to committees. There may, however, be some doubt about whether an Act of Parliament can limit the powers of the Parliament to pass laws.

There is little doubt that the committee system has not been very effective. The General Constitutional Commission made a review of the system in 1980, and it concluded in its final report of 1982 that the committee system was ineffective.[20] As recently as 28 April 2000, it was reported that the committee system had not been operational since 1998 and that the members of the committees were being paid for doing nothing.[21] According to the report, the Clerk of Parliament had reported in his annual report to Parliament that almost all the 28 permanent committees of the Parliament had been inactive for almost two years.[22]

Questions, motions, resolutions and petitions

Parliament is able to probe the government through questions, motions, etc. Section 111 of the *Constitution* enables a Member of Parliament (including a backbencher) to introduce into Parliament (subject to the relevant Standing Orders) a petition, question, Bill, resolution or motion. Redress of "individual grievances" are often dealt with through questions asked of Ministers, but the main function of "questions" is to probe the executive's performance and its activities. The right to introduce a Bill is restricted by s 210. This provision prevents any ordinary Member of Parliament introducing any Bill relating to the finances of the country. The freedom to introduce a petition or a motion in Parliament must also comply with the Standing Orders of Parliament.

Disallowance of delegated legislation

Section 100 of the *Constitution* expresses in uncertain terms that the law-making power of the people of PNG is vested in the National Parliament. This legislative power can, however, be delegated to another authority under s 100(2). The range of authorities envisaged by this provision is very wide, and includes the executive and its instrumentalities, and second and third-level law-making bodies. According to the CPC, this provision was included because "many regulations, rules, by-laws and orders are made by the government under the authority of enactments of the legislature"[23] and, therefore, it was imperative that the government was given the anchorage to invoke this power, but at a lower scale.

The *Constitution* puts the exercise of this power by the government under strict scrutiny. According to ss 116 and 258 and Sch 1.18, the Parliament retains the

19 See *Permanent Parliamentary Committees Act* 1994, s 20(2).

20 General Constitutional Commission, *Final Report of the General Constitutional Commission* (Government Printer, Port Moresby, 1982), pp 121-124.

21 One of the country's daily newspapers, *The Post Courier*, splashed this alarming report as its cover story on Friday, 28 April 2000.

22 Ibid.

23 CPC, *Final Report*, p 6/7.

right to disallow a subordinate legislative enactment. For a subordinate legislative enactment to be valid, it must be tabled and received by Parliament.

Approval of treaties

Similarly, although the executive may enter into treaties with foreign states, the Parliament's consent is normally required if PNG is to be bound by a treaty. Section 117 of the *Constitution* sets out the manner in which a treaty may bind PNG. The procedure spelt out by the section is very meticulous, but, according to a commentator, the procedure in its totality is very weak and has been subject to frequent abuse by the executive.[24]

Tabling of reports

Numerous provisions of the *Constitution* and the Organic Laws require various officers and bodies to table annual reports in the Parliament. The CPC did not offer any explanations as to the purpose of the tabulation of these reports in Parliament.[25] However, it is generally understood that in a parliamentary democratic system these reports serve a very important function, and that is to keep the Parliament up to date about the management and affairs of these institutions. Many of the institutions that report to Parliament are usually independent and free from direction and control by any person.[26]

Specific limits and controls in statutes

Parliament can pass laws specifically aimed at controlling executive action. Numerous statutes are in place to achieve this purpose. Most of these statutes relate to the operations of the bureaucracy. The basic thrust of these statutes is the control of the executive and administrative powers of the Minister or the departmental head over the public servants.[27]

Informal control

There are also more informal control measures such as lobbying and the use of the media by Members of Parliament to ensure that the executive is adequately performing its functions. The most effective tool under this head is the use of the media. The media in PNG has been used as a very important tool to bring about the desired changes in the country. The infamous Sandline Crisis of 1997[28] and the National Provident Fund Saga of 2000[29] are just two examples of the many

---

24 For a discussion of some aspects of the treaty-making power, see Kwa, "Treaty Law-Making in Papua New Guinea: After Two Decades *Yumi Stap We?*" (1997) 25 MLJ 43.

25 CPC, *Final Report*, p 6/9.

26 For example, s 220 of the *Constitution* makes it mandatory for the Ombudsman Commission to present its annual report to Parliament through the Head of State.

27 The application of this control mechanism is discussed in Chapter 6 (6.4).

28 In an attempt to end the Bougainville crisis, the government of Sir Julius Chan secretly engaged some mercenaries in 1996, under the Sandline Contract, to train and lead the PNG Defence Force soldiers on Bougainville to crush the rebels on the island. The media exposed this secret deal in early February 1997, and by March 1997 the people took to the streets and destroyed property and almost brought the government of Julius Chan to its knees.

29 The National Provident Fund (NPF) is a superannuation fund created by statute for the benefit of private sector employees. The fund collects and manages members' contributions. Upon the retirement, termination or death of the member, the fund would pay the member the moneys he or she had contributed plus interest. Over the years since 1995, the fund had been making bad investments, and by 1999 the fund was running at a loss. The media again exposed the fund's financial difficulties in early April 2000. Subsequently, the government set up a Commission of Inquiry to investigate the affairs of the fund and recommend possible legal actions against those implicated in the report.

instances where the media has exposed the secret activities of the government. The change in the government after the 1997 general elections is mainly attributed to the media hype that was created by the Sandline Crisis. The effectiveness of the media in exposing the weakness in government has always been a concern to those in government.[30]

5.4 LEGISLATIVE POWERS

The power to make laws is usually regarded as the principal constitutional function of the legislature.[31] In PNG, s 100 of the *Constitution* vests the law-making power of the people in the National Parliament. This provision and s 109 reflect the views of the CPC. The CPC was strongly of the view that the Parliament's primary role was to make laws for the peace, progress and welfare of PNG.[32] The initiation of the law-making process was, according to the CPC, not restricted to the government of the day, but also to private members.[33] The nature and procedures for the making of laws are discussed below.

Vesting of legislative power outside the National Parliament

Section 100(1) of the *Constitution* vests the "legislative power of the people" in the Parliament. The vesting of this law-making power is, however, subject to the *Constitution*. The *Constitution* allows for the transfer of this law-making power of the legislature to another or other authorities.[34] Section 100(3), however, prevents the "permanent" transfer or divesting of legislative power. It has been suggested that the vesting of "exclusive" legislative powers in provincial governments, by ss 26 and 29 of the *Organic Law on Provincial Government* (repealed), offended s 100(3).[35] This view was confirmed by the Supreme Court in *SCR No 7 of 1992; Re Forestry Act 1991* [1992] PNGLR 514.

Nature of the legislative powers

According to s 109(1) of the *Constitution*, the legislative powers are "plenary". The formula was discussed in *Croft v Dunphy* [1933] AC 156. An almost identical formula (the words peace, welfare and good government) has been held by an Australian court to be words of limitation.[36] This is clearly not the intent in PNG, because of the clear words of s 109(3)(a).[37] The same or a similar formula is used in the constitutions of a number of Pacific Islands.[38]

---

30 See, eg, "Headline Grabs Members Ire", *Post Courier* (4 May 2000), p 2, where the government was upset over the manner in which the *Post Courier* carried a story in which it was reported that the Parliament was on a possible collision course with the judiciary.

31 Lynch, "Legislatures in Some Pacific Constitutions" in Sack, *Pacific Constitutions* (ANU Printing Services, Canberra, 1982), p 156.

32 CPC, *Final Report*, p 6/7.

33 CPC, *Final Report*, p 6/8.

34 See s 187C(6) of the *Constitution* (as amended), which permits the transfer of law-making powers to the provincial governments and local-level governments.

35 Goldring, *The Constitution of Papua New Guinea* (Law Book Co Ltd, Sydney, 1978), p 84. Sections 26 and 29 of the repealed *Organic Law on Provincial Government* have now been assimilated into the new *Organic Law on Provincial Governments and Local-level Governments*.

36 See *Building Construction Employees and Builders Labourers' Federation (NSW) v Minister for Industrial Relations* (1986) 7 NSWLR 372 (Street CJ and Priestley AJ).

37 The issues involved are discussed further by Lynch, "Styles in the Drafting of Some Pacific Constitutions" in Ghai (ed), *Law, Politics and Government in the Pacific Island States* (USP, Suva, 1985), p 231 and Ghai and Regan, *Law, Politics and Administration of Decentralisation* (Monograph 30, National Research Institute, Port Moresby, 1992), pp 140-141.

38 Cook Islands' *Constitution*, Art 39; Solomon Islands' *Constitution*, s 59; Fiji's former *Constitution*, s 52; Vanuatu's *Constitution*, s 16; Kiribati's *Constitution*, s 66; Nauru's *Constitution*, s 27.

Section 109(3)(b) of the *Constitution* stipulates that legislation can have "extra-territorial" effect, and s 110(2)(b) states that a law can have a retrospective effect. Although the legislative powers are, in theory, plenary, these powers are exercised subject to the constitutional laws and the limits imposed by them. For instance, s 110(2)(b) is restricted by s 37(7). The latter provision prevents the Parliament from enacting laws creating criminal offences or dealing with criminal penalties for acts that were not criminal in nature at the time of their commission.

The exercise of the legislative power is also scrutinised by the judiciary. The power of the courts to supervise the exercise of legislative power is provided by ss 18, 19, 57 and 158(1) of the *Constitution.* The major limits are contained in the human rights provisions. The courts have been very quick in invoking this power, as indicated in cases such as *Constitutional Reference No 3 of 1978; Re Inter group Fighting Act 1977* [1978] PNGLR 421, *SCR No 2 of 1982; Re Organic Law* [1982] PNGLR 214 and *SCR No 2 of 1984; Re New Ireland Provincial Constitution* [1984] PNGLR 81.

The constitutional limits include restrictions on the legislature exercising judicial authority under the guise of legislation, an issue involving the application of the doctrine of separation of powers. This concern has been occasionally highlighted by the Supreme Court, as in the case of *SCR No 1A of 1981; Re Motor Traffic Act* [1982] PNGLR 122 at 134-136 (Kearney DCJ). The Supreme Court is aware, however, of the need to avoid usurpation for the role of the legislature, a point firmly stressed in *Peter v South Pacific Brewery* [1976] PNGLR 537 (at 546, Frost CJ) and (at 560, Kearney J), and in *SCR No 2 of 1981; Re s 19 of the Constitution* [1981] PNGLR 518 (at 528-529 Miles J).

Procedures for exercise of legislative powers by Parliament

The procedures of the Parliament are set out in the Standing Orders of Parliament and the *Parliamentary Powers and Privileges Act* (Ch 24). The quorum for parliamentary meetings is specified by s 113 of the *Constitution.* This provision spells out that a quorum of Parliament is a third of all the seats. If a member draws the attention of the Speaker to the lack of a quorum, and a quorum is not present within two minutes, Parliament is adjourned.[39] It is not clear whether or not the Speaker of Parliament is a part of the quorum. This issue has been determined, but on a provincial constitution and a provincial standing order. This issue arose in the election of the Madang Provincial Premier in 1985. When the matter came before the National Court in *Angmai Bilas v Kamindai* [1985] PNGLR 20, Barnett AJ ruled that the Speaker of the Provincial Assembly can be counted as part of the quorum. The principle of the case is clear – the Speaker can be counted as part of the quorum, because he or she represents an electorate that is counted as "one third of the number of seats in Parliament".

The Parliament requires a "simple majority" vote to pass an ordinary Act. Section 114 of the *Constitution* defines simple majority as a majority of members "present and voting". The Speaker does not normally have a vote. However, the Speaker may vote in special circumstances as specified under s 114(2) and (3).

By certifying the law under s 110 of the *Constitution*, the Speaker provides conclusive evidence that a Bill has become law. The law comes into effect on a date as determined in accordance with this section. By virtue of s 134, the certificate of

39 Standing Orders, ss 37-41.

the Speaker issued under s 110 is conclusive evidence of what transpired in the Parliament.

Distinction between "making" and "coming into effect"

Once a law is made, it must be certified. Under s 110(1) of the *Constitution* a law normally comes into effect on certification by the Speaker. Section 110(2) provides that the Act itself may provide the manner in which the law will come into effect. The distinction was a significant basis for the leading majority decision of Hinchliffe and Andrew JJ in *Kaseng v Namaliu and The State* [1995] PNGLR 481. According to their Honours (at 518), "certification operates to bring a law into operation, rather than the making of the law". It is suggested that the second limb of this proposition is not correct because of two fundamental points. These points are exposed by s 110(1). First, according to this provision, certification proves that the law was made by the Parliament. This position is strengthened by s 134, which provides that the certification of the Speaker is conclusive evidence that the law was made by Parliament. Taken from this perspective, it becomes obvious why the question of whether the Parliament complied with its procedures is non-justiciable.

The second point is that s 110(1) expressly states that where the Act is to come into force in a manner provided for under s 110(2), then certification by the Speaker does not bring the law into force. To say that certification by the Speaker only operates to bring the law into force and not the making of the law, is clearly wrong.

5.5 CONTROL OF THE RAISING AND EXPENDITURE OF FINANCE

The traditional roles of the two main arms of the government on this subject were that the executive arm formulated the budget and the legislature approved it. The *Constitution* provides that the Parliament shall authorise and control the raising and expenditure of finance by the national government. This includes the imposition of taxation and the raising of loans, but is clearly not restricted to them.

Under ss 209-212, the *Constitution* mirrors the distinct roles of the executive and the Parliament. Section 210(1) authorises the executive to initiate laws or other measures for the imposition of tax, the raising of loans or expenditure of public moneys. The Parliament can reduce, but cannot increase or re-allocate the amounts or incidences of, or change the purpose of, proposed taxes, loans or expenditure.

Increased role of the Parliament

In 1988, the traditional roles of the executive and the legislature were slightly altered in PNG by *Constitutional Amendment No 10* 1988. This law amended ss 209(2), 210(2), 211 and 212(1) of the *Constitution*. Under the new arrangement, the Parliament can increase the proposed expenditure for the services of the Parliament or the judiciary if the executive had reduced them from the estimates originally submitted by the Chief Justice or the Speaker, and the amounts of the estimates introduced by the executive are adjudged inadequate. The Parliament has, in reality, been given the power to re-allocate the funds: see s 209(3) and (4) as amended in 1988. This significant change increased the role of Parliament at the expense of the executive. There are practical difficulties likely to be caused by the increases in the appropriations estimated for the Parliament and the judiciary.

Methods of control

Section 209(2) of the *Constitution* has a wide scope, and covers taxation laws, laws approving loans, annual and supplementary budgets and appropriation laws. Since 1988, there is a requirement for separate appropriation Acts for the services of Parliament, the services of the judiciary and the general public services.

The power to impose tax has been taken seriously by the courts, as reflected in *Mairi v Tololo (No 2)* [1976] PNGLR 125 and *James Saleng Mileng v Tololo* [1976] PNGLR 447. Both cases involved the same facts. In these cases, the National Executive Council (NEC) authorised all multi-racial schools to impose "economic fees" for the purposes of improving educational facilities and for discouraging Papua New Guinean parents from demanding Australian-based curriculums. In a nutshell, the Supreme Court ruled that the imposition of the fees by the schools upon the direction of the NEC was in violation of s 209 of the *Constitution*, as the Parliament had not authorised the imposition of these fees.

Expenditure without approval by the Parliament

If, for any reason, an appropriation Act has not been passed by the beginning of the fiscal year, s 212 of the *Constitution* provides for automatic appropriation (without parliamentary approval) of a third of the total of the budgeted expenditure for the previous fiscal year. It is suggested that the purpose of s 212 is mainly to avoid the possibility of blocking of funds (refusal of supply) by the Parliament where the Opposition has the numbers to block the budget but cannot remove the government in a vote of no confidence.

5.6 MEMBERSHIP, POWERS AND PRIVILEGES OF THE LEGISLATURE

The *Constitution* sets out very intricate procedures for membership to the Parliament. To be able to become a Member of Parliament, one must comply with a number of strict requirements in the *Constitution*, the Organic Laws and Acts of Parliament. Many of the processes involved have been defined and clarified by the courts.

Composition

In its report to the House of Assembly, the CPC recommended that the membership of the legislature should comprise only elected members who should represent not more than 107 electorates and not fewer than 101 electorates. The CPC strongly opposed the idea of "regional seats" and "nominated members".[40] The CPC explained that the majority of the people rejected the idea of "regional seats", because they felt that the members holding these seats were usually unknown to them and that they were represented twice. The CPC also explained that "nominated membership" was not very popular with the people, and that the people were of the firm view that the legislature should be comprised of elected

40 CPC, *Final Report*, pp 6/1-6/2.

members only.[41] As will be seen below, the *Constitution* has diverged from the CPC's recommendations.

The Parliament, as the third arm of the government, is a constitutional institution. It is a single-chamber Parliament consisting of 109 elected members who represent 89 open electorates and 20 regional or provincial seats: s 101. These members are elected to the Parliament in accordance with ss 125 and 126 of the *Constitution* and the *Organic Law on National and Local-level Government Elections* 1996.[42]

A third category of members is provided for under ss 101(1)(c) and 102 of the *Constitution*. This special category of members is called "nominated members" or unelected members. This provision has not been implemented since independence.

The practice of nominating members to the legislature existed at the time of the CPC under the *Papua New Guinea Act* 1949-1971. This Act was amended in 1971 to enable the Administrator to appoint seven non-elected members comprising of four official members and up to three other members in addition to the 100 elected members. In 1973, upon attaining self-government, the appointment of four officials ceased. Although the CPC opposed the retention of this category of membership, the government succeeded in persuading the House of Assembly to maintain the practice.[43]

Qualifications for and disqualification from membership

The CPC considered this aspect of the legislature very seriously, because of the "importance of the role of the Parliament in the new system of government"[44] it proposed. The CPC recommended that for a person to qualify to be a Member of Parliament, he or she must be a citizen, a resident of the electorate and above the age of 23. It rejected "educational qualification" as a ground for election to Parliament.[45] These qualifications are set out in ss 50, 103(1) and 103(2) of the *Constitution* respectively. However, s 103(2) varied the age requirement to 25 years and above.[46]

In re Moresby North East Parliamentary Election (No 2) [1977] PNGLR 448 defined the term "residence" under the second qualification under s 103. The court held that Mr Lowa did not meet the tenets of residence as required by the *Constitution*, and therefore his election was absolutely null and void. According to the court, merely owning a property in an electorate for investment purposes, without any constructive residency, did not amount to residence.[47]

Section 103(2) was amended in 1991 by *Constitutional Amendment No 15* 1991. Another condition was added to the existing three by requiring a nomination fee of K1,000. The increase in the fees has been very controversial. At independence,

---

41 CPC, *Final Report*, p 6/1.

42 The *Organic Law on National and Local-level Elections* 1996 replaced the former *Organic Law on National Elections*. The new Organic Law became operational in the 1997 national elections.

43 Government of Papua New Guinea, *Government Paper: Proposals on Constitutional Principles and Explanatory Notes* (Government Printer, Port Moresby, 1974), p 24. The government had actually proposed that the Parliament be allowed to appoint only two members.

44 CPC, *Final Report*, p 6/2.

45 CPC, *Final Report*, pp 6/2-6/3.

46 In *Re Simbu Provincial Election* [1983] PNGLR 28, the petitioner (Mr Iambakey Okuk) disputed the election results of the Simbu Regional Seat, arguing that the candidate who came third in the elections was under-age and his participation in the polls made a difference in the elections. He argued that because the candidate was under-age and his votes affected the results, the election should be declared null and void. The Court of Disputed Returns rejected this argument.

47 See also *SCR No 3 of 1984; Kevin Masive v Iambakey Okuk* [1984] PNGLR 390 and *SCR No 2 of 1985; Re Masive v Okuk* [1985] PNGLR 263.

the nomination fee was only K100.[48] In 1981, the Parliament amended s 86(c) of the *Organic Law on National Elections* by increasing the nomination fee from K100 to K1,000. The Ombudsman Commission challenged this increase in nomination fees in the case of *SCR No 2 of 1982; Re Organic Law* [1982] PNGLR 214. The Ombudsman Commission challenged the increase on two grounds. The first ground was that the amendment was unconstitutional, as it did not comply with the requirements of s 14 of the *Constitution.* The second ground was that the increase in nomination fees violated the rights of citizens to stand for elections under s 50 of the *Constitution.* The Ombudsman Commission was successful on both counts.

In 1991, exactly a decade after the first attempt to increase the nomination fees, the Parliament again amended s 86(c) of the *Organic Law on National Elections* and increased the nomination fee to K1,000.[49] Again, the Ombudsman Commission challenged the increase in fees in *SCR No 1 of 1992* [1992] PNGLR 73. This time the Supreme Court held that the amendment was in order, as it complied with the relevant constitutional requirements.[50]

To be eligible to stand for elections, a qualified person is required to comply with the procedures for elections set out in ss 105 and 126 of the *Constitution* and the *Organic Law on National and Local-level Elections.*[51] A candidate who complies with these requirements and wins become a Member of Parliament. A successful candidate who violated the requirements of the Organic Law or the *Criminal Code* can be disqualified as a duly elected Member of Parliament. This was highlighted by the two cases of *In re Menyamya Open Parliamentary Election* [1977] PNGLR 298 and *John Jaminan v The State* [1983] PNGLR 122.

An elected Member of Parliament is required to uphold the integrity of the office that he or she occupies. Strict codes of discipline and other mandatory obligations are imposed on him or her. The Member of Parliament is subject to ss 26-31 of the *Constitution*, the *Organic Law on Duties and Responsibilities of Leadership* (*Leadership Code*) and the *Organic Law on the Ombudsman Commission.* Any breach of the duties and obligations imposed under these laws may result in the Member losing his or her membership of the Parliament. Some of the cases which are on point include *The State v The Independent Tribunal; Ex parte Sasakila* [1976] PNGLR 491, *Re Sigulogo* [1988-1989] PNGLR 384, *State v Ramoi (No 2)* [1990] PNGLR 136, *Balakau v Ombudsman Commission* [1995] PNGLR 70, *Nilkare v Ombudsman Commission* (1995) N 1344.

A Member may also relinquish his or her position in Parliament if he or she falls under any of the categories listed under s 103(3) of the *Constitution.* These include:

- non-eligibility to vote;
- unsound mind;
- sentenced to death or imprisoned for more than nine months; and
- disqualified under the *Constitution.*

48 This was provided for under s 86(c) of the *Organic Law on National Elections.*

49 *Organic Law on National Elections (Amendment No 1)* 1991.

50 By the same amendment, voters were required to be photographed and then to use their identity cards to vote in the elections. The Ombudsman Commission challenged this requirement in *SCR No 5 of 1992* [1992] PNGLR 114. The Supreme Court ruled that for a voter to be entitled to vote only if he or she had an identification card was a violation of the right to privacy under s 49 of the *Constitution*, and therefore this limb of the amendment was null and void.

51 A losing candidate in an election who is alleged to have committed an offence under the election law can be convicted of the offence, as was the case in *The State v Manasseh Voeto* [1978] PNGLR 119.

Terms of the Parliament

Prior to independence, the term of the House of Assembly was four years. When considering the term of the Parliament, the CPC proposed that the same practice be retained after independence.[52] The House of Assembly did not accept the CPC's proposal. Instead, the Assembly agreed that the term of Parliament should be increased to five years. Section 105 of the *Constitution* reflects this position.

The CPC also considered the question of the dissolution of Parliament, and rejected the idea of early dissolutions resulting in "snap elections".[53] However, it proposed that the Speaker could bring the term of Parliament to an abrupt halt under two circumstances. The first circumstance was if the Prime Minister was voted out of office through a successful vote of no-confidence. This option could, however, be exercised *only* in the final year of the Parliament. The second situation was where extraordinary circumstances existed to warrant dissolution of the Parliament. The CPC did not identify or define what it meant by "extraordinary circumstance".

The Constituent Assembly accepted the first recommendation, but rejected the second one. The Parliament can, therefore, be dissolved within the last year of a current Parliament if:

- a vote of no-confidence against the government is successful; or
- a vote of confidence in the government is not successful; or
- the Parliament, by an absolute majority vote, agrees to dissolve the Parliament.[54]

Two important observations must be made here. First, the vote of no-confidence referred to under this provision is very special. Unlike the usual motion of no-confidence *where an alternative Prime Minister is nominated* and voted pursuant to s 145(2)(a) or (4) of the *Constitution*, a vote of no-confidence against the government under s 105 *does not contain the name of an alternative Prime Minister*. The Parliament basically decides to vote the government out of office and dissolve Parliament. Secondly, the *Constitution* does not specify the circumstances that will warrant the dissolution of Parliament under the third option. It is suggested that this ambiguity follows from the uncertainty the CPC found itself in when it failed to define "exceptional circumstances" when it proposed that the Parliament be dissolved under these circumstances.

The strength of the *Constitution* on this issue was tested in March 1997 during the Sandline Crisis. According to the general public, the crisis could only be resolved by the resignation of the Prime Minister, Sir Julius Chan, and the dissolution of Parliament. The government and Parliament rejected these two demands outright, on the basis that the existing constitutional framework did not permit these demands (resignation and dissolution of Parliament).

In fact, the dissolution of Parliament is permitted by the *Constitution* and, in reality, the Parliament could have voted out the government and dissolved Parliament under s 105, given the fact that the crisis was in March and the election was in June 1997. The Parliament could have easily dissolved Parliament and brought the election forward.

---

52 CPC, *Final Report*, Ch 6, p 6/14.
53 Ibid, p 6/13.
54 *Constitution*, s 105(1).

Elections to Parliament

Section 50 of the *Constitution* guarantees every citizen the right to stand for election to any elective office, including the National Parliament. Apart from the main limitations set out in s 103 of the *Constitution*, any male or female citizen can stand for elections to the National Parliament. The conduct of the elections to the National Parliament is regulated through the *Organic Law on National and Local-level Government Elections* 1996 (OLNLLGE). The Electoral Commission, established by s 126 of the *Constitution* and s 5 of the OLNLLGE, administers elections to the Parliament.[55]

Having decided to continue with a variant of the Westminster system, the constitution-makers tended to assume that the Parliament would operate similarly to Parliaments in Westminster variants elsewhere. Of course, it has been the emergence of strong political parties that has largely determined key aspects of the operation of the Westminster system in the United Kingdom and the older colonies, such as Australia, New Zealand and Canada. In the early 1970s, it tended to be assumed that political parties would continue to grow in strength and importance in PNG, and would be the main basis for mobilising political support for election into, and for the organisation of, groupings of Members within the Parliament.

The limited progress towards mass-based parties lapsed upon independence, largely made redundant by the first-past-the-post electoral system that the *Constitution* introduced to replace the optional preferential voting system. The failure of parties to develop as expected has tended to produce a Parliament that operates quite differently from those of Westminster variants in countries with strong political parties. Important reasons for the weakness of parties lie in the nature of the Papua New Guinean society and economy. Society is based on a multitude of small language and clan groups. The economy is still largely subsistence, with limited links between the traditional subsistence sector and the small externally dominated modern sector. As a result, there are few major cleavages in the society around which political parties can mobilise mass support. Parties cannot pretend to represent a large working class, or a large middle class, as they once did in England and Australia. Nor can they represent large ethnic or religious groups contending for state power, as they have in many parts of Africa and Asia. Rather, in PNG, parties tend to be small, elite-dominated organisations mainly directed towards the organisation of groupings within the Parliament, rather than how the Members get to Parliament. While originating in the structures of society and economy, this tendency has undoubtedly been exacerbated by the first-past-the-post electoral system, which means there is little need in most electorates to seek support beyond particular ethnic and sub-ethnic groups (clan and sub-clan).

55 On elections, see CPC, *Final Report*, Ch 6, pp 6/13-6/14, paras 88-91; pp 6/15-6/18, paras 100-123; *Constitution*, National Goals Nos 1-3 and 5; ss 104-106 and 126. As to election funding and campaign conduct, see *Constitution*, ss 129 and 130 as well as the General Constitutional Commission, *Final Report of the General Constitutional Commission* (Government Printer, Port Moresby, 1982), pp 124-125; Goldring, *The Constitution of Papua New Guinea* (Law Book Co Ltd, Sydney, 1978), pp 8-9, 42 and 46. As to fees for candidates, see *SCR No 2 of 1982; Re Organic Law* [1982] PNGLR 214 and *SCR No 1 of 1992* [1992] PNGLR 73. As to use of voter identity cards in conduct of elections, see *SCR No 5 of 1992* [1992] PNGLR 114. The following cases represent a sample of the many judicial decisions on different aspects of the conduct of elections: *Imbakey Okuk v Electoral Commissioner* [1983] PNGLR 80; *SCR No 2 of 1982; Re Organic Law* [1982] PNGLR 214; *SCR No 5 of 1982; Hugo Berguhauser v Joseph Aoae* [1982] PNGLR 379; *In the matter of the Organic Law on National Elections; Kuberi Epi v Tony Farapo* (1983) SC 247; *Billy Jababa v Okuk* [1983] PNGLR 69; *Okuk v Electoral Commissioner* [1983] PNGLR 80; *Alan Ebu v Roy Evara* [1983] PNGLR 201; *Malipu Balakau v Paul Torato* [1983] PNGLR 242; *SCR No 2 of 1985; Re Masive v Okuk* [1985] PNGLR 263; *Malapu v The Electoral Commission* [1987] PNGLR 128.

As a result, political parties have developed specialised strategies for manipulating the electoral system and the rules for the operation of Parliament. The focus of party resources is on gathering support from those whom the often rather unpredictable clan based electoral politics throws up as elected members, rather than on mobilising support on the basis of policies.

Meetings of the Parliament

Prior to independence, the *Papua and New Guinea Act* required the House of Assembly to meet at least once a year. The CPC was aware that constitutions of many countries in the Commonwealth required a minimum of one annual meeting for the legislatures.[56] The CPC said that it considered the once-a-year parliamentary meeting inappropriate for PNG. It therefore recommended that the Parliament should meet at least three times in a year, and each meeting should be conducted over a period of at least three weeks.[57]

The CPC's proposal was easily accepted by the Constituent Assembly. The recommendation is reflected in s 124(1) of the *Constitution*. The *Organic Law on the Calling of Meetings of the National Parliament* supplements this provision. The Organic Law has only five sections, and sets out the procedure for calling meetings of Parliament after an election, in a state of emergency and for the normal parliamentary meetings.

Section 124(1) of the *Constitution* is in the following terms:

> "The Parliament shall be called to meet not more than 7[58] days after the day fixed for the return of the writs for a general election, and shall meet not less frequently than three times in each period of 12 months, and, in principle, for not less than nine weeks in each period."

This provision has twice become involved in controversy. The first time was in 1990, and the second in 1999. In the first instance, the Supreme Court was asked by the Attorney-General, in *SCR No 4 of 1990* [1994] PNGLR 141, to define the requirements of s 124. In that case, the Parliament had adjourned for seven months from 7 November 1990 to 16 July 1991. The Opposition, being unhappy with the decision of Parliament, began proceedings in the National Court challenging the validity of the adjournment.

The Supreme Court ruled on a number of matters. First, it held that the year of a Parliament begins from the day after the return of the writ after a general election. Secondly, it ruled that s 124 has three main requirements. These are:

(a) the Parliament must meet at least three times in a parliamentary year;

(b) a meeting of Parliament may extend for three weeks; and

(c) s 124 is directory only.

Thirdly, s 124 does not impose a duty on any person.

In the second instance, the Parliament again adjourned for seven months from November 1997 to July 1998.[59] This time the Ombudsman Commission challenged the validity of the adjournment in *SCR No 3 of 1999; Re Calling of*

---

56 CPC, *Final Report*, op cit, Ch 6; *SCR No 2 of 1985; Re Masive v Okuk* [1985] PNGLR 263; *Malapu v The Electoral Commission* [1987] PNGLR 128 at 6/13.

57 Ibid.

58 In 1992, s 124(1) of the *Constitution* was amended to reduce the number of days Parliament could meet after a national election from 21 days to seven days.

59 The adjournment was necessary to enable the Skate Government to consolidate its position in preparation for a possible vote of no confidence that was imminent after the veil of protection (12 months grace period) was removed in December 1998.

Parliament (unreported, 1999). A full bench of the Supreme Court (seven judges) heard this case. By a majority of six to one, the Supreme Court overruled the decision of the Supreme Court in *SCR No 4 of 1990* [1994] PNGLR 141. Essentially, the Supreme Court held that the provisions of s 124 were mandatory. It also ruled that a breach of s 124 could attract penalties that would be determined by the National Court. The majority also defined the nine weeks of sitting days as 63 days in a period of 12 months. This particular segment of the decision is quite radical because it ties down the Parliament and, in practical terms, it forces the Parliament to meet not less than 63 days in a year.

This latter decision has caused great concern for the Parliament. Some Parliamentarians have complained that the Supreme Court has encroached on the doctrine of separation of powers, by directing the Parliament to perform its functions, when the judiciary has no right to do so.

Officers of the National Parliament

The Parliament, as an institution of government, is headed by the Speaker of Parliament. The clear stipulation of s 107 of the *Constitution* is that the Office of the Speaker is a constitutional office. As a constitutional office holder, the Speaker is subject to the *Organic Law on the Duties and Responsibilities of Leadership* (*Leadership Code*). Section 108 of the *Constitution* states that the fundamental role of the Speaker is "for upholding the integrity of Parliament, maintaining order in it and regulating its proceedings and administering its affairs".

The Speaker administers the day-to-day operations of the Parliament through the Clerk of Parliament. The Clerk of Parliament is a constitutional office holder as defined under s 221 of the *Constitution* and s 1 of the *Organic Law on Certain Constitutional Office-holders*. The qualifications and criteria for appointment of the Clerk of Parliament are provided under ss 7-9 of the *Organic Law on Certain Constitutional Office-holders*.[60]

There are other officers of the Parliament who are of lesser status than the above three constitutional officers. These officers are members of the Parliamentary Service, and are answerable to the Speaker through the Clerk of Parliament. The duties and responsibilities of these officers are provided for by the *Parliamentary Services Act* (Ch 26), which itself is provided for under s 132 of the *Constitution*.

The principal functions of the Parliamentary Service are stipulated under s 3 of the *Parliamentary Services Act*. These include the provision of secretarial services, research, legal and other advisory services, reporting services and adequate library facilities. Members of the service are deemed to be public servants under s 11 of the Act and, thus, enjoy certain rights and privileges accorded to public servants.

Note the enhanced powers of the Speaker flowing from *Constitutional Amendment No 8* 1988 and *Constitutional Amendment No 9* 1988.

Procedures

The proceedings of Parliament are spelt out by the Standing Orders of the Parliament as provided for under s 133 of the *Constitution*. The Standing Orders set out in detail the manner and order of proceedings of Parliament. The *Constitution*, however, provides some clear limits and directions on a number of matters

60 The specific roles and functions of the Clerk of Parliament during Parliamentary sittings are set out in Standing Orders 2, 5, 12-18, 19-22 and 36-40 of the of the National Parliament.

relating to the proceedings of Parliament. For instance, s 113(1) states that the quorum for a sitting of Parliament is "one-third of the number of seats in the Parliament". Section 114 stipulates that, except as otherwise provided for in a constitutional law or the Standing Orders, all questions before Parliament are to be decided by a simple majority vote. According to s 112, the meetings of Parliament must always be chaired by the Speaker or, in his or her absence, the Deputy Speaker. The same provision prohibits the Ministers from chairing parliamentary meetings. Section 111 of the *Constitution* stipulates that, apart from a few limitations, any Member of Parliament has a right to introduce a Bill, petition, motion or resolution in Parliament. The enactment and the effectual date of a law are regulated by s 110 of the *Constitution*. The procedures for disallowing delegated legislation and binding PNG under international law are defined by ss 116 and 117 respectively.

According to s 134 of the *Constitution*, the proceedings of Parliament and its committees are non-justiciable. In the case of *James Eki Mopio v The Speaker of the National Parliament* [1977] PNGLR 420,[61] a Member of Parliament sought a declaration that the election of Mr Michael Somare as the Prime Minister was null and void. The Supreme Court hastily decided that the proceeding was barred by s 134 of the *Constitution*. This decision was readily followed by the National Court in relation to provincial legislatures in *Kaguel Koroka v Kapal* [1985] PNGLR 117. These two cases, especially *James Eki Mopio v The Speaker of the National Parliament*, were distinguished by the National Court in *Haiveta v Wingti (No 1)* [1994] PNGLR 160.[62] In that case, Sheehan J correctly found that the non-justiciability under s 134 must be read subject to other constitutional provisions. He concluded that the question before him was therefore justiciable. This portion of Sheehan J's judgment was not considered in any depth by the Supreme Court in *Haiveta v Wingti (No 3)* [1994] PNGLR 197. The obiter dicta is that the National Court was correct on the issue of non-justiciability of parliamentary proceedings.

Parliamentary privileges

The CPC was of the view that detailed provisions of the privileges and immunities of Parliamentarians should be left to ordinary legislation. However, it was also of the view that to strengthen the freedoms of speech, debate and proceedings in Parliament, the privileges and immunities of Parliamentarians should be protected by the *Constitution*.[63]

The CPC's views are reflected in some detail in s 115 of the *Constitution*. This provision spells out a number of privileges and immunities of the Members of Parliament. These privileges include:

- freedom of speech, debate and proceedings in Parliament;
- freedom from suit in any court relating to matters raised in Parliament;
- freedom from arrest for civil debts during Parliamentary meetings; and
- freedom from service of any writ within the precincts of Parliament.

These privileges and immunities are also expanded in the *Parliamentary Powers and Privileges Act* (Ch 24)[64] and the Standing Orders of the National Parliament.

61 The validity of the views expressed in this case are discussed in Goldring, *The Constitution of Papua New Guinea* (Law Book Co Ltd, Sydney, 1978), pp 44-45.

62 *Haiveta v Wingti (No 1)* [1994] PNGLR 160 (Sheehan J).

63 CPC, *Final Report*, Ch 6, p 6/8.

64 See *Parliamentary Powers and Privileges Act*, ss 3, 5 and 6.

Conditions of employment of Members of Parliament

Members of Parliament are technically employed by the government to be legislators. The nature of their position and role in society sets them apart from the rest of the public sector. It is for this reason that the CPC noted that "the salaries and allowances of Members of Parliament are frequently the cause of controversy".[65]

In order to avoid or reduce the potential for controversy, the CPC proposed that the terms and conditions of employment of Parliamentarians be scrutinised by an independent body set up by the *Constitution*. The CPC proposed that this authority should comprise a judge or a magistrate, an experienced accountant and a member of the Public Services Commission.

Generally, the recommendations of the CPC were reflected in s 131 of the *Constitution*. From independence until 1988, the Parliamentary Salaries Tribunal considered the salaries and conditions of the Members of Parliament. The Tribunal was solely responsible for the fixing from time to time of the salaries, allowances, pensions and other financial benefits of the Parliamentarians. In 1988, s 131 was repealed and replaced by s 216A, with the passage of *Constitutional Amendment No 9 of 1988 – Salaries and Remunerations Committee*. The underpinning of the change was that Parliament was given greater control over the process of determining the salaries and other financial benefits of Parliamentarians. This is reflected in the membership of the committee, which comprises of the Speaker of Parliament, the Prime Minister, the Leader of the Opposition, the Chief Justice, the Secretary for the Department of Personnel Management and the Secretary for Industrial Relations.

The *Salaries and Remuneration Commission Act* 1988[66] supplemented the 1988 constitutional amendment. The amendment to the *Constitution* enabled the inclusion of judges, other constitutional office-holders and provincial politicians under the umbrella of the Salaries and Remunerations Committee. The committee, like its predecessor, is mainly responsible for fixing the salaries, allowances and other benefits of the national and provincial Parliamentarians, judges and other constitutional office-holders.[67]

The *Leadership Code* also regulates the employment of Members of Parliament. Under ss 7, 8 and 9 of the *Leadership Code*, leaders, including the Members of Parliament, are prohibited from being employed as company directors, engaging in paid employment or holding shares in companies that are likely to compromise their positions.

5.7 CONCLUSION

The CPC's aims for the Parliament were, to some extent, based on assumptions about how the legislatures work in "developed" countries. It is the complex relationship of law and the society within which it operates that determines the outcomes of a legal system. It can, therefore, be expected that the operation and outcomes of laws creating the basic institutions of government will tend to depend on the political, economic and cultural forces at work in any particular society. In PNG, the strength and roles of the state, the nature of economic

65 CPC, *Final Report*, Ch 6, p 6/6.
66 *Salaries and Remuneration Commission Act* 1988 (No 1 of 1988).
67 Ibid, ss 10, 11, 12 and 13.

relations and the nature of civil society are all dramatically different from those of the developed countries upon whose experience the CPC tended to draw.

The Parliament in PNG continues to play a pivotal role in the development of the country. Its biggest challenge was the Sandline Crisis. In the midst of severe threats, intimidation and danger to the lives of the individual Members of Parliament by the public and the dissenting soldiers, the Parliament was able to display great courage and strength as an institution, maintain its independence and rise up above the crisis.

Since then, the Parliament has been able to exert its position as a very powerful institution in government. The change in government in 1998, and the current tension between the Parliament and the judiciary in relation to the operations of Parliament, are reflective of the growing awareness by Parliament of its powers and functions and its role in the development of PNG.

Chapter 6

THE EXECUTIVE

6.1 INTRODUCTION

The executive is the second arm of government provided under the *Constitution* of Papua New Guinea (PNG). It is the branch of government responsible for "securing the carrying out of policy and applying principles and rules of law to cases, as contrasted with the legislature, whose function is to settle policy and makes rules of law, and the judiciary, whose function is to decide disputes as to the meaning or application of rules of law".[1] The term "executive" can also mean "the total government bureaucracy, the politically responsible officials who direct it and the chief of state".[2]

The executive performs a number of functions. In broad terms, the typical roles of the executive are:

- executing (carrying out) the laws;
- policy formulation (including formulation of proposed legislation for submission to the legislature);
- initiation of revenue-raising and expenditure proposals;
- making delegated legislation;
- supervision of the bureaucracy and the services it provides;
- (maintenance of public order, exercising powers of mercy, management of government property, and conduct of military operations;
- conduct of international affairs; and
- dealing with emergencies.

The position of the executive in the *Constitution* of PNG is consistent with Duchacek's view on the role of constitutions in relation to the executive. Duchacek[3] has stated:

> "Most constitutions determine and describe the form and structure of the national executive and its relationship to national legislatures according to one of two basic models:
>
> (1) A *cabinet*[4] system in which the executive issues from the legislature and, in principle, remains linked with and responsible to it.

1 Walker, *The Oxford Companion to Law* (Clarendon Press, Oxford, 1980), p 449.

2 Gould and Kolb (eds), *A Dictionary of the Social Sciences* (Tavistock Publications, UNESCO, 1964), p 249.

3 Duchacek, *Power Maps: Comparative Politics of Constitutions* (ABC-Clio Press Inc, Santa Barbara, 1973).

4 The term "cabinet" is a French word that means "a private room set aside for interviews". In governmental terms, it refers to a room or cabinet where meetings are conducted in secret.

(2) A *presidential* system in which the national executive and the national legislature are given separate mandates of power by the people and remain separately accountable to the people."[5]

The executive in PNG is based on the *cabinet* system and is entrenched in the constitutional framework. Its position, composition and role in government differs drastically from the original views of the Constitutional Planning Committee (CPC). The CPC had proposed an executive arm of government without the office of the Governor-General and with no more than 20 ministries. The final stage of the *Constitution* and practice since independence have departed, to a large degree, from the recommendations of the CPC.

Since independence, the executive has become more powerful, and has expanded its scope of operations and membership. The role of the executive in the development of the country has also be refined and clarified by the judiciary and the processes of government. As PNG is a developing country, the executive has also faced a number of serious challenges to its existence. This chapter focuses on the operation of the executive, examines its relationship to the other two arms of government and discusses the various struggles between the executive and the other two arms of government.

6.2 THE POSITION OF THE EXECUTIVE IN PNG

When considering the issue of the executive, the CPC was very critical of the role the executive would play in the development of PNG. It was gravely concerned about the potential for abuse of power by the executive arm of government. The CPC, therefore, began its discussion on this subject by proposing that:

> "The Committee proposes that the first part of our *Constitution* should include an article which states: 'Power belongs to the people and it shall be exercised in accordance with this *Constitution*.'"[6]

According to the CPC, this stipulation was necessary because:

> "We believe it is important to make clear in this way that the power exercised under the *Constitution* is derived from the people. In the great majority of the societies that make up our nation, it was from the people rather than from kings or chiefs that power was taken by the colonial rulers. It is therefore appropriate that it be the people to whom that power should be returned."[7]

The CPC considered the proposal for an executive headed by a Head of State, and rejected the proposal because "neither kings and queens, nor governor-general or presidents, have any traditional place in our societies".[8] The CPC recommended that the executive power of the people be vested in the National Executive Council (NEC), which would be headed by a Head of Government called the Prime Minister. This proposal showed a "lack of respect for the useless trappings of tradition, [and] were apparently too radical for those in power".[9]

The government at that time rejected the views of the CPC, and moved for the inclusion of the Head of State in the *Constitution*. Ghai explains that one of the reasons for this move by the Somare Government was "clearly the wish to reassure

---

5 Duchacek, op cit n 3, p 174.
6 Constitutional Planning Committee, *Final Report of the Constitutional Planning Committee 1974 (Part 1)* (Government Printer, Port Moresby, 1974) (CPC, *Final Report*), p 7/1.
7 Ibid.
8 Ibid.
9 Goldring, *The Constitution of Papua New Guinea* (Law Book Co Ltd, Sydney, 1978), p 48.

the Papuans and the Highlanders who approached Independence with considerable suspicion".[10] Goldring, drawing from the parliamentary Hansard, gives the other reasons for the inclusion of the Head of State in the system of government for PNG as including:

- provision of some continuity during the changes of government;
- convenience in diplomatic representation; and
- the settling of disputes between Ministers etc.[11]

The CPC also recommended that the executive should be drawn from the Parliament. This recommendation was easily accepted by the Constituent Assembly. Thus, the concept of responsible government was implanted into the *Constitution*. The CPC further recommended that the Cabinet should contain at least 15, but not more than 27, members. The CPC was concerned that it would be quite expensive to increase and maintain a large number of ministries in light of its proposal for the introduction of the provincial government system in the new era.[12] According to the CPC, the ideal number for the Cabinet would be 20 Ministers. It proposed that any extension beyond 20 Ministers should be approved by Parliament by an absolute majority vote.[13]

The CPC also made sweeping recommendations on the election of the Prime Minister, the formation of government, the composition and function of the NEC, departments and changing governments. Most of these recommendations, either in their original form or in modified versions, are reflected in the *Constitution*.

The National Executive

Section 138 of the *Constitution* declares that the executive power of the people is vested in the Head of State acting in accordance with the advice of the NEC. Section 139 clarifies that the National Executive consists of the Head of State and the NEC. These two institutions are interdependent and need each other for the day-to-day governance of the country. However, in reality, the NEC is more powerful than the Head of State. The position of the Head of State in this relationship was described as "a rubber stamp" by Kidu CJ in *Kila Wari v Ramoi and Dibela* [1986] PNGLR 112. Kidu CJ said (at 116):

> "As has been pointed out under s 86(2) of the *Constitution* the Head of State acts solely on the advice of the NEC or other body designated by written law. He or she does not determine anything. He or she merely affixes his or her signature to documents approved by the NEC or a body designated by written law. The Head of State has no personal power. He or she is a mere figurehead – a rubber stamp is not an inappropriate description of the nature of his or her function."

It is the NEC that is in total control of the government machinery.

The Head of State

The inclusion of this institution in the *Constitution* is a fundamental departure from the recommendations of the CPC. The inclusion of the monarchy in PNG's

10 Ghai, "Executive and Legislature" in Sack (ed), *Pacific Constitutions* (Australian National University, Canberra, 1982), p 216. For comparative purposes, Ghai gives a very good exposition of the systems in the Melanesian region in this paper and also in Ghai, "Systems of Government II" in Ghai (ed), *Law, Politics and Government in the Pacific Island States* (USP, Suva, 1988), pp 76-105.

11 Goldring, op cit n 9, p 48.

12 CPC, *Final Report*, Ch 7, p 7/3.

13 Ibid, p 7/7.

system of government finds its semblance in the Australian *Constitution*. However, unlike Australia, where the Queen is seen to be an integral part of the Commonwealth and the States, in PNG the Governor-General plays a largely ceremonial role.[14]

The position of the Head of State is found in s 82 of the *Constitution*. This provision declares that the Head of State of PNG shall be Her Majesty, Queen Elizabeth II, the Queen of the United Kingdom of Great Britain and Northern Ireland. The Queen's heirs are guaranteed succession and rule over PNG under s 83. To some extent, Sch 1.21 of the *Constitution* duplicates the provisions of s 83. It goes a little further by explaining that the "reference to the 'Head of State' is a reference to the Queen and the Head of State of PNG for the time being and includes a reference to the person or persons exercising sovereignty over the United Kingdom of Great Britain and Northern Ireland". It is clear that, in the event of the Queen vacating the throne, the person occupying the position is deemed to be the Head of State for PNG. A person other than an heir of the Queen, who occupies the throne, is deemed by these two provisions to be the Head of State for PNG.

Governor-General

The Governor-General, who is appointed by Parliament under s 88 of the *Constitution*, represents the Head of State in the country: s 82(2). To be eligible, a person must be a citizen who is qualified to be a Member of Parliament and who is mature and has good standing in the community: s 87. The appointment of the Governor-General, as specified under s 88(2), is "by a simple majority vote, in an exhaustive secret ballot in accordance with an Organic Law". The relevant Organic Law is the *Organic Law on the Nominations of the Governor-General*. Under this law, the Clerk of Parliament is vested with the responsibility of conducting the election of the Governor-General. This is a shift from the normal proceedings of Parliament, which are usually presided over by the Speaker or the Deputy Speaker of Parliament. This criterion has been adopted to allow the Speaker and the Deputy Speaker, who are both Members of Parliament, to exercise their right to cast their votes in favour of their preferred candidates. Another explanation may be that this provides the opportunity for the incumbent Speaker or Deputy Speaker to contest for the job.

Section 91 of the *Constitution* provides that the normal term of office is six years. According to s 87(5), the incumbent is eligible for reappointment only for a second term with the absolute support of two thirds of the Members of Parliament.

The *Organic Law on the Terms and Conditions of Employment of the Governor-General* governs the Head of State's terms and conditions of employment. Section 1 of the Organic Law states that the NEC fixes the Governor-General's salary. The simple criterion for calculating the Governor-General's salary is that it must not be less than the Speaker's salary. Special entitlements of the Governor-General are set out in ss 3 and 4 of the Organic Law. These include:

- rent-free accommodation;
- one motor vehicle free of charge for his or her personal use;
- domestic, gardening and other staff for himself or herself free of charge;
- an official free telephone; and
- an annual retirement pension.

---

14 For comparative purposes, see Hanks and Cass, *Australian Constitutional Law: Materials and Commentary* (6th ed, Butterworths, Sydney, 1999), p 418.

The Governor-General holds the office for only six years. Within this period, he or she may resign from office following the procedure under s 92 of the *Constitution*. The Governor-General's term in office may be cut short either by the NEC or the Parliament pursuant to s 94 of the *Constitution*. Section 94 provides a number of interesting observations. First, although the Governor-General is appointed by Parliament through a lengthy secret process, the NEC can easily remove him or her. Secondly, the Parliament that appointed the Governor-General can only remove him or her by an absolute majority vote. The provision is silent on the grounds of removal. The only ground explicit under the provision is medical. A Governor-General may be removed if he or she is unfit to conduct the affairs of state.

The absence of any specification of grounds does not, in itself, mean that the Governor-General can be removed only if he or she is medically unfit. The alternative view is that this vacuum exists to enable the NEC to remove a Governor-General who may become an obstacle to the progress of government. The executive is given very wide powers to discipline and terminate the Governor-General. Apart from removal, the Governor-General may be suspended from office pursuant to s 94. Again, the *Constitution* does not specify any grounds for suspension. The reasons expanded above apply here equally.

The powers and functions of the Head of State are generalised under s 86 of the *Constitution*. Generally, the Governor-General's powers and functions are as determined by the NEC and the authorities empowered under legislation to give directions to the Governor-General. For instance, under the *Leadership Code*, a Leadership Tribunal can recommend to the Head of State to dismiss a leader found guilty of misconduct in office under the Organic Law. Thus, in *The State v The Independent Tribunal; Ex patre Sasakila* [1976] PNGLR 491, the Supreme Court held that a Leadership Tribunal did not have the power to dismiss a leader found guilty under the Organic Law. It only had powers to recommend to the Governor-General to dismiss a leader.

Prosecutions

The function of the Head of State, as expressed in s 86 of the *Constitution*, does not extend to prosecutions. The Supreme Court decided, in *The State v Mogo Wonom* [1975] PNGLR 311,[15] that the Head of State had no power to prosecute criminal cases. In the words of Raine J (at 316):

> "But these functions, etc of the Head of State are as prescribed under Constitutional Laws and Acts of Parliament (s 86(1)). (No prosecution function is prescribed). ... Functions thus expressly limited in their exercise can no longer be considered as part of the prerogative."

Williams J was more forthright in his description of this function. According to his Honour (at 318):

> "The traditional role of the monarch as 'the foundation of justice and general conservator of the peace of the kingdom' is not recognised by the *Constitution* of this country and a reading of the whole of the *Constitution* makes this abundantly clear to me."

The power of prosecution lies with the Public Prosecutor. This was made clear in *SCR No 1 of 1989: Re The State v Saul* [1988-1989] PNGLR 337.

---

15 See Chalmers, "Constitutional Autochthony: The Position of the Head of State in an Independent Papua New Guinea" (1978) 27 ICLQ 672.

Advice to Governor-General

Section 86(2) of the *Constitution* specifically states that the Governor-General can "act only with, and in accordance with, the advice of the National Executive Council, or some other body or authority prescribed by a Constitutional Law or an Act of Parliament". Given that the Governor-General is only a "rubber stamp", the question of whether or not the Governor-General acted according to lawful advice is non-justiciable. In *The State v The Independent Tribunal; Ex Parte Sasakila* [1976] PNGLR 491 at 504, Saldanha J, referring to this concept, seems to say that if the Governor-General acted within the ambit of lawful advice, the question of whether or not his or her action was lawful is non-justiciable. This view was reaffirmed and expanded by Greville Smith J in *Minister for Lands v Frame* [1980] PNGLR 433 at 439:

> "Because the Governor-General acts, under s 20 of the Act, only with and in accordance with the advice of the National Executive Council, and by virtue of s 86(4) of the *Constitution* the question 'What advice was given?' is non-justiciable, the court cannot examine this advice to see if it was correct or incorrect, by whatever standards, because this court is not allowed to concern itself with what that advice was."[16]

However, Saldanha J was really saying that if the Governor-General acted beyond the lawful advice received, the constitutional veil would not protect. In *Kila Wari v Ramoi and Dibela* [1986] PNGLR 112 at 118, Kapi DCJ said:

> "The exercise of such discretion containing the advice cannot be questioned by a court of law by virtue of s 86(4) of the *Constitution*. It was lawful exercise of discretion.
>
> What is the extent of this protection? As I have pointed out, where advice is given to the Head of State within the discretion given by law, that advice is non-justiciable. Where the advice falls outside the power or discretion given to the person or authority by the law, that advice is not protected by s 86(4) of the *Constitution*."

Thus, where an advice given to the Head of State is in excess of the legal limits, that advice can be reviewed by the courts. Similarly, where the Governor-General acts in violation of a lawful order, he or she cannot seek protection under the constitutional veil.[17]

Future

The future of the Head of State in PNG is a very controversial issue. The issue has its beginning with the creation of the CPC. The CPC was very adamant that this colonial institution should be discarded at independence. Since independence, this controversy has emerged on many occasions, with the latest in 1995. Prior to that, in 1982, the General Constitutional Commission, which was set up under s 260 of the *Constitution* to review the operations of the *Constitution*, also recommended that the present system be replaced to enable PNG to become a republic with a citizen as Head of State.[18] In 1995, the issue again arose and became

16 Kapi J also came to the same conclusion at 469.

17 See the discussion of this issue in Baker, "The Executive and the Courts" in Regan, Jessep and Kwa (eds), *Twenty Years of the Constitution* (Lawbook Co, Sydney, 2001).

18 See the analysis and discussion on the work of the General Constitutional Commission in Goldring, "The Executive Government: Power, Politics and Responsibility" in DeVere, Colquhoun-Kerr and Kaburise (eds), *Essays on the Constitution of Papua New Guinea* (Government Printer, Port Moresby, 1985), p 69.

critical when the NEC directed the Constitutional Review Commission[19] to review the position of the Head of State and recommend possible changes to the government structure in PNG. After studying the issue for about six months, the Constitutional Review Commission reported to Parliament that it could not adequately address the issue. It stated that because the issue was sensitive, the commission needed more time to conduct wide consultation before it could make some final recommendations to the Parliament. This issue has not re-emerged since 1996, nor was the commission tasked to continue on this project.

The National Executive Council

The executive under the *Constitution* is the offspring of the British parliamentary system, which evolved over 250 to 300 years ago. The roles and functions of the executive evolved in time with the changing circumstances. In PNG, these various roles and functions have been given constitutional status, because they are contained in the *Constitution*.

The NEC

The executive, headed by the National Executive Council (NEC), exercises its powers and functions in various ways and through various government agencies. It is the power base of the government process. The NEC is the single most powerful and accessible institution of government. In describing the influence of the NEC on government, Goldring said:

> "Real executive power would formally and in fact be vested in the National Executive Council or Cabinet, which would be representative of and responsible to Parliament, which, as the representative of the people, has final control."[20]

The NEC is established by s 149 of the *Constitution*. The NEC or the Cabinet is made is made up of all the Ministers, and the Prime Minister who is the chairperson of the NEC. Section 141 prohibits any person from being appointed as a member of the Cabinet unless he or she is a Member of Parliament. This proviso extends to Cabinet members who have been dismissed as Members of Parliament by a Leadership Tribunal, such as in the case of Gabriel Dusava, and those whose elections have been declared null and void by the Court of Disputed Returns under the *Organic Law on National and Local-level Government Elections* (OLNLLGE), such as in the case of *Kandep Malapu v Electoral Commission and Jimson Sauk v Electoral Commission* [1987] PNGLR 128.

The *Organic Law on the Integrity of Political Parties and Candidates* 2000,[21] which was enacted on 30 November 2000, also imposes stringent conditions on the Members of Parliament who aspire to become Ministers or Vice-Ministers in government.

---

19 The Constitutional Review Commission was a political institution established under the *Constitutional Commission Act* 1993. It was an offshoot of the General Constitutional Commission, which is a constitutional institution. It has now been replaced by the current Constitutional Development Commission.

20 Goldring, op cit n 9.

21 The provisions of the Organic Law that are cited in the text are derived from the Bill as gazetted on 17 July 2000. Between 17 July 2000 and its eventual enactment on 30 November 2000, there were a number of controversial meetings organised by the creator of the law, the Constitutional Development Commission (CDC). The CDC had promised to incorporate those views in the law before the second and final reading on 30 November 2000. The author is of the firm view that the provisions as cited are intact, because there were no amendments in the first reading of the Bill. The rule is clear that at the second and final reading of the Bill, there can be no further amendments to the Bill.

Section 75 of the Organic Law prevents a Member of Parliament who breaches the Organic Law, especially s 72, from becoming a Prime Minister, Minister, Vice-Minister, Chairman or Deputy Chairman of a Permanent Parliamentary Committee during the term of the Parliament to which he or she has been elected. The offences under s 72 are:

- resigning from a political party unlawfully;
- joining another political party in contravention of the Organic Law; and
- voting for a Prime Minister, the national budget and a constitutional law against the resolution of his or her political party.

The powers and functions of the NEC are stipulated in s 149(3) of the *Constitution*. This provision is in very broad terms, and states that the function of the NEC is "to be responsible, in accordance with this *Constitution*, for the executive government of Papua New Guinea". Other powers and functions of the NEC may be provided in other laws. The various powers and functions of the executive are discussed below.

The CPC recommended that the executive power of the people be vested in the NEC, which would be headed by a chief executive – the Prime Minister. The General Constitutional Commission echoed the same views. In contrast, Deklin warns that vesting too much power in the executive can be counterproductive. In his analysis, he argues that a balance must be struck between limited freedom to the executive to deliver the social goods that the people expect of it on the one hand, and, on the other hand, the desire to control the executive so that it does not abuse the rights of the citizens.[22] The balance is found within the law. It is the law that separates these two competing interests through the control of the exercise of discretion by the executive. In the case of PNG, the *Constitution* and various pieces of legislation have placed restrictions on the executive in the exercise of its discretion. A former Prime Minister has described these limitations as very restrictive and "unknown in other parliamentary constitutions".[23] Sir Julius Chan proposed an easing of these restrictions to allow the executive to exercise greater freedom in dealing with the country's many problems. Chan's frustrations with the constitutional restrictions on the executive probably explain the manner in which his government attempted to deal with the Bougainville Crisis by secretly engaging mercenaries to crush the rebellion on Bougainville in 1997.[24]

The CPC recommended that the total number of Cabinet members should be at least 15 and should not exceed 20. These figures were modified slightly by the *Organic Law on the Number of Ministers*. Section 2 of the Organic Law sets the minimum threshold at 18 members. To entrench the maximum figure would have been unduly strenuous on the political process. Section 1 of the Organic Law gives the Prime Minister the freedom in determining the total number of Ministers. The total number of Cabinet members over the years has ranged from 21 to 27.

---

22 Deklin, "The Legal Control of the Executive in Papua New Guinea" in Sack (ed), op cit n 10, p 175.

23 A former Prime Minister has complained that the constitutional restrictions on the executive made it difficult for him to properly manage the country: see Chan, "Experience with the Papua New Guinea's Constitution: A Prime Minister's Reflections" in Ghai (ed), *Law, Politics and Government in the Pacific Island States* (USP, Suva, 1988), p 246.

24 See the chronology of the Sandline Affair and the wider impacts of the crisis on the country in Dinnen, May and Regan (eds), *Challenging the State: The Sandline Affair in Papua New Guinea* (Australian National University, Canberra, 1997).

Ministries and government departments

Ministries or government departments find their existence under ss 141, 189 and 195 of the *Constitution*. Section 141, in the true sense, does not create departments, but talks about Ministers of government. The Ministers are empowered by the above provisions to carry out the executive functions of government. The specific roles of Ministers are as determined by the Prime Minister from time to time. These roles and responsibilities of the Ministers are usually published in the *National Gazette*.[25] The Prime Minister can, from time to time, revoke and vary these functions depending on the aims and objectives of the government. The Ministers performs these functions through their departments. These departments are part of what the *Constitution* calls "State Services". The state services include the:

- National Public Service;
- Police Force;
- PNG Defence Force; and
- Parliamentary Service.

Apart from the Defence Force, s 189 of the *Constitution* requires that civilians control all these state services. The appointment of the leadership of these services is to be made by the NEC in consultation with the Public Services Commission (PSC), which is established under s 190 of the *Constitution*. The structures, employment and terms and conditions of employment of members of the state services are as determined by Acts of Parliament: s 195. One such Act is the *Public Services (Management) Act* 1995. This piece of legislation sets out in details the appointment, terms and conditions of employment of public servants working in state services.

The National Public Service consists of all the government departments and the various statutory and other governmental organisations operating at the national, provincial and local levels. As a general rule, "all organs of government must be the responsibility of a department, or some other part of the Government, for which the Prime Minister or another Minister is politically responsible".[26] At the time of writing, the ministries were: Health, Treasury, Police, Department of Defence, Home Affairs, Provincial and Local-level Governments Affairs, Attorney-General (Justice), Correctional Institutions Services, Petroleum and Energy, Mining, Planning and Implementation, Rural Development, Communications, Education, Lands, Forests, Foreign Affairs, Trade and Industry, Environment and Conservation, Tourism, Works, Transport, Civil Aviation, Corporate Affairs, Labour and Employment, Agriculture and Housing. Some of these departments take on different names and sizes depending on the priorities of the government of the day. At different times, some of these departments have been either merged or abolished.

In a strange twist, s 144 of the *Constitution* provides for the creation of other ministries apart from those created by s 141. This provision allows for the appointment of other Ministers. The provision is very clear, and states that the Prime Minister may appoint no fewer than six and no more than 27 Ministers. This provision is in sharp contradiction to the views of the CPC. The CPC recommended against a large Cabinet. However, this provision has expanded the discretion of the Prime Minister to appoint, apart from the Ministers selected under s 141, his or her cohorts, to retain their support for him or her and

25 This is the official newsletter of the government.
26 Goldring, op cit n 9.

consequently expand the Cabinet. Duchacek has described the underpinning of s 144 eloquently:

> "Prime ministers sometimes find it necessary to create new ministries in order to satisfy the ambitions of some important personalities or groups within the majority party or within the coalition. Those ministers are not given administrative responsibility but they can participate in cabinet deliberations, share in the collective responsibility for policy, and enjoy the emoluments that symbolise the top of the power pyramid."[27]

In 1994, the Parliament enacted the *Vice-Ministers Act*[28] to enable the Prime Minister to appoint certain Members of Parliament as Vice-Ministers to assist the Ministers in running the departments. The central argument for the creation of this category of Ministers was that the Ministers had a lot of work to do, and they required assistants to reduce their workload. Since the enactment of the legislation, several Members of Parliament have been appointed as Vice-Ministers to assist the Ministers. In the same year, the maximum number of Vice-Ministers to be appointed by the Prime Minister was set at 12 by the *Vice-Ministers (Amendment) Act* 1994.[29] The amendment was quickly introduced and passed by Parliament to ensure that a Prime Minister would not unduly exercise his or her discretion under s 2 of the Act to unnecessarily appoint too many Vice-Ministers.

The powers and functions of a Vice-Minister, as spelt out in s 3 of the *Vice-Ministers Act*, are to:

- assist the Minister or Ministers as are designated by the Prime Minister;
- be a supportive spokesperson in Parliament on subject matters affecting the department to which he or she is assigned;
- exercise delegated legislative powers;
- conduct ceremonial functions in relation to the portfolio; and
- carry out such functions as are assigned to him or her by the Prime Minister.

Although the Act does not stipulate its origins, it is suggested that when this legislation is read together with s 144 of the *Constitution*, the legislation finds its support from this constitutional provision.

The NEC and ministries

An important distinction needs to be made between the NEC and the ministries. The powers and functions for the NEC are different from those of the ministries. The powers and functions of the executive are exercised on a corporate basis. In the terms of s 141(1) and (2) of the *Constitution*, the Cabinet is "collectively answerable to the People" and can be collectively dismissed from office. In contrast to the ministry, a Minister operates as an individual and is the political head of the department. The Minister acts as the agent of the NEC in his or her department. In *Kila Wari v Ramoi and Dibela* [1986] PNGLR 112, the Supreme Court clarified the relationship between the Minister and the NEC. In this proceeding, the appellants, who were members of the Post and Telecommunications Corporation Board, sought an injunction against the Minister and the Governor-General from dismissing them. In the National Court,

---

27 Duchacek, op cit n 3, p 178.

28 *Vice-Ministers Act* 1994 (No 19 of 1994). The Act was later amended by *Vice-Ministers (Consequential Amendments) Act* 1994, and was further amended by the *Vice-Ministers (Amendment) Act* 1994.

29 Only s 2 of the principal Act was amended to replace the phrase "not exceeding the number of Ministers" with "not exceeding 12".

the judge refused their application and dismissed their case. The appellants then appealed to the Supreme Court.

The Supreme Court dealt with a technical point on the case. The judges had to decide whether the defendants were correctly enjoined in the proceeding. The judges unanimously agreed that the Minister and the Governor-General were wrongly joined as parties to the proceeding. Therefore, the proceeding was misconceived. The court held that the correct party was the state, acting through the NEC. Kidu CJ (at 114-115) explained that:

> "The Minister is a member of the National Executive Council (NEC) (see s 149(2) of the *Constitution*) but if an injunction had been granted (interim or permanent) it would not have been binding on the National Executive Council as it was not, and still is not, a party to the proceedings."

Amet J (at 120) gives a clear description of this relationship:

> "The first feature to note therefore is that whilst the Minister has the power and indeed the obligation to make recommendations to the National Executive Council for its advice to the Head of State as to candidates for appointment to the Board under s 7(3)(a), he has no corresponding legislative role to play on a member's termination.
>
> Technically, therefore, the Minister has no legislative power or role in the termination of the appointment of the members of the Board.
>
> The 'advice' to the Head of State is thus from the National Executive Council and not the Minister. In my opinion, it should therefore be the National Executive Council which is the principal party and not the Minister, Gabriel Ramoi. The Minister has no power to do anything under the Act in relation to termination which he needs to be restrained from carrying through to completion."

The NEC, as a corporate body, must act "in its primary role as the National Executive body constituted by s 149 of the *Constitution* with responsibility to carry out the executive government of Papua New Guinea": *SCR No 3 of 1986; Reference by Simbu Provincial Executive* [1987] PNGLR 151 (at 181 per Barnett J). The NEC is serviced by a secretariat, which is headed by a Secretary whose position is created by s 150 of the *Constitution*.

Prior to 1989, the Secretary for Justice was, pursuant to s 156(1)(a) of the *Constitution*, the Principal Legal Adviser to the NEC. However, this arrangement was modified in 1989 by the *Attorney-General Act* 1989.[30] Under the Act, where the Minister for Justice is a lawyer recognised under the *Lawyers Act* 1986, he or she shall be the Attorney-General of PNG and the Chief Legal Adviser to the NEC. Where the Minister is not a lawyer, the Secretary to the Department shall be the Attorney-General. The position of Attorney-General became a controversial issue when a former public servant, who had already retired from the public service, was appointed the Secretary for Justice by the NEC. The national lawyers employed by the government reacted angrily against the government and went on strike. They requested their union, the Public Employees Association, to challenge the appointment in court. The matter went before the National Court, and it ruled that the appointment was null and void as it was contrary to the *Public Services (Management) Act* 1986 and the *Public Service Standing Orders*. On appeal, in *NEC v PEA* [1993] PNGLR 264, the NEC and Lucas (the appointee) requested the Supreme

30 *Attorney-General Act* 1989 (No 17 of 1989). The Act repealed the *Legal Aid Act* (Ch 53) and the *Principal Legal Adviser Act* (Ch 54). The Act also created the Office of the Solicitor-General, whose sole responsibility is to defend the state in civil suits.

Court to overturn the decision of the National Court. The Supreme Court rejected the appellants' arguments and upheld the decision of the National Court.

The decisions and acts of the NEC are protected under s 153 of the *Constitution*. As a collective body, its procedures are not subject to review by the judiciary: s 153(2). This position was affirmed in *The Waterboard v The NCDIC and The State* (1990) N 864. In this case, the NCDIC sought to call the Secretary of the NEC as a witness to disclose certain matters to the court. The court ruled that:

> "It could be improper for this Court to allow general far-ranging questions of the Secretary, NEC on matters of executive policy. It will only cause confusion and appear to impinge on the executive workings of this Government. It is not a valid exercise of the powers of this Court to summons witnesses in this case to enquire into the executive workings of the Council."[31]

The deliberations on the report of the Power of Mercy Committee by the NEC are also non-justiciable: *Constitution*, s 153(3). Moreover, no act of a Minister is subject to review on the ground that he or she had no power to do the act: s 153(4). The protection provided by these provisions does not apply to the Ombudsman Commission (see *The State v Allan Ebu Marai* [1992] PNGLR 53) or a leadership tribunal (s 153(5)), and they are subject to "any Constitutional Law or Act of the Parliament": s 153(1). Thus, where the Minister acts ultra vires his powers under the *Forestry (Private Dealings) Act* (Ch 217),[32] his or her action can be reviewed by the National Court, as in *Mcdui Development v Genia* [1992] PNGLR 49. Similarly, where the NEC's decision is in breach of a constitutional right, as in *The State v NTN Pty Ltd* [1992] PNGLR 1, the decision of the NEC can be reviewed.

However, the main weapon used by aggrieved parties to erode the non-justiciability principles in s 153 of the *Constitution* is the concept of "principles of natural justice" provided under s 59. Numerous cases have illustrated the need for the NEC and its agent, the Minister, to be mindful of the principles of natural justice.[33]

The Prime Minister

The office of the Prime Minister is established by s 142(1) of the *Constitution*. The Prime Minister is appointed by the Parliament after a National Election, which is held every five years, or through a vote of no-confidence under s 145, or after a resignation of the Prime Minister under s 146. The Prime Minister, therefore, holds the position at the pleasure of the Parliament. If the Parliament wants to remove him or her, it can move a vote of no-confidence under s 145, and replace him or her with another person.

The first case to test the validity of the appointment of a Prime Minister was *James Eki Mopio v The Speaker of the National Parliament* [1977] PNGLR 420. In this case, Mopio challenged the election of Michael Somare as the first duly elected Prime Minister after the first general elections after independence, claiming that Somare's election offended s 142(4) of the *Constitution*. Mopio contended that, according to s 142(4), the Speaker of Parliament should have been elected first,

---

31 See the discussion of this case by Baker, "The Executive and the Courts" in Regan, Jessep and Kwa (eds), *Twenty Years of the Constitution* (Lawbook Co, Sydney, 2001).

32 Repealed by the *Forestry Act* 1991.

33 On many occasions the courts have ruled that, where an act of the NEC or the Minister violates this principle, the protection under s 153(2), (3) and (4) of the *Constitution* will not prevail. See, eg, *Re Gegeyo v Minister for Lands* [1987] PNGLR 331; *Re Application of NCDIC* [1987] PNGLR 339; *NCDIC v Crusoe Pty Ltd* [1993] PNGLR 139; and *Nuia v Sabumei* [1992] PNGLR 90.

before the election of the Prime Minister, and not vice-versa. This argument was dismissed by the court because, in its opinion:

> "These are matters which concern the conduct of the business of the Parliament and its procedure. Accordingly as the issue before the Court involves the question whether that procedure has been complied with, and also the exercise of the freedom of proceedings of Parliament and the functions and duties of the Speaker, this Court has no jurisdiction to entertain the case now before it."

The Supreme Court was timid. It briefly looked at s 134 of the *Constitution*, which states that proceedings of Parliament are non-justiciable, and made no attempt to examine the relationship of this section with the other provisions of the *Constitution*. The reasons expanded by the court were clearly subject to other constitutional provisions. This provision was tested again after 17 years in 1993 in *Haiveta v Wingti (No 1)* [1994] PNGLR 160. After examining all the relevant cases and considering the relevant constitutional provisions and the relationship between ss 134 and 142, the National Court (Sheehan J) concluded (at 177):

> "Even s 134 of the *Constitution*, which defines proceedings of the Parliament as non-justiciable, expresses itself to be subject to the *Constitution*. It reads: ...
>
> The net effect of all this is that the proceedings within the Parliament are non-justiciable unless there is a procedure specifically provided by a Constitutional Law that must be followed in the conduct of any parliamentary action. ... Examples of such Constitutional Laws relating to procedure within Parliament would be ss 13 and 14 ... Section 142 is another such Constitutional Law. In the event of a vacancy of Prime Minister, it prescribes *inter alia*, the time when an election shall be held and even the priority it shall take on the Parliament's agenda for that day. ... It may be seen, therefore, that a justiciable issue arises, and it is here that the Supreme Court's decision in *Mopio's case* must be examined. I would add, with respect, that what follows is not a critique of that decision but only the reasons that this Court holds that it should be distinguished."

Sheehan J practically disagreed with the Supreme Court's decision in *James Eki Mopio v The Speaker of the National Parliament*. Sheehan J's ruling on this point of law was not disputed nor rejected by the Supreme Court on appeal in *Haiveta v Wingti (No 3)* [1994] PNGLR 197.

The second case to question the election of a Prime Minister was the case of *Bill Skate v Sir Julius Chan* (unreported, Sheehan J, OS 468, 12 April 1995). In that case, in an apparent reversal of positions, Wingti's allies challenged the election of the predecessor of Wingti, Julius Chan, as Prime Minister. Skate argued that Chan should not have been elected on the same day as the Speaker, because the election conflicted with the ruling in *Haiveta v Wingti (No 3)* where the court laid down the rules that a Prime Minister must be elected on the next sitting day after Parliament is informed of the vacancy. The National Court (Sheehan J) dismissed the proceeding on the grounds that it was vexatious and an abuse of the process.

In the performance of his or her powers and functions, the Prime Minister is required to operate within the ambit of the law. In relation to policy matters, the Prime Minister has wide discretion, and can influence the direction of the country in pursuit of his or her government's policy. In this regard, the Prime Minister is given the freedom to appoint and remove Ministers who will assist the Prime Minister in achieving the government's goals. This unfettered power has been used indiscriminately by Prime Ministers to discipline and remove rebellious Cabinet members.

The Prime Minister can be removed from office only through a vote of no-confidence or by a Leadership Tribunal for misconduct in office as specified under the *Leadership Code*: *Constitution*, s 142(5). The procedure for removing the Prime Minister through a vote of no-confidence is provided under s 145 of the *Constitution*. Section 145(2)(a) prohibited the removal of the Prime Minister in the first four years after independence. In 1976, in *Reference No 2 of 1976* [1976] PNGLR 228, the Parliament requested the Supreme Court to explain the meaning and application of this provision. After considering s 145(2)(a) with s 269(4), the court held that this prohibition was not applicable to the first Parliament (1975-July 1977), and further held that the provision applied only to a motion of no-confidence in the second Parliament (1977-1982).

After the second Parliament, a Prime Minister who was appointed after a national election, or through a vote of no-confidence, or after the resignation or death of a Prime Minister, was protected from removal through a vote of no-confidence for only six months. The provisions on votes of no-confidence have been used very successfully since independence. What has been coined the "grace period" was proved to be very short for a Prime Minister to effectively carry out the policies of his or her government. The process was being abused by politicians to pursue their own selfish interests in the pretext of providing a better government for the country. The frequent use of the system to change governments was in direct conflict with the visions of the CPC, which had thought the six months grace period would bring stability to government. In the words of the CPC:

> "in order to ensure some stability in government, such a motion may not be moved unless the Prime Minister has been in office for at least six months".[34]

This problem was very vivid in the minds of the members of the General Constitutional Commission, which was set up by Parliament pursuant to s 260 of the *Constitution* to review the *Constitution*. The General Constitutional Commission recommended that the grace period be extended to 12 months from the present six months. Parliament turned a deaf ear to the proposals of the General Constitutional Commission. The Parliament, however, responded to the problem in 1991 by amending s 145(4) of the *Constitution* and increasing the grace period to 18 months. The expansion of the grace period has not deterred the politicians from applying the provision to change an existing government. This is manifested in three cases that were politically sensitive to the country. The first was the case of former Prime Minister Paias Wingti, who, after being appointed as Prime Minister after the national elections in 1992, resigned from the post and was re-elected a few months before the end of the 18 months period in 1993.[35] Wingti had hoped that by resigning and getting re-elected, he would add another 18 months to his term in office. By adding the extra 18 months, Wingti would have been in office for 36 months. Wingti's ploy must be set against s 145(2)(b). This provision prevents the removal of a Prime Minister 12 months before the date of the next election. Thus, by adding 36 months to 12 months, it would amount to 48 months. Given that there are 60 months in a five-year parliamentary period, Wingti would have been under no protection for 12 months.

The second case, involving a close political ally of Wingti, was that of another former Prime Minister, Bill Skate. Skate's case is almost a replica of the Wingti case. However, Skate went a little further than Wingti. After the national election in

---

34 CPC, *Final Report*, Ch 7, p 7/6.

35 The details of what has been dubbed the "constitutional coup" are contained in *Haiveta v Wingti (No 1)* [1994] PNGLR 160. The matter was later adjudicated by the Supreme Court in *Haiveta v Wingti (No 2)* [1994] PNGLR 189 and *Haiveta v Wingti (No 3)* [1994] PNGLR 197.

1997, Skate was appointed Prime Minister. As Wingti had been, Skate was protected, by s 145(4), from removal from July 1997 to January 1999. After January 1999 and beyond, Skate was open to challenge by aspiring prime ministerial candidates. To extend the government's term in office, it successfully moved for an adjournment of Parliament from 2 December 1998 to 13 July 1999, giving Skate breathing space for another seven months.

The adjournment of Parliament to avoid votes of no-confidence is not new. Earlier in 1990, the government had successfully moved and adjourned Parliament for seven months from 7 November 1990 to 16 July 1991. The next election was to be held in May-June 1992. When considered against s 145(2)(b), the government was protected for 18 months rather than just 12 months, the extra six months being added because of the adjournment. To save face, the NEC requested the Supreme Court, in *SCR No 4 of 1990* [1994] PNGLR 141, to give its opinion on, amongst other issues, whether it had met the minimum requirement of s 124, which stipulates that, in principle, the Parliament must meet three times in a 12-month period. The court held that the Parliament must, in principle, meet three times in a 12-month period. It further ruled that the requirement was only directory and not mandatory. Moreover, it held that whether the three sittings were held within the first six months or spread through the 12-month period, was the prerogative of the Parliament.

Skate's attempt to adjourn Parliament for seven months to avoid the vote of no-confidence must be considered in the light of the court's decision in the above case. Skate and his government thought that the adjournment was in order and proper. The adjournment was, however, challenged by the Ombudsman Commission in *SCR No 3 of 1999* (1999) SC 628. By an overwhelming majority of six to one, the Supreme Court overturned the decision in *SCR No 4 of 1990*, and held that the provision of s 124 is mandatory and that Parliament is required to meet 63 days in a 12-month period. It further ruled that where the Parliament breached this mandatory requirement, the National Court could impose sanctions on the Parliament. Kapi DCJ, delivering the key judgment, alluded to this matter when he said:

> "To give effect to this principle, s 124 requires the Parliament to sit in principle for duration of not less than nine weeks to perform its constitutional functions. To come to the contrary view is to fail to give effect to the intention and the underlying philosophy of the *Constitution*. If Parliament loses its focus then it is the duty of this Court to point the Parliament in the right direction."

In the third case, the government of Sir Mekere Morauta deliberately defied the decision of the Supreme Court, and successfully moved the Parliament to adjourn from 30 November 2000 to 16 July 2001. Prime Minister Morauta made this move to save his government and maintain power into the election year - 2002. The constitutional veil that protects the Prime Minister lapsed on 14 January 2001. From 15 January 2001 to 15 July 2001, a vote of no-confidence can be moved against Prime Minister Morauta. By adjourning Parliament to 16 July 2001, the Morauta Government was safe to go into the 2002 elections without any threats of removal.[36]

---

36 The successful ploy by the Morauta Government may be short-lived because the Supreme Court has now been asked to review its own decision in *SCR No 3 of 1999* (1999) SC 628. Counsel for both parties have already made closing submissions on the case and are awaiting a ruling by the Supreme Court. In a separate case, the Head of State has also requested the Supreme Court to reconsider its decision in *SCR No 3 of 1999*.

In a further attempt to rectify some of the anomalies relating to the election of a Prime Minister under s 145, the Morauta Government boldly introduced a controversial Bill in Parliament, called the *Organic Law on the Integrity of Political Parties and Candidates* 2000. The Bill, which was passed into law on 30 November 2000, seeks to control the membership of politicians to political parties, their conduct in Parliament during their term in Parliament, the manner of voting in Parliament on certain issues and their dismissal from Parliament.

The sections of the *Organic Law on the Integrity of Political Parties and Candidates* that relate to election of the Prime Minister are ss 71, 72, 73, 75, 76, 77 and 78. Section 71 departs dramatically from the current practice of election of a Prime Minister. This provision empowers the Governor-General, acting on the advice of the Electoral Commissioner, to invite the registered political party with the greatest number of elected members to form government. Where no single political party masters the numbers, the Governor-General, acting on the advice of the Electoral Commissioner, may invite two or more political parties to form government.

The invitation to form government encapsulated by the Organic Law renders the election of the Prime Minister under s 142(2) of the *Constitution* meaningless. Although s 71(4) of the Organic Law permits the Members of Parliament to vote for the Prime Minister after a national election, it restricts the list to only the leader of the party invited to form government, or a person chosen by the parties invited to form government, to be the Prime Minister. The Organic Law has, in practical terms, shifted the responsibility for electing the Prime Minister from the Parliament, as espoused by the *Constitution*, to the Electoral Commissioner and the Governor-General.

On the other hand, s 72 of the Organic Law promotes certainty of leadership by outlawing "political yo-yoing", and nullifies "horse-trading" or "politicians-trading" under s 82, which have become trademarks of PNG politics. A Member of Parliament who votes for the Prime Minister in contravention of s 72 will have his or her vote nullified under s 73. An independent Member of Parliament who does not join a political party after the national election is not eligible to vote for a Prime Minister in a motion of no-confidence: s 77.

The Prime Minister can also be removed from office if he or she is medically unfit to run the government. This procedure is available under s 142(5)(c) of the *Constitution*. Under the authority of this provision and s 143 (which provides for the office of the Acting Prime Minister), the *Prime Minister Act* (Ch 27) was enacted. Section 5 of the Act makes provision for the suspension of the Prime Minister and the manner in which he or she may be removed for health reasons. Since independence, this provision of the *Constitution* and this aspect of the Act have not been effected.

The Prime Minister can also elect to vacate the office by resigning from the post under s 146 of the *Constitution*, thereby avoiding any embarrassment through a vote of no-confidence or suspension or dismissal by a Leadership Tribunal. Two former Prime Ministers attempted this mechanism (Wingti in 1993 and Skate in 1999) during their terms as Prime Ministers. They had hoped that by resigning they would attract the sympathy of the Members of Parliament to win back their positions, but both of them failed to achieve the intended result.

A new convention that seems to have been developed by Prime Ministers is the idea of "stepping aside" in the face of allegations of a kind that may amount to misconduct in office. This practice was started by Somare, and later Chan, in 1997.

The *Constitution* does not contain any provision that allows for the "standing aside" or "standing down" of the Prime Minister pending an investigation into a matter in which he or she has been directly or indirectly involved and which may amount to a misconduct in office pursuant to s 27 of the *Constitution* and the *Organic Law on the Duties and Responsibilities of Leadership.*

It is suggested that the act of "stepping aside" or "standing down" from office by a Prime Minister is unconstitutional. The *Leadership Code* is very clear on the type of leaders that have to lead PNG. The standard of leadership required by the people of PNG is very high. The Supreme Court made this clear when it was hearing the case against Julius Chan in *SCR No 5 of 1988; Re Sir Julius Chan v Investigating Authority into the Placer Pacific Ltd Share Issue* (1988) SC 350. Kapi DCJ, giving the leading judgment, recited s 27(1) of the *Constitution*, and stated the principle as follows:

> "The integrity of our leaders is a matter of great significance and is protected by s 27 of the *Constitution*. ... In a morally corrupt society we need to protect the leadership of our nation."

It is imperative that the person who is appointed as the Prime Minister is a person of impeccable character. It therefore follows that, where the integrity of a Prime Minister is brought into question, the *Constitution* makes available to him or her *only* two courses of action. The Prime Minister has to either resign under s 146, or be suspended by Parliament pursuant to s 145(6). There is no room for stepping aside or standing down. To promote and encourage this convention is to depart from the spirit of the *Constitution* and lowers the standard of leadership required of a Prime Minister.

Ministers

Ministers are members of the Cabinet or the NEC, and are appointed by the Prime Minister. The Ministers hold office at the pleasure of the Prime Minister, as highlighted in *The State v The Independent Tribunal; Ex Parte Sasakila* [1976] PNGLR 491. In this matter, the Leadership Tribunal dismissed Sasakila as a Member of Parliament after it found the Minister guilty of misconduct in office. Sasakila sought a review in the Supreme Court of the decision of the Leadership Tribunal. His case rested on two grounds. The first ground was whether the Tribunal validly dismissed him as a Member of Parliament, and the second ground was whether he was validly dismissed as a Minister. The court held that his dismissal as a Member of Parliament was null and void, but his dismissal as a Minister was valid. Frost CJ (at 499), pronouncing the law, said:

> "Turning now to the Instrument of Dismissal by the Governor-General, the Minister can have no redress insofar as his dismissal from office as Minister is based on the invalid recommendation by the Tribunal. The reason is that the Instrument not only recites the recommendation from the appropriate Tribunal, but goes further and recites, as an additional ground, that the Governor-General has acted with, and in accordance with, the advice of the Prime Minister, and as any question concerning the nature of that advice is beyond the power of this Court the prosecutor's dismissal from his ministry must stand."

The Ministers are chosen from the Members of Parliament, usually on political party lines. In adopting this selection process, the CPC rejected two other options that were submitted to it. The first was the proposal to have nominated members, especially people with special skills, to join the Cabinet. The second proposal was to maintain the system at that time, whereby a parliamentary committee was to nominate the Minister and they, in turn, would appoint the chief Minister. The CPC rejected these two proposals because it believed that "an elective procedure which will directly involve the Parliament and yet cope with a possibly fluid political situation"[37] was more appropriate.

The Ministers are to perform the duties and responsibilities assigned to them by the Prime Minister. This constitutional mandate is given by s 148 of the *Constitution.* The Ministers have political control over their departments and other organs of the government that are placed under their control. Section 148(3) limits the power of the Minister to direct and control his or her department. This provision became controversial in *SCR No 1 of 1982; Re Bouraga* [1982] PNGLR 178. In that case, the Police Commissioner and Secretary refused to entertain the direction of the Police Minister, and he was consequently charged and disciplined by the Public Services Commission (PSC). A Board of Inquiry was set up under the *Public Service Act,* with the task of investigating the truth of the disciplinary charges. The board completed its investigations and, before it could present its findings to the PSC, it sought the views of the Supreme Court on a number of issues. One of the issues was whether the Police Minister had the power of direction and control of the Police Commissioner. In answer to this question, the Supreme Court declared that the Minister or other persons, except the NEC, had no power of direction and control of the Commissioner.

The decision was severely criticised by Ghai and Hegarty as an intrusion by the judiciary into the executive realm.[38] The politicians responded to this decision by proposing, through the General Constitutional Commission in 1981, that s 148 be amended to give Ministers more power and control over their departments.[39] This proposal, and others by the General Constitutional Commission, have not been implemented.

Section 141(b) of the *Constitution* states that Ministers, as a collective body, are answerable to Parliament.[40] To keep them under check, the Parliament has been given the prerogative under s 45 to remove a Minister or the whole ministry if Parliament is unhappy with their performance. Emy explains the rationale of this concept in this way:

> "Ministerial responsibility is a product of British constitutional theory. The idea behind this doctrine is that it is up to parliament to see that ministers, apart from being called to account for their mistakes and those of their officials, also behave 'responsibly' in exercising power. ... Responsible government contains an injunction that ministers and public servants, as wielders of coercive power, should use that power in a certain way. ... Responsible government therefore includes a normative statement about how men should properly rule other men, as well as a more specific doctrine of accountability."[41]

To compare and contrast the value of the relationship between the Minister and his or her officials, Saffu conducted a short survey in 1982 to ascertain this value.

---

37 CPC, *Final Report,* Ch 7, p 7/3.

38 Ghai and Hegarty, "Ministerial and Bureaucratic Power in Papua New Guinea: Aspects of Dutton/Bouraga Dispute" in Sack (ed), op cit n 10, p 247. Note: The page numbering of this article is confusing.

39 Goldring, op cit n 18, p 77.

40 See the discussions by Goldring, "Responsibility of the Executive Government: To Whom and For What" (1981) Mel LJ 116.

41 Emy, *The Politics of Australian Democracy: Fundamentals in Dispute* (2nd ed, MacMillan, Sydney, 1978), pp 246-247.

When asked about the characteristics that they would like to see in their Ministers, many departmental heads said that:

> "Adequate level of education ... an ability or willingness to listen and learn. The ability to communicate ideals and inspire people to perform and some experience in government services. ... appropriate training in the area covered by the ministry they headed."[42]

Saffu found that most of the Ministers were not optimally performing their duties in the ministries because of:

- inadequate educational background and necessary apprenticeship in politics;
- lack of interpersonal skills (the Ministers do not respect departmental staff, are not transparent and employ "wantoks" and campaign managers to duplicate or tamper with the work of the bureaucrats); and
- frequent ministerial changes.[43]

In the final analysis, Saffu concluded that:

> "But for any long-term strategy of ending departmental rule, and ensuring that popular participation in politics will affect policies made by ministerial or cabinet system and move things more rapidly in the direction of the Eight Aims and the National Goals, the establishment of open, vigorous but disciplined, nation-wide mass parties would seem to be a *sine qua non*."[44]

6.3 THE BUREAUCRACY

The bureaucracy has been described as the "institution that carries out the functions and responsibilities of the state. It is the engine room of the state".[45] The bureaucracy in a modern state comprises government departments and is "a large, multi-tiered organisation, containing enormous knowledge and experience in its specialist area. Departments, like all other organisations, develop their own ways of proceeding, their own priorities, and their own 'house view'."[46] The bureaucracy in PNG is made up of a number of what the *Constitution* terms *state services*. These state services are part of the "executive government" of PNG. The description of the executive government by Kidu CJ in *SCR No 1 of 1982; Re Bouraga* [1982] PNGLR 178 at 186 is noteworthy:

> "The executive government is a conglomerate of Ministers, public officers, statutory bodies, the police force, defence force, etc."

Detailed provisions regarding the state services are set out in the *Constitution* and the statutes. In general, they make it clear that the ultimate responsibility for direction and control of the state services rests with the National Executive Council. Kidu CJ confirmed this in *SCR No 1 of 1982; Re Bouraga* [1982] PNGLR 178 at 186, when he said:

> "The only body in the country that can hold this mass of men, etc together is the National Executive Council."

42 Saffu, "Bureaucrats and Ministers" in King, Lee and Warakai (eds), *From Rhetoric to Reality (Papers from the Fifteenth Waigani Seminar)* (UPNG Press, Port Moresby, 1985), p 189.
43 Ibid, pp 190-191.
44 Ibid, p 195.
45 Hague, Harrop and Breslin, *Comparative Government and Politics: An Introduction* (MacMillan Press Ltd, London, 1992), p 342.
46 Ibid, p 344.

The bureaucracy is at the core of the modern government and "consists of an administrative staff of permanent officials organised in career service. They are appointed and promoted on merit, and perform specialised roles in a hierarchical structure which formally invests officers with specific set of duties for the performance of which they are responsible to their superiors".[47] It is the bureaucrats who run the day-to-day operations of the state services. The bureaucracy is a very powerful organisation and can, at times, stifle the direction and aspirations of a new government. As Hague, Harrop and Breslin observed:

> "[A]ll this complicates the task of political control. It means that steering a department in a new direction is a slow and complicated business which needs sustained effort from the minister."[48]

In a modern democratic state, the bureaucrats have become dominant and are now formulating and implementing policies. After reviewing the working relationship between the Ministers and heads of departments in PNG in 1982, Saffu concluded that "largely by default, bureaucrats have dominated the policy-making process, being the real initiators and selectors of policy, and herein lies one of the major strengths and weakness of the PNG political system".[49] The bureaucrats have become the policy makers by default because:

> "Determination of policy is the function of ministers, and once a policy is determined it is the unquestioned and unquestionable business of the civil servant to strive to carry out that policy with precisely the same good will whether he agrees with it or not."[50]

The disputes that arise between the Ministers and the bureaucrats are usually focused on the control of the bureaucracy.[51] This is the main field of contention. The CPC was well aware of this struggle, and tried to put the parties in their proper stations. The CPC held the view that public servants, including the bureaucrats, were to be *implementers* of policy and *not initiators*. The CPC accepted that:

> "It is on these people [public servants] that governments rely for much of their professional and technical advice, and it is they who are responsible for implementing government policies. Their role is particularly important in new nations where governments are usually more actively and directly involved in the development process."[52]

The CPC was aware that effective government machinery was the key to success in the new nation state. The CPC was mindful about the size of the bureaucracy. These concerns were genuine, given the fact that "the huge bureaucracy of modern Papua New Guinea has grown, even exploded since 1950".[53] The growth of the bureaucracy is a global trend,[54] and PNG was not exempt from this process. However, given the size and character of the emerging state, with its concomitant deficiencies in administrative infrastructure, skilled and experienced labour and funds, the CPC pushed for the downsizing of this huge white elephant. The CPC recommended that the size of most departments should be reduced, and that they

---

47 Powles, "The Relationship between the Executive and the Public Service in Pacific Constitutions" in Ghai (ed), op cit n 10, p 135.
48 Hague, Harrop and Breslin, op cit n 45, p 196.
49 Saffu, op cit n 42, p 195.
50 Quote from Jennings, *Cabinet Government* (3rd ed), cited by Kidu CJ in *SCR No 1 of 1982; Re Bouraga* [1982] PNGLR 178 at 187.
51 See Hague and Harrop, *Comparative Government: An Introduction* (3rd ed, MacMillan Press Ltd, London, 1982), p 196.
52 CPC, *Final Report*, Ch 12, p 12/1.
53 Goldring, op cit n 9, p 52.
54 Hague and Harrop, op cit n 51, p 184.

should be decentralised to the provinces under the proposed provincial government system.[55]

The CPC and the government were not bothered about restructuring the bureaucracy, but were more concerned about the localisation and decentralisation of the public service. According to Ballard, this shift in emphasis "meant that the public services survived decolonisation intact as the embodiment of the state".[56] The implementation of the CPC recommendation did not auger well in the provinces. In their findings, Ghai and Regan found that:

> "The colonial administration had not properly prepared for a decolonisation process which occurred much earlier and faster than anyone anticipated. ... In many provinces, localisation programs were limited, so that by the time the provincial government system was being established, poorly trained staff were often filling relatively senior positions as expatriate officers departed. ... They had no training for such roles and received little assistance from national agencies to develop necessary skills. As a result, there was a huge gap in the personnel resources needed to enable provincial governments to operate as envisaged by the OLPG."[57]

The large size of the bureaucracy has been a thorny issue for successive governments since independence. In 1998, in a bold move, the Skate Government introduced a radical scheme to drastically reduce the size of the public service from the estimated 60,000 public servants. The government argued that in the prevailing economic conditions, and with an inefficient and costly public service, there was difficulty delivering quality goods and services to the people. Prime Minister Mourata put the move on hold in 1999. It was realised that the decision of the previous government was premature without a financial package. In a surprise move, the Mourata Government agreed, in 2000, to proceed with the trimming of the public service with financial backing from the World Bank. These attempts highlight the seriousness of the government to reduce the public service to a manageable level. Goldring warns that these attempts may be encouraging, but "it is unlikely to diminish greatly in numbers, because it is the main source of employment for university and other tertiary graduates, of whom there is now a number and whose political influence is great".[58]

6.4 THE MAIN STATE SERVICES

The bureaucracy is made up of a number of state services, some of which are clearly identified by the *Constitution*, while others are created by specific legislation. The state services are specified under s 188 of the *Constitution*.

The first of these is the Public Service. The public service consists of the Ministers, who are the political heads of the departments, the public servants, who work in these departments, and the Public Services Commission (PSC).

The terms and conditions of public servants and their rights and duties are spelt out under the *Public Services (Management) Act* 1995. This legislation, which was enacted as a consequence of the *Organic Law on Provincial Governments and Local-level Governments* (OLPGLLG), repealed and replaced the *Public Services (Management) Act* 1986. Under the old provincial government system there were

55 CPC, *Final Report*, Ch 10, p 10/20.
56 Ballard, "The Public Service" in Sack (ed), op cit n 10, p 242.
57 Ghai and Regan, *The Law, Politics and Administration in Papua New Guinea* (Monograph 30, National Research Institute, Port Moresby, 1992), pp 223-224.
58 Goldring, op cit n 9, p 32.

two categories of public servants – those employed and operating at the national level, and those public servants assigned to the provinces from the national level. Although assigned public servants were employed by the public service, s 47(2) of the *Organic Law on Provincial Governments* (repealed) empowered the provincial government to direct and control them.

The introduction of the OLPGLLG has removed the classification of public servants in the provinces. Under ss 75 and 76 of the OLPGLLG, public servants at the national level can be assigned to the provinces and local-level governments on a permanent basis. Unlike the previous arrangement under s 47 of the old *Organic Law on Provincial Governments*, all personnel assigned to the provinces and local-level governments remain under the direction and control of the national departments. Section 76(3) of the OLPGLLG states that the general terms and conditions of public servants provided under the *Public Services (Management) Act* 1995 equally applies to the assigned officers. Similarly, teaching staff in the provinces have been streamlined to fall under the national Education Department. According to s 77 of the OLPGLLG, the management and movements of the teaching staff are to be covered separately under the *Teaching Service Act* 1988.

Public Services Commission

In acknowledging the huge size of the public service, the CPC said that:

"We believe that the two different kinds of demands:

- a career service in which there is reasonable protection for individual public servants; and
- firm government control over the management of the public services;

are best met by dividing personnel and management matters between the two bodies we have proposed."[59]

The CPC proposed that all personnel matters should be controlled by the Public Services Commission (PSC), which it recommended to be a constitutional office, guaranteeing it freedom from direction and control from any person. The CPC proposed that a department be established to look after all management matters. The CPC was of the view that the government should control management matters such as organisational structures, creation of positions, localisation and training and policy issues. The CPC stressed that these two institutions should cooperate to avoid confusion and conflict between the two organisations.[60]

The CPC's recommendations were integrated into the *Constitution* under ss 190-192. *Constitutional Amendment No 8 – Public Services Commission* amended these sections in 1986. The PSC is established under s 190 of the *Constitution*. The PSC shall consist of three members who are appointed for a term of five years. Under the old section, membership of the PSC was set at four members, and the term of appointment was not specified. The amendment to s 190 clarified these ambiguities.

The members of the PSC must be former top public servants. This requirement is made clear in s 190(3). Under the original section, the only requirement was that all the members of the PSC be citizens. The 1986 amendment contains the additional requirement that the member must "have gained substantial

59 CPC, *Final Report*, Ch 12, p 12/5.
60 Ibid.

experience in the National Public Service". The original functions of the PSC were to:

- ensure the efficient management and control of the National Public Service;
- be responsible for all personnel matters connected with the National Public Service;
- keep the state services under continuous review; and
- advise, on its own initiative or on request, the NEC and any other state service on organisational matters and the coordination of effort in relation to conditions of employment to avoid wastage and duplication of resources.

These functions were very broad and gave the PSC enormous powers over the public service. This *power to review* does not apply to the Office of the Public Solicitor and other constitutional offices, because they are creatures of the *Constitution* and not part of the state service. The Supreme Court clarified this issue in *Constitutional Reference No 1 of 1978 (s 19)* [1978] PNGLR 345. In this case, the Ombudsman Commission sought the opinion of the Supreme Court on two important questions. The first question was whether the Ombudsman had the power to investigate the Public Solicitor or an officer of the Public Solicitor on complaint or on its own initiative. The second question was whether the Public Solicitor was required to release any documents on a matter being investigated by the Ombudsman Commission.

The majority (Prentice CJ and Wilson J) answered in the negative. The dissenting judge (Pritchard J) argued that the Public Solicitor should be open to the scrutiny of the Ombudsman Commission.[61] Prentice CJ said (at 350):

> "The *Constitution* and Organic Laws have created and vested powers and responsibilities in certain organisations and offices, such as the Public Prosecutor, Public Solicitor, Committee of Mercy and Public Accounts Committee.
>
> Insofar as such bodies are created independent of direction and control, they would seem to be exercising the power of the people given to them as a direct grant by the *Constitution* and Organic Laws and their exercise of powers could not I think be said to be an exercise of power 'by the National Government' in such a sense as would by itself constitute any of them 'an arm' of the National Government, or department or agency or instrumentality thereof within the meaning of s 219 and Sch 1.2 of the *Constitution*.
>
> An 'arm of Government' would normally be an instrumentality which acts on behalf of the government. An arm acts under the control of the body of which it is part. For myself I cannot see how as a matter of fact, the Public Solicitor in carrying out his duties to advise and represent clients can be envisaged as carrying out work on behalf of or for the government."

In the majority, Wilson J said (at 359-360):

> "Is the Public Solicitor a 'State Service' by reason of s 219(1)(a)(i) of the *Constitution* whose conduct the Ombudsman Commission has jurisdiction? To answer the question it is necessary to look to the provisions of s 188 of the *Constitution*. It is to be noted immediately that the Public Solicitor is not included as one of the State Services thereby established, and no act of the Parliament has made provision for or in respect of the Public Solicitor as a State Service. The Public Solicitor could hardly be said to be a member of the National Public Service and therefore a member of the State Service (see

61 Consider the analysis of this case in Ntumy, "Separation of Powers" in Regan, Jessep and Kwa (eds), op cit n 31.

> s 188(1)(a)). It is to be noted that his office is established by, the manner of his appointment is laid down in, his functions are set out in, and the circumstances of his removal from office, are specified in s 176 to s 178 of the *Constitution*."

In regards to the employees of the Public Solicitor, Prentice CJ said (at 352):

> "In one sense, employees of the Public Solicitor are members of a State Service by virtue of their having been recruited into the National Public service, and being subject for conditions of service to the *Public Service (Interim Arrangements) Act* 1973. But I consider one must bear in mind what I regard as the expressed intention that the Ombudsman's powers of investigation and overseeing are directed towards administrative affairs of the bureaucracy rather than to the professional duties carried out by deputies and subordinates."

Pritchard J (at 388) conceded that officers of the Public Solicitor:

> "are in fact employed in a State Service, the Public Service, I am satisfied that whilst they are employed in the office of the Public Solicitor, by virtue of s 13 of the *Organic Law on the Guarantee of the Rights and Independence of Constitutional Office-holders*, ... whatever immunity to investigation is enjoyed by the Public Solicitor must of necessity be enjoyed by them whilst serving him".

In *Limitopa v PNG* [1988-1989] PNGLR 364, Brunton AJ agreed with the decision of Pritchard CJ in *Constitutional Reference No 1 of 1978*. Brunton AJ was of the view that, although the Public Solicitor was not a State Service, it "is a part of the National Government in the broad sense," stating (at 371) that:

> "In the absence of any statute like the *Public Prosecutor (Office and Functions) Act* which makes State Prosecutors, officers and employees of the Public Service, and in the absence of a statute which gives the Public Solicitor's Office corporate status capable of suing and being sued in its own name, in matters other than those designated by the *Constitution* as the particular functions of the Public Solicitor, it is clear that the Public Solicitor is part of the National Government. Accordingly, in those matters and for purposes which are not described in s 176(2) of the *Constitution*, the Public Solicitor is part of the State. In particular, tortious actions and actions in contract brought against individual lawyers employed in the Public Solicitor's Office in the course of their employment, may by virtue of the doctrine of vicarious liability of an employer be brought against the State."

Brunton AJ's position must be considered against the background of the case. In this case, the plaintiffs sued the state for the negligence of lawyers from the Public Solicitor's Office. The lawyers admitted that they had failed to adequately represent the plaintiffs in two motor vehicle accident claims against the Motor Vehicles Insurance Trust. To attach liability, the court had to identify the nexus between the lawyers employed in the Public Solicitor's Office and the state.

There are differences between *Constitutional Reference No 1 of 1978* and *Limitopa v PNG*. In the first case, the issue was one of review of one constitutional office by another constitutional office. In the second case, the issue was one of liability of officers of a constitutional office. The principle is that, in the conduct of their official duties, the officers of a constitutional office are not subject to review by another constitutional office. In the second case, the principle appears to be that where, in the conduct of their official duties, the officers of the constitutional office are negligent or reckless, they cannot escape liability.

It is clear from these cases that constitutional office-holders and their offices are not subject to review by the PSC. This protection applies to employees of the constitutional officers in the conduct of their official duties. However, the PSC is permitted to review administrative (personnel) matters, such as appointments, promotions, demotions, transfers, suspensions and termination of employment, without any restriction.

In its endeavour to perform its functions, the PSC was not subject to the control and direction of any person. This protection, however, did not give the PSC the power to direct and control the public service. The PSC was also required to comply with any policy direction from the NEC. The limitation contained in s 191(3) of the *Constitution*, according to the Supreme Court in *SCR No 1 of 1982; Re Bouraga* [1982] PNGLR 178, also extended to disciplinary matters. The court found that the PSC did not have any power to discipline a departmental head under the *Constitution* or the *Public Service Act* (Ch 67).[62] The PSC, however, had the power to discipline public servants other than departmental heads under s 85 of the *Public Service Act*. Thus, in *PEA v PSC* [1983] PNGLR 206, the Supreme Court held that where public servants took part in a strike action which was deemed a disciplinary action under the Act, the PSC correctly exercised its powers under the Act in dismissing them for the breach of the Act.

Constitutional Amendment No 8 1986 drastically reduced the powers and functions of the PSC. The amendment removed the power of the PSC to ensure the efficient management and control of the National Public Service, and the PSC's responsibility for all personnel matters connected with the National Public Service. The amendment also collapsed two other functions of the PSC into a single and mundane responsibility. Under this limb of the amendment, the PSC has the power to continuously review the state services and advise the NEC or a state service only on organisational matters. This amendment reduced the once-powerful PSC to a less powerful constitutional institution. Apart from organisational matters, the PSC has no power to coordinate the affairs of state services, review the terms and conditions of employment of public servants, or advise on wastage or duplication of functions and roles of state services. The personnel matters over which the PSC has responsibility are defined under s 194 of the *Constitution* as:

> "decisions and other service matters concerning an individual whether in relation to his appointment, promotion, demotion, transfer, suspension, disciplining, cessation or termination of employment (except cessation or termination at the end of his normal period of employment as determined in accordance with law), or otherwise".

Where the PSC has exercised acts on a personnel matter and makes a recommendation to the appropriate authority, that authority can reject or accept the PSC's recommendation. If the authority refuses to accept the recommendation of the PSC, the authority must give an explanation for refusing to act on the recommendation of the PSC. Failure to give an explanation can be contested. This requirement was built into the process by *Niggints v Tokam* [1993] PNGLR 66. Niggints, who was a senior officer within the Department of Correctional Services, was dismissed by the Commissioner for improper conduct. After completing his investigations, the internal investigator recommended against the termination of

62 This legislation was replaced by the *Public Services (Management) Act* 1986, which was also repealed and replaced by the *Public Services (Management) Act* 1995.

the officer. The Commissioner, however, refused to accept the recommendation of the investigator.

Niggints then appealed to the PSC to review his case. After reviewing the applicant's case, the PSC recommended that the applicant be reinstated. The Commissioner refused to accept the PSC's recommendation and, instead, reaffirmed his decision without giving any reasons. The applicant then applied to the National Court to review his dismissal. The court stated the principle as follows:

> "The statement of principle I now enunciate is that the departmental head who decides in his discretion, on proper consideration of the Public Services Commission's recommendation, not to accept it should state the reasons for not accepting the recommendation ... If no reasons are stated other than this kind of statement, it leaves the court no option than to conclude that there were no good reasons at all. Public officials discharging public duties are required for public accountability to provide reasons for their actions and decisions."

One of the principal functions of the PSC that remains unaffected by the amendment, is its *right to be consulted* before the NEC makes appointments to senior positions in the public service: *Constitution*, s 193. The PSC has been very protective over this function, and has used it to influence a number of government decisions. For instance, in *Geno v PNG* [1993] PNGLR 22, Geno and the two other members of the PSC sought a declaration in the National Court by way of a judicial review that, because the NEC did not consult them in its appointment of departmental heads, the appointments were null and void. The National Court refused to make the declaration, on the grounds that the matter was an administrative matter and involved two departments or services of the state and should be settled out of court. On appeal, the Supreme Court held that the trial judge erred in holding that the matter was one of policy and administration. The court correctly ruled that the issue was one of constitutional law (s 193) and, therefore, the court had the power to determine the case. The Supreme Court then proceeded to grant leave to the PSC to apply for judicial review. This decision was followed Salika J's decision in *Public Services Commission v PNG* [1994] PNGLR 603. In that case, the NEC again failed to consult the PSC when it made certain appointments for departmental heads. The National Court ruled that the consultation process was mandatory and, where the NEC failed to comply with this rule, its decisions would be null and void.

The case clearly illustrates the significance of the PSC's right to be consulted on appointments under s 193 of the *Constitution*. On the other hand, even where the NEC has consulted the PSC and an appointment is made pursuant to s 193, other interested parties can challenge that appointment. This was clearly demonstrated by two cases. The first case was *NEC v PEA* [1993] PNGLR 264. In that case, the NEC, after consulting the PSC, appointed a retired public servant as the head of the Attorney-General's Department. Lawyers, who worked within the department and were members of the Public Employees Association (respondent), requested the union to challenge the appointment. The main ground for their contention was that, under s 51 of the *Public Services (Management) Act* 1996, the appointee had already reached the mandatory age of retirement from the public service and was not eligible for appointment to the position. The PEA successfully challenged the appointment, and the appointee was removed from the position.

The second case was *SCR No 1 of 1984; Re Morobe Provincial Government v PNG* [1984] PNGLR 212, in which the Morobe Provincial Government challenged the appointment of the Provincial Secretary by the NEC. The evidence revealed that the PSC had been consulted pursuant to s 193 and it had agreed to the appointment. At the hearing, the evidence also showed that the appointee's name was never on the list submitted to the NEC by the provincial government. Moreover, the NEC proceeded to appoint the Provincial Secretary without consulting the provincial government. As in *NEC v PEA*, the Supreme Court ruled, inter alia, that, although the PSC had consented to the appointment by the NEC, the NEC did not follow the correct procedure in appointing the Provincial Secretary. The court held that the NEC abrogated the procedure stipulated under s 50 of the *Organic Law on Provincial Governments* by not appointing a person from the list provided by the provincial government.

It was settled in *Constitutional Reference No 1 of 1978 (s 18)* [1978] PNGLR 460 that a person appointed under s 193 of the *Constitution*, whether he or she is on a permanent, temporary, acting or short term appointment, falls within the ambit of s 26(1)(f) of the *Constitution* and is, consequently, subject to the *Leadership Code*.

The Disciplined Forces

The other arms of the state services are the Defence Force and the Police Force. According to s 207 of the *Constitution*, the Police Force, the Defence Force and other forces or services set up under statute are the disciplined forces. The members of these disciplined services are not members of the public service per se. They are not covered under the *Public Services (Management) Act* 1995 and are not subject to the control of the PSC.

The primary role of the disciplined forces is to obey lawful orders. This is a constitutional duty under s 208 of the *Constitution*. The same provision protects the members of the disciplined forces in the conduct of their lawful duties. This section envisages the enactment of an Organic Law to cover the liability of members of the disciplined forces. No such law has been enacted yet. The absence of this legislation does not preclude the members of the disciplined forces from liability under other provisions of the *Constitution*, such as the human rights provisions, and other statutes. Where the members of the disciplined forces breach such provisions, as in the case of *David Wari Kofewei v Augustine Siviri* [1983] PNGLR 449, they can be held personally liable for the breach.

Defence Force

The powers and functions of the Defence Force are set out in ss 200-206 of the *Constitution*, while the conduct and terms and conditions of the members of the Defence Force are covered under the *Defence Act*, *Defence Force Code of Military Conduct*, *Defence (Period of Service) Regulation* and the *Defence (Aid to Civil Power) Regulation* 1988.[63]

Section 202 of the *Constitution* empowers the Defence Force to:

(a) defend PNG;

(b) assist in the fulfilment of PNG's international obligations; and

(c) assist the civilian authorities in a civil disaster and during public disorder.

The first function relates to war against PNG by another country or countries, where PNG responds by declaring war under s 227 of the *Constitution*. The second

63 The historical background of the PNG Defence Force is recorded in Sinclair, *To Find a Path: The Papua New Guinea Defence Force & The Australians to Independence* (Crawford House Press, Bathurst, 1992), Vol 2.

function is very broad and can sometimes cause difficulties in interpretation. This is highlighted in *SCR No 4 of 1980 (No 2); Re petition of MT Somare* [1982] PNGLR 65.[64] The third function has been used frequently by the government over the years in dealing with natural disasters and internal strife, such as the Bougainville Crisis. For the members of the Defence Force to be deployed to assist the civilian authorities, s 204 of the *Constitution* requires that they must be "called out" by the Governor-General (acting on the advice of the NEC). Section 204 has been simplified by the *Defence (Aid to Civil Power) Regulation* 1988. The Regulation clearly provides that when the members of the Defence Force are called out, they are to be controlled by the civilians. This requirement expands the scope of s 201 of the *Constitution*, which states that the Defence Force is to be controlled by the NEC.

In the conduct of their duties, the members of the Defence Force are given special protection under s 208 of the *Constitution*. This protection is very limited and relates only to the conduct of lawful duties. Section 203 of the *Constitution* exposes the members of the Defence Force to the scrutiny of other laws, such as the *Criminal Code* and similar legislation, where their conduct is not within their lawful duties. Soldiers who disobey lawful orders of their superiors can be disciplined by their superiors. Where proper disciplinary procedures were followed, the court cannot assist a dissatisfied soldier.[65] Soldiers whose conduct is in breach of the *Defence Force Act* and the *Code of Military Discipline* can be prosecuted and imprisoned by the National Court, as realised by the three soldiers in *State v Ugunnie* [1988-1989] PNGLR 101. Conversely, all forms of protection given to other people under other laws equally apply to the members of the Defence Force. Thus, in *Nuia v Benias Sabumei* [1992] PNGLR 90, the court held that the principles of natural justice enunciated under s 59 of the *Constitution* must also be accorded to an army colonel before being dismissed by the Defence Council.

Police Force

The Police Force is a constitutional institution and comes under the direct control and supervision of the NEC. Section 196(1) of the *Constitution* delegates the NEC's powers over the Police Force to the Police Minister. The primary functions of the Police Force, as enumerated under s 197, are:

(a) to preserve peace and good order in the country; and

(b) to maintain and, as necessary, enforce the law in an impartial and objective manner.

In terms of the first function, the Police Force is given very wide-ranging powers. The second function requires the Police Force to be objective and fair in the enforcement of the laws of the land. Being custodian of the laws, the Police Force is directed by the *Constitution* to enforce the law fearlessly and fairly. This is a very high calling, and requires all members of the Police Force to be diligent, honest and prudent in the performance of their constitutional functions. This duty extends to the laying of charges against offenders of the law. Akuram J, commenting on this power, said in *Ignote v Hualupmomi* [1996] PNGLR 308 at 319, that the duty contained an:

---

64 See the analysis of the decision from two different perspectives by Kwa, "Treaty Powers", and Wolfers, "Foreign Relations", both in Regan, Jessep and Kwa (eds), op cit n 31. See also Kwa, "Treaty Law-making in Papua New Guinea: After Two Decades *Yumi Stap We?*" (1997) 25 MLJ 43.

65 *Benas Openefa v Willie Karai Wagera* [1980] PNGLR 188.

> "unfettered discretion to charge any person for breaches of the laws of this country of which no superior officer or another person of high ranking can direct him or her to charge a person alleged to have broken the law".

Section 50A of the *Criminal Code Act* (Ch 262) makes it a criminal offence for anyone to create their own police force, and prohibits the creation of unauthorised forces. This section must be distinguished from s 200 of the *Constitution*. Section 50A of the *Criminal Code Act* is very wide, and covers the prohibition of military, paramilitary and police, or an organisation purporting to exercise military, paramilitary or police powers and functions. Section 200 of the *Constitution*, on the other hand, is very specific, and prohibits the creation of unauthorised military or paramilitary forces. Section 200 is apparently a restatement of s 50A, which was a pre-independence provision. Apparently, s 200 cut down the scope of s 50A and confined it to the Defence Force.

In 1977 and 1979, the East New Britain Provincial Government, responding to the Mataungan Association, secretly established a "Mataungan Security Police" and a Mataungan court to deal with law and order in the East New Britain Province. The Premier and Deputy Speaker, who were active members of the association, were arrested and charged under s 50A of the *Criminal Code Act* for establishing an unauthorised force. The two pleaded guilty and were convicted by the National Court. They appealed to the Supreme Court against their sentences. The Supreme Court, in *Koniel Alar and Hosea Biu v The State* [1979] PNGLR 43, considered the appeal and dismissed it. In the Supreme Court, the central issue was whether the sentences were excessive. The court did not considered the issue of whether there was any relationship between s 50A of the *Criminal Code Act* and s 200 of the *Constitution*. The National Court had alluded to it, but said no more than that. Although the decision would not have changed, it is suggested that the Supreme Court was concerned with the common law and then the constitutional law of PNG. It also reflects the apathy of the judges at that time to the *Constitution*.

The Police Commissioner, whose office is created under s 198 of the *Constitution*, heads the Police Force. The Police Commissioner is "responsible for the superintendence, efficient organization and control of the Police Force in accordance with an Act of the Parliament". The *Police Force Act* (Ch 65) outlines the Commissioner's responsibilities, the appointment, terms and conditions of employment of the members of the Police Force, and the processes and procedures of the Police Force. In 1993, the *Police Force Act* was amended to give more powers to the Police Commissioner, enabling him or her to hire and fire officers from the Police Force.

In the exercise of his or her powers and functions under the Act, the Police Commissioner is not subject to the direction and control of his or her political head, the Minister for Police. This statement of the law was enunciated in *SCR No 1 of 1982; Re Bouraga* [1982] PNGLR 178.[66] In the exercise of his or her powers and functions, the Police Commissioner is bound by the rules and principles of law laid down in the *Constitution* and other statutes. In *Farapo v Commissioner of Police* [1996] PNGLR 17, the court found that the Commissioner did not accord the applicant the principles of natural justice adopted by s 59 of the *Constitution*. Therefore, the Police Commissioner's order to dismiss the applicant from the Police Force was quashed by the court, and the applicant was reinstated to his previous position.[67]

---

66 The intervention of the judiciary in this case, and the impacts of this decision on the workings of the bureaucracy, have been severely criticised by Ghai and Hegarty, "Ministerial and Bureaucratic Power in Papua New Guinea: Aspects of Dutton/Bouraga Dispute" in Sack (ed), op cit n 10.

67 A similar ruling was made by the same judge in *Tuma v Commissioner of Police* [1996] PNGLR 430.

Other state services

There are other components of the state services envisioned by the *Constitution*. These categories of services are established by various specific pieces of legislation. These services include:

- the Teaching Service created by the *Teaching Service Act* 1988;
- the Parliamentary Service established by the *Parliamentary Service Act* (Ch 26);
- the National Fire Service provided by the *Fire Service Act* (Ch 64);
- the Probation Service promulgated under the *Probation Service Act* (Ch 381); and
- the Legislative Drafting Services created by the *Legislative Drafting Service Act* (Ch 80).

These state services are either administered by government departments or, in the case of the Parliamentary Service, are within the control of the Speaker and the Clerk of Parliament. For instance, the Fire Service and the Legislative Drafting Service fall under the Prime Minister's Department, and the Probation Service comes under the control of the Attorney-General's Department. The employees of these state services are members of the public service. Although their terms and conditions are contained under specific legislation, the provisions of the *Public Services (Management) Act* 1995 generally encompass these public servants.

Statutory bodies

There are also a number of statutory organisations that do not constitute state services. They operate as autonomous organisations outside the ambit of the National Public Service, but they are agents of the state and provide specific services to the public. Examples include:

- the Electricity Commission, which provides electricity to the public and operates under the auspices of the *Electricity Commission Act*;
- Post PNG, which provides postal services in accordance with the *Postal Services Act*;
- Telikom, created under the *Telecommunications Act*, which is responsible for the provision of telecommunication services to the nation;
- the University of Papua New Guinea, established under the *University of Papua New Guinea Act*; and
- the other state universities created under their specific pieces of legislation, which are responsible for providing university education to the people of PNG.

Some of these statutory organisations are managed by boards whose members are appointed by the government. The board members hold office at the pleasure of the government: *Kila Wari v Ramoi and Dibela* [1986] PNGLR 112.

6.5 CONCLUSION

The working of the executive government in PNG has not been smooth sailing. The executive arm of the government, like the judiciary and the legislature, has undergone some difficult challenges. The most significant challenge to the executive's authority has been the decisions of the Supreme Court in *SCR No 1 of 1982; Re Bouraga* [1982] PNGLR 178 and the *Haiveta v Wingti* cases. The tensions between the two separate arms of government are inherent in these cases. They reflect the jealousy of the judiciary in asserting its authority as the custodian of the *Constitution* and the enforcer of the rule of law.

The *Constitution* set out deliberately and in detail many of the executive's powers and functions, which are covered by unwritten conventions found in other countries applying the Westminster system of government. These include the relationship between the executive and the Head of State, the relationship between the executive and the judiciary and the legislature, and the supervision of the bureaucracy. It is no wonder a former Prime Minister complained that:

> "A major pre-occupation of those who framed the *Constitution* was their desire to keep the Executive – the Government – under what they regarded as proper democratic control. Having chosen the basic model of a parliamentary or Westminster type system, with the Executive drawn directly from Parliament and depending on a parliamentary majority for its continuation in office, they imposed a large number of specific restrictions on it, many of them unknown in other parliamentary constitutions."[68]

The size of the bureaucracy has been a major concern for successive governments. This is more significant in light of the devolution of powers and functions to the rural areas under the OLPGLLG. Its reduction will be a gradual process. Apart from the obvious problems of funding, the exercise is a manifestation of the salient struggle between the politicians and the bureaucracy. The bureaucracy has become too dominant and arrogant, and needs to be taken head-on by the politicians. The centralisation of the bureaucracy, under the leadership of the department head under the OLPGLLG, drastically eroded the powers of the politicians over the public servants.

In PNG, the politicians need to control their level of interference in the work of the public servants, so that the bureaucracy can perform its role efficiently and with satisfaction. The Mourata Government seems to have taken a very strict line on this matter, with the sacking of two Ministers who conspired to remove the Police Commissioner because of petty political reasons.[69] If this trend is followed with the improvement in other areas of the executive branch of government, the bureaucracy will be strengthened, and the executive will, in the long term, begin to bring some credibility into the operations of government.

---

68 Chan, "Experience with Papua New Guinea's Constitution: A Prime Minister's Reflections" in Ghai (ed), op cit n 10, p 246.

69 *Post Courier* (15 December 2000).

Chapter 7

THE JUDICIARY

7.1 INTRODUCTION

The position of the judiciary, and the role it plays in contemporary Papua New Guinean society, has been pivotal in the constitutional development of Papua New Guinea (PNG). The judiciary has faced numerous challenges from its beginnings[1] to the present.[2] These challenges have been met, and the judiciary has not shrunk from its responsibility to administer justice over the last 25 years. Its fundamental character as an independent and impartial institution has been, and continues to be, an inspiration to many people within and outside the country.[3]

In PNG, the judiciary is regarded as "a vital part of the foundations of which our people seek freedom, fulfilment and total development, both personal and national".[4] The Constitutional Planning Committee (CPC) was of the view that the judiciary would occupy a very important position in the new state. That position was not only to be the "third pillar of the government", but also the custodian of the *Constitution.*

Many of the traditional roles of the judiciary, such as: keeping the peace; deciding controversies; judicial law-making; review of constitutionality of laws and actions of the executive and of other institutions and persons; enforcement of human rights; review of administrative actions on grounds other than constitutional grounds; procedural rule-making; and enforcement of judicial decisions, have been given constitutional status in PNG, unlike other common law jurisdictions.[5]

This chapter examines the role of the judiciary in the development of PNG in the last 25 years, its powers and functions, its structure and the manner in which it performs its responsibilities. In PNG, the judiciary's performance is clearly determined by its history.[6]

7.2 THE SOURCE OF JUDICIAL AUTHORITY

It has been said that:

> "the courts are the instruments and guardians of the national legal system. They protect the citizens against unlawful practices and in some countries,

1 This is exemplified in the famous Rooney Affair, which is discussed elsewhere in this book.

2 The recent controversy between the judiciary and the legislature about the sittings of Parliament as defined by the Supreme Court in *SCR No 3 of 1999; Re Sittings of Parliament* (1999) SC 628 is on point.

3 For a detailed historical account of the judiciary in PNG prior to independence, see Chalmers, *Full Circle: A History of the Courts of Papua New Guinea* (LLM Thesis, UPNG, 1978).

4 Constitutional Planning Committee, *Constitutional Planning Committee Final Report (Part 1)* (Government Printer, Port Moresby, 1974) (CPC, *Final Report*), p 8/1.

5 Regan, "Constitutionalism, Legitimacy and the Judiciary" in James and Fraser (eds), *Legal Issues in a Developing Society* (UPNG, Faculty of Law, Port Moresby, 1992), p 28.

6 James and Fraser (eds), Ibid, p 4.

> protect the constitution itself against alterations by unconstitutional laws, and executive orders or acts".[7]

Where is the source of authority for the judiciary?

In many countries, it is the constitution itself that vests the judicial authority on the judiciary. In the case of PNG, as with other countries, it is not merely the *Constitution* that confers this authority. It is the will of the people that underlies and bestows authority on the judiciary. This was declared by the Supreme Court in *The State v Wonom* [1975] PNGLR 311. In that case, the defendant was arrested and charged before independence on 16 September 1975. On 19 September 1975, the defendant pleaded guilty. Before sentencing, the defendant's counsel argued that the accused was wrongfully indicted, as the indictment was in the name of the "state" and not the Crown. The National Court reserved its ruling and sought the advice of the Supreme Court. The Supreme Court ruled that the indictment was properly worded and, therefore, there was no irregularity or illegality. Raine J (at 318) correctly stated the principles as follows:

> "For the reasons given earlier, The People having judicial authority lodged in them, and having vested it in the National Judicial System, it is appropriate and correct for the proceedings to be brought in the name of the State."

Williams J (at 320), agreeing with Raine J, was more explicit and said:

> "The power of the judicature in this country lies in the people at large. This has been invested by the people in the courts established under the *Constitution*. I think it is inappropriate that proceedings of a criminal nature should be brought in the name of the court, nor do I think that proceedings should be in the name of the Public Prosecutor, whose functions are defined in s 177 of the *Constitution*, which, in their terms appear inapt to meet the present situation. In my view it is appropriate that proceedings be brought by the people in their collective corporate name 'The State'."[8]

The Supreme Court decision in the above case was easily followed by the National Court in *Yamba v Geru* [1975] PNGLR 322. Both decisions are based on s 158(1) of the *Constitution*. This section declares that the "judicial authority of the People" is vested in the National Justice System. The National Justice System, as defined in s 115(1), is the various levels of courts, from the Supreme Court to the Village Courts. The Parliament reacted to this decision in November 1975 by enacting the *Legal Process by and Against the State Act* 1975. This Act removed any doubts in relation to the description of the state. Under s 3 of the Act, all criminal proceedings were to be brought in the name of the state.

However, the *Constitution* does not define "judicial authority". In PNG, it is important to know exactly what "judicial authority" means. This definitional exercise should be seen in the context of the doctrine of separation of the powers and functions of the three main arms of government in s 99(3) of the *Constitution*. The judiciary guards its sphere of authority, as highlighted in the case of *SCR No 1A of 1981; Re Motor Traffic Act* [1982] PNGLR 122. In addressing this issue, Kearney DCJ, delivering the main judgment, stated (at 134) that:

> "It is clear from its structure that the *Constitution* contemplates a general separation of powers between the three principal arms of government – the

7 Duchacek, *Power Maps: Comparative Politics of Constitutions* (American Bibliographical Center – Clio Press Inc, Santa Barbara, 1973), p 214.

8 For an analysis of this case, see Chalmers "Constitutional Autochthony: The Position of the Head of State in an Independent Papua New Guinea" (1978) 27 ICLQ 672; and Brunton, "The State v The Queen: In the Matter of the State against John Wonom of Jigi" (1976) 4 MLJ 126.

> legislature, executive and the judiciary; see the *Constitution*, s 99. As a parliamentary system with an executive responsible to Parliament, the separation of powers between the arms cannot be rigid. But the separation principle remains of basic importance in the *Constitution* and prohibits incursions by one arm of government upon basic functions of another. The legislation presently in question, I think, is an example of the legislature having gone too far in prescribing rules which control judicial decisions in certain cases, thus invading the realm of judicial power."[9]

The principle of separation of powers is reinforced by specific limits on the extent to which the "judicial authority" can be conferred on persons or bodies other than those within the National Judicial System. Section 159(1) of the *Constitution* permits vesting of judicial authority on persons or bodies other than courts. The conferral of judicial power on other bodies is, however, very restricted. A major restriction is imposed by the fact that any vesting of judicial authority must be done by an Organic Law or statute by the legislature. Equally important, s 159(3) declares that judicial authority in respect of criminal matters cannot be vested in a person or body other than a court.[10]

Vesting of judicial authority outside the courts is permitted to avoid the constitutional problems that have arisen in Australia in attempts to vest judicial authority in bodies other than courts.[11] Hence, the vesting of judicial power outside the judicial system is not intended to offend the principles involved in the doctrine of separation of powers, but rather to provide some flexibility, especially in respect of the vesting of powers in "arbitral or conciliatory tribunals" outside the National Judicial System, as specifically mentioned in s 159(1) of the *Constitution.*

As s 157 of the *Constitution* guarantees the independence of courts and their members from directions from any person or authority outside the National Judicial System concerning the exercise of "judicial powers or functions", directions might be given to the courts about other matters (for example, organisation of its staff).[12]

The central aspect of the exercise of judicial authority involves the resolution of disputes. Almost all cases decided by courts ultimately involve disputes of one kind or another. Disputes may take various forms, and arise in relation to a number of matters, such as criminal matters, civil matters (contracts, torts, equity etc), allegations of breaches of human rights, etc. Such disputes may be between:

- one person and another; or
- persons and governments; or
- different levels of government.

These disputes are usually resolved by applying the law to the facts involved in the dispute. As the judiciary is an arm of the state, the exercise of judicial authority involves the power of the state to determine disputes (controversies) between persons (citizens and others) and between the state and persons.[13] The definition

---

9 The other three judges (Kidu CJ, Andrew and Kapi JJ) endorsed the Deputy Chief Justice's exposition of the law.

10 However, note the exceptions in relation to disciplinary offences: detention and other punishments (not including death) imposed in relation to members of the disciplined forces; punishments (other than death or detention) imposed on members of the state services; and penalties (other than death or detention) imposed on association members for breaches of rules of the association.

11 Goldring, *The Constitution of Papua New Guinea* (Law Book Co Ltd, Sydney, 1978), pp 122-123.

12 There is an exception to the protection from direction. The Parliament can provide direction through legislation as specified by s 157 of the *Constitution*.

13 *Huddart Parker Pty Ltd v Moorehead* (1909) 8 CLR 330 at 357.

of judicial power in that case emphasises that judicial power is exercised in relation to:

- a dispute (controversy);
- about rights or duties under law of one kind or another (whether it be to life, liberty or property); and
- involves the making of a binding determination to end the dispute.

There are, therefore, clear distinctions between the nature of legislative and executive powers, on the one hand, and judicial power, on the other hand. The CPC discusses this role in the first few paragraphs of Ch 8 of its final report. The courts in PNG have roles in relation to all of the kinds of disputes mentioned above. Relating the dispute resolution function to the jurisdiction of courts, the jurisdiction of a particular court as determined by law is a definition of the limits of the kinds of disputes the court can deal with.

7.3 THE ADMINISTRATION OF JUSTICE

Background

The arrival of Europeans in the South Pacific region had a "dramatic and lasting consequence for the legal and political system".[14] In PNG, the people were exposed to the British, Germans and, later, the Australians. PNG's interaction with these cultures, particularly the Australians, exposed the country to the legal, political and economic structures of that country.[15] PNG, therefore, adopted what it was more accustomed to, that is, the colonial structures. As one commentator observed:

> "The existing legal system is not one of choice. Adopted for colonial needs, it was thrust upon the people without as it often happens, understanding the needs of the recipient society."[16]

Chalmers described the situation thus:

> "It is self-evident that a developed western legal system cannot be transplanted in toto onto Papa New Guinea society without some careful and ingenious adaptation. A foreign legal and administrative system imposed in such an unpalatable form must inevitably lead to difficulties."[17]

The exposure to the "Western" cultures, values and structures, however, did not extinguish the traditional structures and values of the people. At independence, PNG adopted dual legal, political and economic structures. In the legal arena, PNG adopted the "new" system of administering justice through the courts, and accepted the application of both custom and common law as an integral part of the new legal order. The CPC was aware that:

> "With the establishment of modern institutions in our country, the courts of justice, developed elsewhere, are gradually becoming acceptable institutions in our society."[18]

---

14 Powles, "Law, Courts and Legal Services in Pacific Societies" in Powles and Pulea (eds), *Pacific Courts and Legal Systems* (USP, Institute of Pacific Studies, Suva, 1988), p 7.

15 Sakora, "Judicial Law-making under the Papua New Guinea Constitution" in Sack (ed), *Pacific Constitutions* (Australian National University, Canberra, 1982), p 58.

16 Wijetillake, "Integrating the Judicial System and Reviewing the Administration of Justice in Papua New Guinea" (1988) 16 MLJ 34 at 35.

17 Chalmers, op cit n 3, p 1.

18 CPC, *Final Report*, Ch 8, p 8/1.

The CPC, therefore, declared that the courts constituted the third pillar of the government in PNG. The expressions of the CPC are reflected in s 99 of the *Constitution.* The administration of justice, as espoused by s 154 of the *Constitution,* is in the National Judicial System, the Minister for Justice and the Law Officers of PNG. It is not clear why the Minister responsible for Justice is included in the National Justice Administration. Presumably, it is because he or she acts as the link between the National Justice Administration and the executive arm of government. In that respect, it is worth noting the other functions of the Minister provided under the *Constitution.* These include chairing the Judicial and Legal Services Commission (s 183(2)), consulting the NEC on appointment of the Chief Justice (s 169(2)), receiving reports under s 37(14), and appearing in proceedings over conflict of precedents under Sch 2.10(2).

The Law Officers

The Law Officers of PNG are the Public Prosecutor and the Public Solicitor created under s 176 of the *Constitution.* The *Public Prosecutor (Office and Functions) Act* (Ch 338) amplifies the powers and functions of the Public Prosecutor. The Supreme Court considered the powers of the Public Prosecutor under the relevant section in *SC Review No 5 of 1987 (Application by Public Prosecutor)* [1987] PNGLR 216. The court found that the Public Prosecutor did not have standing to seek a judicial review under s 155(2)(b) where no conviction or acquittal was entered against a defendant. The powers and functions of the Public Prosecutor were also brought under the microscope in *The State v The Principal Magistrate* [1983] PNGLR 43. In that case, the Supreme Court was asked to resolve a dispute between the Public Prosecutor and the Principal Magistrate of the Port Moresby District Court regarding the nature and extent of their powers under the *District Courts (Committal Proceedings in Cases of Indictable Offences) Act*[19] and the *District Courts (Hearing of Indictable Offences) Act.*[20]These series of amendments enabled certain indictable offences under the *Criminal Code* to be dealt with by the District Court. The list of offences are contained in Sch 1A to the *Criminal Code.* Both the District Court and the Public Prosecutor have concurrent powers over these offences. However, the Public Prosecutor argued that he had the power to decide, at any time, either to allow the proceedings to proceed summarily or by way of committal. The Principal Magistrate, on the other hand, argued that he had the power to make that decision, and therefore he did not need to wait for the Public Prosecutor's election. After a lengthy discussion, Pratt J, with whom Kapi DCJ and Bredmeyer J agreed, ruled that the magistrate did not have the jurisdiction to deal with the matter summarily. He went on to further say that if the Public Prosecutor did not want the case to be dealt with summarily, the Public Prosecutor had to make his or her decision known before the files were delivered to the defendant.

In *Constitutional Reference No 1 of 1978 (s 19)* [1978] PNGLR 345, the Supreme Court considered that the Public Solicitor is a Law Officer and a constitutional office holder. The Public Solicitor is, therefore, not subject to any direction or control by any person. Conversely, he or she cannot be investigated by any person, including the Ombudsman Commission, in relation to the exercise of his or her official duties and functions. The Public Solicitor, as a "leader" under the

---

19 *District Courts (Committal Proceedings in Cases of Indictable Offences) Act* (No 31 of 1980).

20 *District Courts (Hearing of Indictable Offences) Act* (No 32 of 1980). This Act amended the *District Courts Act* and the *Criminal Code (Amendment) Act,* which amended the *Criminal Code Act* (No 28 of 1980).

cover of the *Organic Law on the Duties and Responsibilities of Leadership*, can be investigated for alleged misconduct in office.[21]

National Judicial System

The National Justice System, according to s 155 of the *Constitution*, consists of:

(a) the Supreme Court;

(b) the National Court; and

(c) other courts established under Acts of Parliament.

The administration of justice in PNG is associated more with the judiciary than the Minister for Justice or the Law Officers. There are two main reasons for this view. First, there is the general assumption that because the judiciary deals primarily with disputes and resolves them, the courts must be the source of justice. Secondly, the roles and functions of the Law Officers are not clearly understood by the community at large and, thus, there is a general misconception that they are not administrators of justice.

The method of achieving justice in the new legal order is through the adversarial system, where the prosecution has to prove the guilt of the defendant.[22] In this system, the judges of the courts act as independent umpires in the dispute.[23] The judiciary has, time and again, been reminded of the importance of this responsibility, as reflected in the following cases: *Kavali v Hoihoi* [1986] PNGLR 329; *Agai v Yarume* [1987] PNGLR 124; *The State v Sari* [1990] PNGLR 48; *Boateng v The State* [1990] PNGLR 342; and *Diro v Amet* [1995] PNGLR 411. These cases show that, where the integrity of the judge is put into question, the judge must disqualify himself or herself. The judges and magistrates of the courts are assumed to be persons of impeccable reputation and standing in society. As the CPC observed:

> "Members of our Judiciary should have integrity, appropriate professional qualifications and experience."[24]

The integrity of the judges is the "golden thread" that holds the whole system of government together in PNG. Because the judges are required to carry out justice and keep the peace through dispute resolution, their independence from any direction and control is crucial. The judiciary must be insulated from the crises of society. The judiciary cannot "directly appeal to the people in national affairs or even in matters relating to itself".[25]

The judiciary must also be careful in the exercise of its judicial powers. The main area of concern is the potentiality of the courts becoming too political in their decisions. This was a major concern for the CPC.[26] It therefore recommended that

---

21 Consider the short commentary on this case in Bayne, "The Constitution in the Courts 1975-1980" in Weisbrot, Paliwala and Sawyerr, *Law and Social Change in Papua New Guinea* (Butterworths, Sydney, 1982), p 220.

22 *Constitution*, s 37(4)(a).

23 The need to ensure impartiality and avoid any appearance of bias is discussed by Nonggorr, "Maintenance of Judicial Independence and Integrity in Papua New Guinea: Some Recent Developments" (1992) (3) *Commonwealth Judicial Journal* 9; and Ntumy., "The Nemo Iudex Principle of Natural Justice" in Regan, Jessep and Kwa (eds), *Twenty Years of the Constitution* (Lawbook Co, Sydney, 2001).

24 CPC, *Final Report*, Ch 8, p 8/2.

25 Wijetillake, "Integrating the Judicial System and Reviewing the Administration of Justice in Papua New Guinea" (1988) 16 MLJ 34 at 37.

26 CPC, *Final Report*, op cit, Ch 8, pp 8/1-8/2.

the independence of the judiciary be protected. Section 157 of the *Constitution* achieves this objective.

However, there are wider issues involved. The political consequences of court decisions are especially important when major constitutional issues are decided. The result can be a significant redistribution of political power. This is exemplified by the cases of *Haivetta v Wingti (No 3)* [1994] PNGLR 197, *Kaseng v Namaliu* [1995] PNGLR 481 and *SCR No 3 of 1999; Re Sittings of Parliament* (1999) SC 628. In the first case, the Prime Minister, Mr Paias Wingti, resigned from office and then had Parliament re-elect him the next day. The Supreme Court decided that the re-election of Wingti was unconstitutional. Therefore, he was deemed to have resigned from the office of the Prime Minister. Because of that decision, a new Prime Minister was appointed to replace Wingti. In the second case, the Supreme Court declared that the *Organic Law on Provincial Governments and Local-level Governments* (OLPGLLG), which replaced the *Organic Law on Provincial Governments* (and ushered in the reformed provincial government system), was constitutional and valid. This was a fundamental decision that permanently changed the political landscape of PNG. The impact of this decision continues to haunt some provinces, such as Bougainville, which does not have a fully-fledged provincial government. In an attempt to rectify the anomaly, the Provincial Governor asked the National Court, in *John Momis v Attorney-General* (2000) N 1951, to assist the Governor establish the provincial machinery required under the OLPGLLG. The court rejected Momis' application, on the grounds that the Organic Law was in force, and the lack of machinery of the province was based on political, rather than legal, reasons.

In some countries, such as the United States, the courts have developed a doctrine under which the Supreme Court refuses to deal with constitutional issues involving political matters. The aim is to ensure that courts are not drawn into political conflict, thereby lowering their standing in the eyes of the people. No such doctrine seems to have developed in PNG, where the courts have been prepared to take on almost any constitutional issue.[27]

7.4 COMPONENTS OF THE NATIONAL JUDICIAL SYSTEM

The National Judicial System consists of the Supreme Court and the National Court, which are the superior courts, and the District Courts and the Village Courts, which are the lower courts. The Supreme Court is established by s 160 of the *Constitution*, and the National Court is created under s 163. The lower courts are allowed under s 172, and are created by specific Acts of Parliament.

In terms of the status of the decisions of the courts within the National Judicial System, there is a hierarchy of courts. The Supreme Court is at the apex. It achieves this status because of a number of reasons. First, its decisions are binding on all other courts, as declared by Sch 2.9(1). Secondly, it has an inherent power to review all the decisions of the National Court (which in turn has an inherent power to review the decisions of any other court). This power is located under s 155(2)(b). Thirdly, it has the power to interpret and apply the constitutional laws, as provided by ss 18 and 19. Fourthly, the combined effect of ss 99(2)(c),

27 However, the Supreme Court has sometimes been criticised for not basing some decisions on such an approach. See Ghai and Hegarty, "Ministerial and Bureaucratic Power in Papua New Guinea: Aspects of the Dutton/Bouraga Dispute" in Sack (ed), op cit n 15, pp 252-255. See also Omar, "Parliament, the Executive and the Court in Papua New Guinea" (1996) 70 ALJ 313 at 323.

155(2) and 160(2) give the Supreme Court unlimited jurisdiction. Finally, s 155(2)(a) declares that it is the final court of appeal.

The National Court is next in the hierarchy of courts, because its decisions are binding on all courts other than the Supreme Court (Sch 2.9(2)), and it has an inherent power of review over decisions of all courts except the Supreme Court (s 155(3)). The Supreme Court and the National Court have other significant roles that make their decisions of much greater significance than those of the other courts. In particular, they have roles in relation to the enforcement of human rights (ss 57-58) and development of the underlying law (s 20 and Sch 2(3) and (5)).

The result is that the lowest levels of the courts (District Courts and Village Courts), which deal with by far the greatest numbers of cases, have little impact on the law. It is the Supreme Court and the National Court that have the greatest impact on the law and, thus, the manner in which judicial authority is exercised. Because of this, the *Constitution* declares, under ss 160(2) and 163(2), that the Supreme Court and the National Court are *courts of record*. A court of record is a court where "the acts and judicial proceedings are enrolled for a perpetual memory and testimony and which has authority to fine and imprison for contempt of its authority".[28]

Composition of the Supreme Court

The Supreme Court is made up of the Chief Justice, the Deputy Chief Justice and the other judges of the National Court. Acting judges are not eligible to sit on the Supreme Court bench. This prohibition is explicit in s 161(1) of the *Constitution*. In a normal case, at least three judges must constitute the court: s 161(2). The exception to this rule is provided by s 162(2). Under this proviso, an Act of Parliament or Rules of Court can specify cases where a single judge may exercise the power of the Supreme Court, such as in the case of *SCR No 3 of 1984; Ex parte Callick and Koroma* [1985] PNGLR 67. The relevant Act is the *Supreme Court Act* (Ch 37), and the relevant court rules are the *Supreme Court Rules*. The Act and the Rules set out in detail matters relating to the conduct of proceedings in the Supreme Court. Under s 2 of the *Supreme Court Act*, a judge cannot sit on an appeal from his or her own decision.

Composition of the National Court

Section 164 of the *Constitution* provides that the National Court shall consist of the Chief Justice, the Deputy Chief Justice and no fewer than four other judges. This provision also provides that an Act of Parliament may provide for the number of judges. The relevant Act is the *National Court (Number of Judges) Act* (Ch 404). Section 2 of the Act stipulates that the number of judges of the National Court, other than the Chief Justice and the Deputy Chief Justice, is to be "not less than four and not more than the number, being not less than six", as is determined by the Head of State, acting with the advice of the National Executive Council. The decision to increase the number of judges can only be made after the National Executive Council has received and considered a report from the Chief Justice.

In the year 2000, the National Executive Council accepted a number of proposals to increase the number of judges from a ceiling of 12 judges to 24 judges. This increase was necessitated as a result of the increasing workload of the courts and

28 *Osborn's Concise Law Dictionary* (8th ed, Sweet & Maxwell, London, 1993).

the limited number of judges who are currently on the bench. As Chief Justice Amet said:

> "The judicial system is faced with an ever-increasing volume of cases and lacks the resources to dispose of them efficiently because the judicial strength has not increased by much over the years. ... in the past two years, the judges ranks at the National and Supreme Court level had thinned from 20 to just 12."[29]

Acting judges can be appointed for various reasons specified under s 165 of the *Constitution*. These judges hold office for 12 months, and are eligible for renewal only for one term. They do not sit on the Supreme Court, nor are they taken into account when calculating the number of National Court judges permitted by s 164(c).

Section 167 made provision for an Act of Parliament to provide arrangements under which Papua New Guinean judges with qualifications less than those required for full National Court judges could be appointed as "assistant judges" as an interim measure towards ensuring localisation of the bench. This was a major issue for some time, even after independence, when there were almost no Papua New Guineans who had been qualified lawyers for the length of time required to enable them to be appointed judges.[30] The provisions of s 167 have never been utilised.

7.5 JUDGES: QUALIFICATIONS AND APPOINTMENT

The CPC was aware of the enormous task the judiciary had in the development of the country. The CPC was also mindful of the role the judges had in influencing government policies and the path of development in dealing with controversial cases. The CPC, therefore, proposed that to be eligible for appointment as a judge, a person must be a person of integrity, a professional lawyer and must have adequate legal experience.[31] The CPC, however, did not define the qualities of a judge in detail. Sections 1 and 2 of the *National Court Act* (Ch 38) fill this vacuum. Section 1 deals with citizen applicants, and s 2 covers non-citizen applicants. Section 1 is in the following terms:

> "Subject to Section 4 of the *Organic Law on the Terms and Conditions of Employment of Judges*, a citizen is qualified for appointment as a judge if:
>
> (a) he:
>
> (i) is a graduate in law of at least six years standing of a university in Papua New Guinea or of a university of another country the degree in law of which is recognised by the Judicial and Legal Services Commission as a sufficient academic qualification for appointment; and
>
> (ii) has practised as a lawyer for not less than four years; or
>
> (b) he:
>
> (i) is a graduate in law of a university in Papua New Guinea or of a university of another country the degree in law of which is

29 Speech by the Chief Justice, ADR Workshop, Granville Motel, 30 October 2000: *The National* (31 October 2000), p 3.

30 See CPC, *Final Report*, Ch 8, p 8/4. See also the discussion in Ross, "A Review of the Judiciary in Papua New Guinea" (1977) 5 MLJ 5 at 13-14.

31 These are the qualities proposed by the CPC. See CPC, *Final Report*, Ch 8, p 8/2.

recognised by the Judicial and Legal Services Commission as a sufficient academic qualification for appointment; and

(ii) has not less than five years experience in Papua New Guinea as a Magistrate Grade IV or a Magistrate III, or partly as a Magistrate Grade IV and partly as a Magistrate Grade II."

It is clear that the legislation departs drastically from the recommendations of the CPC. The provision is also confusing, in that it is not clear to what category of persons paragraph (a)(i) is referring as opposed to paragraph (b)(i). It is more confusing when paragraph (a)(ii) and (b)(ii) are contrasted. It is submitted that paragraph (a) refers generally to lawyers who are not magistrates, while paragraph (b) specifically refers to magistrates. Paragraph (a) is quite ambiguous. It appears, on the face of the provision, to separate the lawyers into practitioners and non-practitioners. Law graduates, who have not practised law for more than six years, may be considered for appointment under paragraph (a)(i). A lawyer who has practised for more than four years may be considered for appointment. Seen from this perspective, it is suggested that when the two limbs of the paragraph are considered as two separate conditions that stand on their own, the whole section opens the door for the appointment of inexperienced lawyers to the bench.

The same arguments can be raised in relation to the criteria in paragraph (b). The CPC envisaged a bench comprising of highly qualified and experienced Papua New Guineans of impeccable character. Section 1 of the *National Court Act* reduces the standard and quality of the bench. It may be argued that the Act must be considered in the light of the lack of qualified and experienced citizens available for appointment to the bench immediately at independence. This argument is no longer relevant. Most of the citizen judges appointed to the bench since independence have been experienced, professional and impeccable.

Sections 1 and 2 of the *National Court Act* must be read together with s 4 of the *Organic Law on Terms and Conditions of Employment of Judges*. The Organic Law sets out the categories of persons who are not qualified to be appointed as judges. These include:

- Members of Parliament;
- members of a provincial government;
- members of a local-level government;
- officers of a registered political party;
- bankrupt persons;
- mentally ill persons; or
- prisoners.

National Court judges are appointed by the Judicial and Legal Services Commission, and not the executive arm of government. This is clearly set out in s 170(2) of the *Constitution*. The only judge appointed by the executive arm of government is the Chief Justice.

Period of appointment of judges

The periods of appointment of judges are determined by the *Organic Law on Terms and Conditions of Employment of Judges*. According to s 2, the term of appointment for citizens in the first ten years after independence was three years, but thereafter became ten years. The term for non-citizens is three years. Both categories of judges are eligible for reappointment.

Under s 7 of the Organic Law, judges must retire at the age of 60. However, a judge's term may be extended beyond 60 years to 65 years only if the Judicial and Legal Services Commission deems it appropriate. If a judge wants to resign, s 6 states that the judge must give three months notice in writing to the Judicial and Legal Services Commission. Since independence, a number of judges have made use of this provision, and have resigned from the bench. The first time it was used was in 1980, when the then Chief Justice and the majority of the judges resigned as a consequence of the famous Rooney Affair.

Remuneration

The remuneration of judges is determined by the Salaries and Remuneration Commission, which is established under s 216A of the *Constitution*. The Commission became a constitutional office after the ninth amendment to the *Constitution* in 1988. The amendment gave the Commission responsibility for determining all aspects of remuneration of the judges, thereby overriding s 3 of the *Organic Law on the Terms and Conditions of Employment of Judges*. The latter provision was eventually repealed by the *Organic Law on the Terms and Conditions of Employment of Judges (Amendment No 1 – Consequential Amendment) Law* 1991.[32]

Other terms and conditions of employment

The *Organic Law on the Terms and Conditions of Employment of Judges* also sets out a number of conditions with which the judges are required to comply. These conditions are spelt out clearly in s 5. This provision states that judges are not permitted to:

- actively engage in politics;
- engage either directly or indirectly in the management or control of a corporation or other body of persons carrying on business for profit;
- acquire, use or hold in any manner any interest in any property in PNG;[33] or
- solicit, accept or receive any other benefit other than those provided for in his or her terms and conditions of employment.

Office of the Chief Justice

The position of Chief Justice in PNG is very important. The Chief Justice must be a judge of impeccable standing in the judiciary. Since independence, three Chief Justices have headed PNG. On independence, an expatriate Chief Justice, Sir Sydney Frost, headed the judiciary. He remained in that position until 1980, when the Chief Justice and other members of the judiciary resigned as a consequence of the Rooney Affair. The first Papua New Guinean Chief Justice, Sir Buri Kidu, was appointed to the position in 1980, and held the post for 13 years until his removal by the government in 1993. The current Chief Justice, Sir Arnold Amet, is the second citizen Chief Justice since independence.

Position and responsibilities of the Chief Justice

The position of the Chief Justice is set out in s 169 of the *Constitution*. Section 169(3) defines the main role of the Chief Justice. The Chief Justice is responsible,

---

32 *Organic Law on the Terms and Conditions of Employment of Judges (Amendment No 1 – Consequential Amendment) Law* 1991 (No 3 of 1991).

33 However, citizen judges may hold interests in land in the same way as any other citizen.

among other powers, functions, duties and responsibilities, for the organisation of the affairs and administration of the business of the Supreme Court and the National Court. There is a proviso in this section. The condition is that this function must be performed only after consultation with the other judges. This requirement is repeated in s 3 of the *National Court Act*. While the *Constitution* speaks in general terms about the consultation process, the Act specifically states that, in determining:

(a) the principal seat of the National Court,

(b) the place and frequency of sittings of the National Court, and

(c) the location and number of registries,

the Chief Justice must consult the other judges of the National Court and Supreme Court. This proviso highlights the need for transparency and openness within the judicial system.

The other powers and functions of the Chief Justice are set out in the *Constitution* and various statutes. Under the *Constitution*, he or she:

- is a member of the Judicial and Legal Services Commission (s 183(2)(b)), the Salaries and Remuneration Commission (s 216A(2)(d)), and the Ombudsman Appointments Committee (s 217(2)(b));
- takes the Governor-General's Declaration of Loyalty (s 90(1));
- must report to the government on delays in criminal trials (s 37(14));
- must forward Rules of Court to the Speaker of the Parliament (s 184(5)); and
- becomes Acting Governor-General in the absence of the Governor-General and the Speaker of the Parliament (s 95(3)).

Some of the powers and functions of the Chief Justice under the statutes include:

- determining of the "principal seat" of the National Court (*National Court Act*, s 3);
- determining the place and frequency of sittings, and the location and number of registries (*National Court Act*, s 4 and *National Judicial Staff Service Act* 1987-1990);
- appointing Leadership Tribunals inquiring into allegations of misconduct in the office of leaders referred by the Public Prosecutor or the Ombudsman Commission (*Organic Law on the Duties and Responsibilities of Leadership*, s 27(7)(d) and (e)); and
- administering declarations of office of all office-holders covered under the *Organic Law on Certain Constitutional Office-holders* (*Organic Law on Certain Constitutional Office-holders*, s 12).

Appointment of the Chief Justice

The Chief Justice is appointed by the Head of State acting on advice of the National Executive Council after consultation with the Minister responsible for National Justice Administration. By contrast with the appointment of other judges, there is no requirement for the involvement of the Judicial and Legal Services Commission. The appointment provisions reflect concerns of the CPC that the Chief Justice should be someone "accepted by all major political groups as being clearly impartial".[34] However, the process in the *Constitution* does not provide for the range of consultation that the CPC envisaged.[35]

34 CPC, *Final Report*, Ch 8, p 8/3.
35 Ibid.

The method of appointment of the Chief Justice opens the process to overtly political considerations. This concern is significant in the light of the fact that the period of appointment of a citizen Chief Justice is ten years, rather than for life. The concern to be reappointed every ten years could result in political pressures being brought to bear on an incumbent Chief Justice. The desire of another judge or of some other person to be appointed Chief Justice could also add to the political pressures leading up to an appointment.[36]

Position and responsibilities of the Deputy Chief Justice

The position of the Deputy Chief Justice is created by s 170(1) of the *Constitution*. Section 171(1) makes this position the second most senior judge of the court after the Chief Justice. Under s 169(4), when there is a vacancy in the office of Chief Justice, or he or she is unable to carry out his or her functions and powers as the Chief Justice, the Deputy Chief Justice performs these tasks. The performance of these duties by the Deputy Chief Justice is non-justiciable: s 169(5).

The Deputy Chief Justice is appointed in the same manner as the other judges of the National and Supreme Court. He or she also enjoys the same benefits and privileges as the other judges.

7.6 THE JUDICIAL AND LEGAL SERVICES COMMISSION

Purpose and composition

The affairs of the judiciary are managed by the Judicial and Legal Services Commission (the Commission) created under s 183 of the *Constitution*. The main functions of the Commission are provided by s 8 of the *Organic Law on the Judicial and Legal Services Commission*. These functions include:

- conducting a continuous review of the jurisdiction, practice and procedure of all courts except the Supreme and National Court;
- making recommendations to the Law Reform Commission for legislative changes to jurisdiction, practice and procedure;
- ensuring adequate staffing for the courts; and
- ensuring that adequate and proper statistics relating to the exercise of the jurisdiction of all courts are compiled and kept.

When considering the role of the Commission, the CPC was concerned about the quality and character of people who would be appointed as judges and magistrates of the courts to perform the above functions. It said:

> "The selection of the Deputy Chief Justice, other judges and magistrates also requires careful assessment of the professional ability and individual character of the potential appointees."[37]

The CPC view

To this end, the CPC proposed the creation of an independent and impartial body to perform this task. The CPC was careful in its proposal on the composition of the

36 For a discussion of the issues in the context of the appointment of the present Chief Justice, see Regan, "Papua New Guinea" in Saunders and Hassall (eds), *Asia Pacific Constitutional Yearbook* (1994 and 1996), pp 195-197.
37 CPC, *Final Report*, Ch 8, p 8/5.

Commission, because it wanted "people who are likely to take into account all" the circumstances of the country. The CPC therefore proposed that the Commission should consist of:

- the Minister for Justice;
- the Chief Justice;
- a lawyer of the National Court;
- the Chief Ombudsman; and
- a lawyer appointed by the Permanent Parliamentary Committee.

Under s 183 of the *Constitution*, the members of the Commission are:

- the Minister for Justice;
- the Chief Justice;
- the Deputy Chief Justice;
- the Chief Ombudsman; and
- a Member of Parliament.

There was considerable divergence from the CPC's proposals. The CPC was of the view that by expanding the Committee to include more lawyers, it would ensure that "persons chosen as judges are thought to be just by people whose concern is the proper administration of justice".[38] The composition of the Committee it proposed was intended to achieve:

> "a middle course between the various systems of appointing judges by politicians alone (as in most countries of the world) on the one hand, and formally excluding politicians from the appointment process by placing it in the hands of members of the judiciary ... on the other hand".[39]

Role of the Commission

The main purpose of the Commission is to insulate the process of appointments of judges, magistrates and high officials involved in the administration of justice from direct political control. The independence of the Commission is reaffirmed by s 183(4) and (5) of the *Constitution*. The Commission is an independent institution and is not subject to any direction and control by any person. However, the inclusion of the Minister responsible for National Justice Administration as Chairman of the Commission, as well as a Member of Parliament as a member, means that politicians are heavily involved in the selection process. This is a deliberate departure from the recommendation of the CPC, whose reasons should be considered in this context. The only positive outcome is that the other members of the Commission, being the Chief Justice, the Deputy Chief Justice and the Chief Ombudsman, outweigh the politicians votes.

When the Commission considers matters as to appointment or removal from office of members of the magisterial service, the Chief Magistrate sits as an additional member of the Commission: s 183(3). Pursuant to s 3(2) of the *Organic Law on the Judicial and Legal Services Commission*, the Member of Parliament holds office at the pleasure of the Parliament.

38 Ibid.
39 Ibid.

Appointment functions of the Commission

The Commission appoints the Deputy Chief Justice, National Court judges and acting judges: *Constitution,* s 170. The Commission also appoints the Chief Magistrate (s 175(2)), the Deputy Chief Magistrate and all other magistrates. The magistrates of the Village Courts are appointed under s 6 of the *Magisterial Service Act* (Ch 43). The Attorney-General's Department administers the Village Courts.

The Commission also appointments the Public Prosecutor and the Public Solicitor: *Constitution,* s 176(2). Pursuant to s 7 of the *National Court Act,* the Commission is empowered to appoint the registrar and other senior administrative staff of the National Court. The Commission is also empowered, under s 259 of the *Constitution,* to provide a list of approved persons to be appointed to independent tribunals.

Section 11 of the *Organic Law on the Judicial and Legal Services Commission* compels the Commission to produce and submit annual reports to Parliament through the Head of State. These annual reports may contain certain recommendations for approval by Parliament. The same section also empowers the Commission to produce other reports for presentation to the Parliament or the National Executive Council for deliberations.

7.7 JURISDICTION OF THE SUPREME COURT AND NATIONAL COURT

Jurisdiction of the courts can be classified in various ways, such as civil, criminal. special (for example, courts martial, or ecclesiastical courts), original (power to hear and decide the issues at first instance), and appellate (power to hear appeals against decisions of courts exercising original jurisdiction, or of lower appellate courts).

In PNG, the jurisdictions of the Supreme Court and National Court are set out in ss 99(2)(c), 155(2) and 160(2) of the *Constitution.* In saying the Supreme Court and the National Court are courts of "unlimited jurisdiction" (s 99(2)(c)), the *Constitution* is not saying that they can deal with any matter at all, but rather there are no limits to the value of cases and to the general subject matter of disputes that can come before them. There are other kinds of limits set in the *Constitution* and statutes.

Jurisdiction can be *unlimited* or *limited* in various ways. Some courts have both civil and criminal jurisdiction, and some have one or the other. Some have both original and appellate jurisdiction, and some have mainly one or the other. Often the highest courts have limited original jurisdiction, and unlimited, or largely unlimited, appellate jurisdiction. Lower courts often have original jurisdiction in both civil and criminal matters, but little or no appellate jurisdiction, and their original jurisdiction is usually limited in area, subject and value.

In essence, jurisdiction concerns the geographic limits, powers of punishment, value of the subject of cases, and subject matter limits on the nature of matters that a court can deal with. Limits on jurisdiction are of crucial importance, because anything done by a court that is in excess of its jurisdiction is a nullity. A higher court can make orders of "prohibition" or "certiorari" to correct a matter. In PNG, a magistrate who exceeds his or her jurisdiction can be sued under s 247 of the *District Courts Act* (Ch 40).

Those parts of the jurisdiction of the Supreme and National Courts that are provided by the *Constitution* are protected from removal except by constitutional amendment. On the other hand, s 157 of the *Constitution* permits the Parliament to give directions to the courts on the exercise of judicial powers or functions, but only by passing legislation. This provision may permit the Parliament to pass laws that place limits on the jurisdiction of the courts. An example of legislation which limits the jurisdiction of these courts is the *Mining (Ok Tedi Restated Eighth Supplemental Agreement) Act* 1995.[40]

Constitutional interpretation

The interpretation of constitutional laws is one of the fundamental responsibilities of the judiciary. In PNG, the *Constitution* vests this power in the Supreme Court.

The CPC considered the advantages and the disadvantages of giving this power to the judiciary, especially the Supreme Court, and said:

> "We consider that the new Supreme Court ... is the appropriate body to be given this primary responsibility for deciding constitutional issues."[41]

The power to interpret the *Constitution* is stated in ss 18, 19 and 162(1)(a). In interpreting the *Constitution*, the Supreme Court is required to take into account the documents enumerated under s 24 of the *Constitution* and the *Constitutional Documents (Manner of Proof) Act* (Ch 5).[42] The Supreme Court is also required, under s 25 of the *Constitution*, to use the National Goals and Directive Principles as a guide in interpreting the *Constitution*.[43] The importance of the Supreme Court's function regarding constitutional interpretation was highlighted by Amet CJ in *Haivetta v Wingti (No 3)* [1994] PNGLR 197 (at 207):

> "Because constitutional interpretation is the sole preserve of the Supreme Court, the highest judicial authority in the nation, as delegated by the People to it through the *Constitution*, the Court has to be responsive to the constitutional values. The social philosophy of the *Constitution* must inspire the judicial decision-making process to adopt a broad goal-oriented and purposive approach directed towards advancing the constitutional objectives when interpreting the *Constitution*."

However, the s 18 power to interpret the *Constitution* does not extend to the interpretation of ordinary statutes. This was made explicit in *SCR No 2 of 1981; Re s 19(1)(f) of the Criminal Code* [1982] PNGLR 150. In essence, the power to interpret the *Constitution* makes the Supreme Court the "guardian" of the *Constitution*. The exclusivity of this power of the Supreme Court has now been extended to the National Court.[44]

Human rights enforcement

The *Constitution* also empowers the National and Supreme Courts to enforce the human rights[45] of the people enshrined in the *Constitution*: ss 57, 58 and 162(1)(b).

---

40 Act No 48 of 1995.

41 CPC, *Final Report*, Ch 8, p 8/16.

42 See Regan and Wolfers, "Aids to Interpretation of the Constitution: Some Preliminary Thoughts" (1986) 14 MLJ at 153-172.

43 See Chapter 3.

44 Regan, "The Jurisdiction of the National and Supreme Courts: The Incidence of the Exercise of Judicial Power" in James and Fraser (eds), *Legal Issues in a Developing Society* (UPNG, Law Faculty, Port Moresby, 1992), p 47. See also *Re s 42 of the Constitution and Jacob Hendrich Prai* [1979] PNGLR 42 and *Ready Mix Concrete Pty Ltd v PNG* [1981] PNGLR 396.

45 This subject is discussed in some detail in Chapter 9.

This jurisdiction is shared between the Supreme Court and the National Court. Under s 57(1), it could be extended to other courts as prescribed by statute. That has not yet occurred, despite the practical problems caused by the fact that constitutional issues arising in the District Court cannot be dealt with there, but instead have to be referred to the National Court. In *John Alex v Martin Golu* [1983] PNGLR 117 at 121, Kapi DCJ called for changes in this regard. He made the following observations:

> "It is apparent that under the *Constitution*, courts other than the National Court and the Supreme Court have no power to make such orders under s 57 of the *Constitution*. This means that in a trial in courts other than the National and Supreme Courts where issues under s 57 of the *Constitution* arise, such courts are unable to deliberate on these issues. In these circumstances, such a court has to adjourn its hearing and allow the defendant to make the relevant application either to the National Court or the Supreme Court. Such a course may in many cases disrupt the trial and cause delays as in this case and, therefore, the Parliament should seriously consider the possibility of prescribing some of the lower courts for the purpose of making orders under s 57 of the *Constitution*."

It is submitted that here would be major advantages, in terms of accessibility of people to enforcement mechanisms, if the higher levels of the magistracy were to have jurisdiction on at least some aspects of enforcement of rights.

Review of National Court decisions

Section 155(2) of the *Constitution* vests the Supreme Court with the inherent power to review all acts of the National Court. The power to review exists even where there is no right of appeal to the Supreme Court from the National Court, such as in relation to National Court decisions on elections, as stated in s 220 of the *Organic Law on National and Local Level Government Elections* (OLNLLGE).

In *Jimson Sauk Papaki v Don Pomb Polye and the Electoral Commissioner* (1999) SC 616, the applicant had applied to the Supreme Court for the stay of the order of the National Court dismissing the applicant as a Member of Parliament. The Supreme Court considered the application, and held that a decision of the National Court under s 220 of the OLNLLGE is final and self-executing and cannot be stayed by the Supreme Court. The Supreme Court further ruled that the only option available to the applicant was for a judicial review under s 155(2)(b) of the *Constitution*. Sir Charles Maino successfully applied this approach (judicial review) in his election petition in *Charles Maino v Moi Avei* (unreported, SC633, 2000).[46] The OLNLLGE has retained s 220 from its predecessor, the *Organic Law on National Elections*. Under the same provisions in the previous law, no appeal lay from the decision of the National Court. However, in *In re Moresby North East Election Petition* [1977] PNGLR 424, the Supreme Court ruled that its inherent power to review all decisions of the National Court could not be prohibited by s 220. Prentice DCJ said (at 432):

> "... counsel might have sought that such an interpretation point be referred, or the Chief Justice might have wished to refer such a point – in compliance with the Supreme Court's 'inherent power to review all judicial acts of the National Court' (s 155(2)(b) of the *Constitution* – this despite s 220 of the *Organic Law on National Elections*, which enacts that 'a decision of the

46 At first instance in the National Court see (2000) N 176. However, Sir Charles Maino's win was short-lived, as another Supreme Court reviewed this decision and overruled the above decision: (2000) SC 648.

> National Court is final and conclusive and without appeal, and shall not be questioned in any way'."

His Honour took this view because, as he rightly pointed out, "[a]n Organic Law must of course be read subject to the *Constitution* (s 10(a) of the *Constitution*)". Pritchard J expressed similar views. Supporting the views of the Deputy Chief Justice, his Honour said (at 442):

> "Although as he says, s 220 of the Organic Law enacts that 'a decision of the National Court is final and conclusive and without appeal, and shall not be questioned in any way' that provision must be read subject to the inherent power of the this Court to review all judicial acts of the National Court entrenched in s 155(2)(b) of the *Constitution*."

This decision paved the way for the review of National Court decisions relating to election disputes.

The power of review can also be invoked when the time for an appeal has expired, as was the case in *Avia Aihi v The State* [1981] PNGLR 81. In that case, the appellant had run out of time to appeal against her sentence of life imprisonment by the National Court. According to s 27 of the *Supreme Court Act* (Ch 37), an appeal had to be filed within 40 days after the date of conviction and sentence. Avia Aihi did not lodge her appeal within the prescribed 40 days and was, thus, barred from making an appeal to the Supreme Court. The appellant then requested the Supreme Court to invoke its powers under s 155(2)(b) to review her case. By a majority (three judges to two), the Supreme Court granted the application for review. Andrew J said, in a clear exposition of the law, that in common law the "inherent jurisdiction" would give way to legislation. However, as the *Constitution* is the supreme law, "the powers given to the Supreme Court by s 155(2)(b) are unfettered". His Honour further said (at 101-102):

> "For these reasons it is my view that it is the grant of power and jurisdiction to the Supreme Court by the *Constitution* in s 155(2)(b) which means that the court has a discretionary power to review the sentence passed upon the applicant. That power cannot be subject to or restricted by the *Supreme Court Act*."

Kearney DCJ, sharing the same views, said (at 92):

> "The word 'inherent' also connotes that within the limits of the subject-matter of the *Constitution*, s 155(2)(b) – 'judicial acts of the National Court' – the power of review of this Court is plenary. In the absence of express constitutional provision, that power and its exercise cannot be restricted by any Act of Parliament."

This decision laid the criteria for an applicant to invoke the power of the Supreme Court under s 155(2)(b). The court ruled that an applicant can succeed in his or her application, if he or she can show one or more of three factors. First, he or she must show sufficient reasons for the failure to use the appeal procedure. Secondly, he or she must show exceptional circumstances, and thirdly, he or she must show that the application for review has merits. These criteria were re-enforced in *Avia Aihi v The State (No 2)* [1982] PNGLR 44 and *Sunu v The State* [1984] PNGLR 305.

However, the precise difference between proceeding by way of appeal or by way of review was not entirely clear. In the above case, Kapi J strongly opposed the views of the majority. According to his Honour (at 107):

> "If this Court ruled that it can give a right to apply to the applicant under s 155(4) of the *Constitution* contrary to s 27 of the *Supreme Court Act* then this

> would have a peculiar effect in that this Court would have power to disregard or override clear provisions of the statutes. This, in effect, would amount to amendment or repeal of legislation by judicial power."

Kapi J reaffirmed his views in the case of *Malipu Balakau v Torato* [1983] PNGLR 242 (at 253):

> "With respect, I consider that the majority decision reads too much into the words 'inherent power to review' under s 155(2)(b). The word 'review' or 'reviewed' has been used constantly in English legislation and judicial decisions to refer to the power of review in the appeal procedure."

The majority in the case (Kidu CJ and Andrew J) reaffirmed the views of the majority in *Avia Aihi v The State*. In *The State v District Land Court* [1981] PNGLR 192, Bredmeyer J held that appeal and review are two different things. His Honour said (at 193):

> "Appeal is prevented by s 61 [of the *Land Dispute Settlement Act* (Ch 45)] but review is open by those sections of the *Constitution*."

In a slight departure from the *Avia Aihi* cases and *Sunu v The State*, the Supreme Court held, in *SC Review No 5 of 1987; Re Central Bank Regs* [1987] PNGLR 433 (at 437), that where the applicant "has no other way", he or she could approach the Supreme Court via s 155(2). In that case, the accused was charged under the *Central Baking (Foreign Exchange and Gold) Regulations* (Ch 138) with unlawfully sending foreign currency out of PNG. In the National Court, the defendant, without taking a plea, argued that the charges were defective. The National Court found that the relevant sections of the Regulation under which the defendant was charged were ultra vires and, consequently, they went on to discharge the defendant. The state applied for a review of the National Court decision.

In the Supreme Court, the defendant argued that the state did not satisfy the criteria set out by the cases of *Avia Aihi* and *Sunu v The State*. In rejecting the defendant's submission, the Supreme Court held (at 437) that:

> "In a case where a person or a party in a proceedings has no other way of coming before this Court in similar circumstances as in this case, s 155(2) is available without the criteria in *Avia Aihi* and *Danny Sunu* being first established. In this case, there is an important point of law to be determined and it is not without merit."

The basis of the court's decision was that, because the defendant did not plead to the indictment, there could not be an acquittal by the National Court. Therefore, the state could not appeal against the decision, as there was no acquittal. The only option open to the state was to seek a review under s 155(2). When the review was conducted under s 155(2)(b) by the Supreme Court in *SC Review No 5 of 1987 (Application by Public Prosecutor)* [1987] PNGLR 216, the Supreme Court ruled that the Public Prosecutor did not have standing to seek the review, because the defendant had neither been convicted nor acquitted.

The Supreme Court decision in *SC Review No 5 of 1987; Re Central Bank Regs* was followed in *SCR No 5 of 1988; Kasap v Yama* [1988-1989] PNGLR 197[47] and *Griffin v Westpac Bank (PNG) Ltd* [1993] PNGLR 352. In the latter case, the Supreme Court allowed the review, because the applicant had no right to appeal against a consent order.

---

47 See also *State v Colbert* [1988] PNGLR 138.

Appeals

It is the *Supreme Court Act* (Ch 37) which gives the Supreme Court its appellate jurisdiction, and not s 155(2)(a) of the *Constitution*. Section 155(2)(a) does not vest jurisdiction, but rather clarifies that there is to be no appeal to a foreign court such as the Australian High Court.[48]

National Court jurisdiction

The jurisdiction of the National Court is stipulated under s 166(1) and (2) and s 155(3) and (5) of the *Constitution*. The main issues as to National Court jurisdiction are similar to those concerning the Supreme Court. The National Court shares original jurisdiction with the lower courts in relation to civil and criminal matters. The precise nature of the jurisdiction of the National Court in relation to such matters is determined by the limits on the lower court jurisdiction – limits set mainly in the various statutes concerning those courts, as well as the *Criminal Code* (Ch 262).

A separate Supreme Court bench?

At present, the membership of the National Court and the Supreme Court is identical, except in terms of the acting judges. The same judges sit on some occasions as National Court judges, and on other occasions as members of the Supreme Court.

Because of the increasing volume of work for the Supreme Court, there are proposals that the Supreme Court be made a separate court. The most senior judges would no longer deal with National Court matters, but would constitute a specialised Supreme Court, dealing only with matters within the Supreme Court jurisdiction (appeals, constitutional matters, etc). Many countries have dedicated appeals courts at the pinnacle of the judicial hierarchy. The main advantage claimed for the proposal is that it would help produce greater consistency and authority in the decisions of the Supreme Court. A constitutional amendment would probably be required to establish a separate Supreme Court in PNG.

7.8 OBEDIENCE TO JUDICIAL DECISIONS: CONTEMPT

Section 155(6) of the *Constitution* declares that:

> "Subject to any right of appeal or power of review of a decision, it is the duty of all persons (including the Law Officers of Papua New Guinea and other public officers in their respective official capacities), and of all bodies and institutions, to comply with and, so far as is within their respective lawful powers, put into effect all decisions of the National Judicial System."

The *Constitution* is very clear. It requires that all state instrumentalities, private individuals and corporate persons must endeavour to give meaning to the orders of the court. This directive is very broad and covers every person in the country.

The failure to comply with a lawful court order may result in the person being charged with *contempt of court*. Contempt of court is a "conduct which interferes with the administration of justice or impedes or perverts the course of justice."[49]

---

48 Goldring, op cit n 11, pp 117-118.

49 *Osborn's Concise Law Dictionary* (8th ed, Sweet & Maxwell, London, 1993).

The Supreme Court and the National Court have the power to punish for contempt of court under ss 37(2), 160(2) and 163(2) of the *Constitution*.

A number of cases concerning both civil and criminal contempt, and involving press reports of cases, have arisen in PNG. The most famous case on contempt of court in PNG is the well known case of the former Minister for Justice, Mrs Nahau Rooney, in *Public Prosecutor v Rooney (No 1)* [1979] PNGLR 403; *Public Prosecutor v Rooney (No 2)* [1979] PNGLR 448.[50]

When considering the issue of contempt, the court must be mindful of the rights of citizens to freedom of expression. In a single bench Supreme Court decision in *SCR No 3 of 1984; Ex parte Callick and Koroma* [1985] PNGLR 67, McDermott J laid down the criteria for determining whether published material is demeaning to the court. His Honour said that the relevant factors to consider are freedom of expression, the nature of material, timing and nature of the publication of the material, and the balance between the right to criticise for public good and the rights of the disputing parties seeking justice in the courts. The imposition of a penalty is basically discretionary.

7.9 OTHER COURTS

The *Constitution* allows for the creation of courts other than the Supreme Court and the National Court. The general permissive provision is s 172 of the *Constitution*. Under the auspices of this provision, a number of other courts were established. These are:

- the District Courts[51] established under the *District Courts Act* (Ch 40); and
- the Village Courts created by the *Village Courts Act* 1989.

These courts, which are not *courts of record*, and are, therefore, called the lower or inferior courts, have special jurisdictions. In *SCR No 1A of 1981; Re Motor Traffic Act* [1982] PNGLR 122, the District Courts (and the then Local Courts) were described by Greville Smith J (at 137) as "courts of summary jurisdiction".

District Courts

By s 5 of the *District Courts (Amendment) Act* 2000,[52] there are two classifications of magistrates: Principal Magistrates (old Grade 5) and Junior Magistrates (old Grades 2-4). Principal Magistrates are entitled to deal with all matters ranging below K10,000, and Junior Magistrates can hear any civil claim where the amount does not exceed K8,000.

The criminal jurisdiction of the District Courts is clearly stated in s 20 of the Act. The jurisdiction under this provision must be read together with the *Summary Offences Act* (Ch 264), which contains the summary offences. The District Courts also have jurisdiction over offences committed under the *Industrial Relations Act* (Ch 174). However, when dealing with an offence under the *Industrial Relations Act*, the court has now laid down the rule in *Keke v PNG Color Laboratories Pty Ltd* [1992] PNGLR 265 at 269 that "the institution of criminal proceeding [under the *Industrial Relations Act*] calls for the professional expertise of a trained lawyer conversant with the duties and responsibilities attaching to such a prosecution".

50 For further reading, see *State v Taua; Re Awaita* [1985] PNGLR 179; *Robinson v The State* [1986] PNGLR 307; *Yap v Tan* [1987] PNGLR 227; *Poka v The State* [1988] PNGLR 218; and *Metta v The State* [1992] PNGLR 176.

51 See *Magistrates Manual of Papua New Guinea* (Lawbook Co, Sydney, 2001).

52 *District Courts (Amendment) Act* 2000 (No 8 of 2000).

The District Courts' civil jurisdiction is set out in s 21 of the *District Courts (Amendment) Act* 2000. The categories of cases with which the District Courts can deal are wide, and cover all personal actions at law or in equity. However, the District Courts have no jurisdiction over:

- cases where validity or effect of a devise or bequest or limitation under a will or settlement is in dispute;
- disputes over infringement of trade names;
- slander of title;
- actions for illegal arrest, false imprisonment or malicious prosecution;
- actions for seduction or breach of promise to marry; or
- bona fide disputes over title to land.

The *District Courts (Amendment) Act* 2000 fused the jurisdiction of the former Local Courts with the District Courts assuming the functions of the Local Courts. This amendment has enlarged the powers of the District Court to hear almost all the matters that the Local Court had powers over. Some matters have gone to the Village Courts.

Village Courts

The Village Courts were originally created under the *Village Courts Act* (Ch 44). This Act came into force in 1974.[53] The "aim of the village courts system was to provide an official mechanism for the settlement of disputes in a manner understood and accepted by village people".[54] Its operation is primarily based on custom. The Village Courts are to conduct their proceedings under the cover of the legislation. On a question of whether the Village Court had power to order imprisonment under s 33 of the Act, the Supreme Court ruled, in *SCR No 2 of 1989; Re Village Court Act* [1988-1989] PNGLR 491, that the Village Court did have the power to imprison a defaulter of its orders. The Village Courts have no power to impose imprisonment at the first instance.

In 1989, the *Village Court Act* 1974 was repealed and replaced by the *Village Courts Act* 1989. The new Act does not deviate much from its predecessor. It encourages the mediation of disputes in the first instance. In the exercise of its jurisdiction, the Village Court is required to observe the minimum requirements of natural justice. Although the Village Court is required to apply custom, where it exercises its powers in excess of the *Constitution*, the National Court can easily set aside its decisions. This was shown in *Maris v Nalik Village Court* [1994] PNGLR 314 and *Re Mark* [1995] PNGLR 234.

Other courts

Other specialised courts have been established under relevant legislation to deal specifically with matters specified by those statutes, and they operate parallel to the District Court. These include the Local Land Court and the District Land Court created under the *Land Dispute Settlement Act* (Ch 45), the Children's Court established under the *Child Welfare Act* (Ch 276), and the Family Court created under the *Deserted Wives and Children Act* (Ch 277).[55] As their names suggest, they

53 For a short history of the village courts system, see Chalmers, "The Village Courts of Papua New Guinea: Their Introduction, history and operation until 1976" (1980) 6 MLJ 56; and Mitchell, "Family Law in Village Courts: The Woman's Position" in King, Lee and Warakai (eds), *From Rhetoric to Reality? (Papers from the Fifteenth Waigani Seminar)* (UPNG Press, Port Moresby, 1985), p 81.

54 Mitchell, op cit n 53, p 82.

55 For further readings on the history, jurisdiction and operation of these two courts, see Jessep and Luluaki, *Family Law in Papua New Guinea* (2nd ed, UPNG Press, Port Moresby, 1994).

are responsible solely for dealing with matters arising specifically under the pertinent legislation. These courts share powers vertically with the District Court and, thus, magistrates of the District Court preside over these courts as well. The rest of the magistrates are appointed under the *Magisterial Service Act* (Ch 43).

Magisterial service

The operations of these courts, especially the District Courts, are the responsibility of the Magisterial Services, established under s 173 of the *Magisterial Service Act*. The Chief Magistrate, whose office is created by s 175, heads the Magisterial Services. The Chief Magistrate is, therefore, a constitutional office holder, and is appointed by the Judicial and Legal Services Commission.

7.10 CONCLUSION

Given the length of time that PNG has been independent, the judiciary in PNG is young. The founders of the country were aware of the difficulties of creating an institution that would be filled and managed by foreigners. To speed up the localisation process in the judiciary, the current laws have not abandoned experience and professionalism in enabling more Papua New Guineans to join the bench.

After 25 years of independence, the founders of the country must be saluted for their foresight and wisdom. The current composition of the judiciary is very encouraging, with almost all of the members being citizens. The first woman has been appointed to the judiciary. Most of these citizen judges joined the bench while they were very young.

However, the overarching imperative for justice and fairness in the contemporary PNG is dependent on the effectiveness of the judiciary, the Law Officers and other constitutional office holders. The judiciary cannot bear the sole responsibility of maintaining order, peace and justice within the community. Its partners are also mandated to perform their duties and functions effectively to achieve the same objectives. This is important because, as Oliver said:

> "A sense of fairness of their society cannot grow within the people unless bodies like the Ombudsman Commission, the Law Reform Commission and the Public Solicitor's Office have enough funds and staff to be effective both as watchdogs and in the role of adapting imported institutions to fit local needs."[56]

56 Oliver, "The Ethics of Development: In Search of Justice" in Thirlwall and Hughes (eds), *The Ethics of Development: In Search of Justice (Papers from the 17th Waigani Seminar)* (UPNG Press, Port Moresby, 1989), p 4.

Chapter 8

DECENTRALISATION OF GOVERNMENT

8.1 INTRODUCTION

At independence on the 16 September 1975, Papua New Guinea (PNG) rejected a system of provincial government that the Constitutional Planning Committee (CPC) envisioned would bring the government closer to the people. At this time, the country moved into a new era with the threat of cessation of Bougainville, which had wanted an autonomous government within the constitutional framework of the independent PNG. The threat of cessation was so serious that the first constitutional amendment, made in 1976, was to enable the establishment of provincial governments in the country. Thus began the process of decentralisation.

This first constitutional amendment was supplemented by the *Organic Law on Provincial Governments* 1976 (OLPG),[1] which set out in detail the gradation of provincial governments within the 19 provinces in the country. The Organic Law came into effect in 1977. In 1995, after 19 years of operation, the provincial government system was reformed by the enactment of the *Organic Law on Provincial Governments and Local-level Governments* (OLPGLLG). This law, which came into effect in 1996, replaced the *OLPG* and ushered in the "new look"[2] provincial government with the local-level governments system.

The process of decentralisation in PNG must be considered against the issue of spatial distribution of powers. Spatial distribution of powers relates to the manner in which powers of government can be distributed vertically to the lower levels of government. Hague, Harrop and Breslin identify three systems whereby government power is distributed. These are:

(a) the highly centralised unitary systems;

(b) the relatively decentralised federal systems, where authority is shared between the central and lower governments; and

(c) the highly decentralised confederal systems.[3]

A fourth system is the "quasi-federal" system, which is an offshoot of the federal and unitary systems.

This chapter examines the various provisions of the OLPGLLG and the various structures created under the Organic Law. A short history of the OLPG will be considered, as well as the work of the CPC on decentralisation. The OLPGLLG is a very complex and difficult law and is still in its infancy. The Organic Law

---

1 On Organic Laws, see Chapter 4.

2 It is a new-look system in that, apart from the provisions on local-level governments, much of the provincial structures remain somewhat intact.

3 Hague, Harrop and Breslin, *Comparative Government and Politics: An Introduction* (3rd ed, MacMillan Press Ltd, London, 1992), p 268.

establishes a number of institutions and empowers them. The exercise of the powers and functions of these institutions are not only set out under this Organic Law, but also in a number of statutes, many of which are yet to be enacted by the National Parliament. The discussion on this subject will focus more on the existing provisions of the Organic Law than on its application.

8.2 DECENTRALISATION IN PNG

The subject of decentralisation is not new in PNG. As far back as the 1960s the idea of establishing some sort of regional, provincial or district structure was mooted.[4] The issue was not seriously considered at that time. It was only after the establishment of the CPC that decentralisation became quite a controversial issue.[5]

The CPC members were men who had long-standing experiences with the colonial administration and had the unique experience of living under an oppressive and difficult regime. Some of the members, including John Momis, the de facto chairman of the CPC, had "had long, often bitter-sweet encounters with the colonial masters that had resulted in their holding a common conviction – get rid of them".[6]

In their discussions with the people, the CPC discovered that "[t]here is widespread discontent with the present distribution of power in our country, and a deep yearning among our people for a greater say in the conduct of their affairs."[7] The CPC lamented with the people because they were powerless and frustrated with the existing system of government, whereby many decisions that could be made locally were being made at Konedobu. Against this backdrop, the CPC proposed that:

> "Power must be returned to the people. Government services should be accessible to them. Decisions should be made by the people to whom the issues at stake are meaningful, easily understood and relevant. The existing system of government should therefore be re-structured, and power should be decentralised, so that the energies and aspirations of our people can play their full part in promoting our country's development."[8]

The system of government that the CPC proposed was a decentralised system of government, whereby central government powers would be devolved to the provincial governments.

In *Re Provincial Government Grants* [1990] PNGLR 532, the Supreme Court observed (at 538) that:

> "Careful reading of these provisions [*Constitution*] and the Organic Law clearly shows that the provincial government system is not a federal system like the USA, Australia and Canada. However, substantial legislative and executive powers are given to provincial governments by the Organic Law."

---

4 Tadabe, "The Constitution and Provincial Governments" in De Vere, Colquhoun-Kerr and Kaburise (eds), *Essays on the Constitution of Papua New Guinea* (Government Printer, Port Moresby, 1985), p 87.

5 For a detailed discussion on the provincial government system in PNG under the old system, see Ghai and Regan, *The Law, Politics and Administration of Decentralisation in Papua New Guinea* (Monograph 30, National Research Institute, Port Moresby, 1992).

6 Narokobi, "The CPC, Nationalism and Vision" (Paper presented at the Twenty Years of the Constitution Conference, Granville, Port Moresby, 1996).

7 Constitutional Planning Committee, *Constitutional Planning Committee Final Report (Part 1)* (Government Printer, Port Moresby, 1974) (CPC, *Final Report*), p 10/1.

8 Ibid.

The Supreme Court was alluding to the fact that PNG had a "quasi-federal" system of government. PNG opted for the quasi-federal system, whereby some governmental powers were given exclusively to the provincial government while the national government retained *veto powers* over certain matters. The distribution of power became a controversial issue just a few months before independence, with the government mustering the votes to throw out the provincial government system.

As a contingency plan, the government enacted the *Provincial Governments (Preparatory Arrangement) Act* 1974 to appease emerging separatist movements in different parts of the country. The Act provided a step-by-step procedure for attainment of provincial governments by the districts. The rejection of the provincial government system by the Constituent Assembly before independence resulted in a backlash by the Bougainvilleans. The Bougainvilleans threatened to secede from PNG. The post-independence government succumbed to the pressure from Bougainville, and in 1976 amended the *Constitution* to usher in the provincial government system.

8.3 CONSTITUTIONAL FRAMEWORK ON DECENTRALISATION

The result of the first amendment to the *Constitution* was the insertion of a new Pt VIA. Part VIA was effectively misplaced in the constitutional structure, and contains ten sections (ss 187A-187J).

The first section under Pt VIA (s 187A) provided for the *establishment of the provincial government system.* Section 187B provided for the enactment of the Organic Law, which would set out in detail the criteria for granting a provincial government status to a properly organised body for that purpose. The grant of provincial government was to be on a gradation basis. This was clearly mandated by s 187G. The OLPG was enacted for that purpose. The criteria for granting provincial government status were spelt out under Pt II (ss 2-7) of the OLPG. The constitution, powers and functions of the provincial governments, as envisaged by s 187C of the *Constitution,* were spread out throughout the OLPG. Each year the Minister responsible for provincial affairs was required, under s 187J of the *Constitution,* to present a report to Parliament on the operations of provincial governments. Where a report revealed that there was widespread corruption and mismanagement in the administration of the province, a provincial government would be suspended according to the procedure set out in s 187E. A suspension could be lifted and a provincial government could be re-establishment under s 187F. Where there was any conflict of laws, s 187D set out the rules for determining the status of the laws.

The OLPG was very comprehensive, and covered almost all the areas that were envisaged by the constitutional provisions. The provincial governments scheme must be seen in the context of the whole *Constitution*: *SCR No 3 of 1986; Reference by Simbu Provincial Executive* [1987] PNGLR 151 (at 173-174, Barnett J). Seen from this perspective, it becomes apparent that the decentralisation process incorporates the values and aspirations of Papua New Guineans found throughout the *Constitution,* starting with the National Goals and Directive Principles and ending with the provisions on law reform found in Schs 2.13 and 2.14.

The OLPG encapsulated a broad spectrum of values and ideas that had been carefully considered by the CPC. The decentralisation process was an intrinsic part of the whole constitutional process, which was geared towards the development of PNG as a prosperous and wealthy nation. The OLPG was to be the vehicle to empower, strengthen and deliver the basic goods and services to the people at the local level.

In a sever attack on the provincial government system, the architect of the OLPGLLG and Chairman of the Constitutional Review Commission (CRC), Ben Micah, reported to Parliament that:

> "The Provincial Government System was created as an instrument of the State in 1977 for the purpose of assisting the majority of Papua New Guineans living in rural communities to improve their welfare. Facts over the last twenty (20) years of the life of the system show quite clearly that the decentralisation system has not really met the full expectations of the ordinary people of Papua New Guinea.
>
> The problems, and these are urgent problems, can be easily identified in the rural areas where the majority of our people live. There is virtually no proper infrastructures and development services for our people."[9]

These assertions were not supported by analysis of the provincial government system existing at that time. In comparison with the CPC, the CRC did not engage in thorough and wide consultation with the vast majority of the people to gauge their views on the subject. There was much rhetoric by the CRC. The report continued:

> "Our people have suffered enough. Twenty years onwards and they remain with no lifestyle changes.
>
> Our people for far too long, have been struggling to come to their Government. For far too long we have defied them their rights to an effective government. They have been walking over the mountains, and crossing the oceans to come to the door steps of their Government.
>
> Time has come for us to rest those weary feet and arms, and bring to them what is rightfully theirs. Time has come for us to build up their capacity and the capacity of the Government closest to them so that there is one more little step towards modernisation."[10]

The CRC asserted that the provincial government system was not meant for the people of PNG, except for the Bougainvilleans. The CRC said the decentralisation was not suited to the rest of PNG. It therefore declared that its review of the provincial government system was to adjust "it so that the lower-level government system can operate more effectively".[11]

The period leading up to the passage of the OLPGLLG was filled with widespread controversy. Events outside the Parliament and inside the corridors of Parliament were sometimes filled with tension and frustration. The record of proceedings of the Permanent Parliamentary Committee on Justice reveals widespread discontent and suspicion by Members of Parliament.[12] Strong opposition came from the members of the provincial governments, political parties such as the Melanesian Alliance and Pangu Pati, and regional groups such as the Islands Premiers Council.

---

9 Micah, *Brief on the Proposed Bill for an Organic Law on Provincial Governments and Local Governments for Members of the National Executive Council and other Members of the National Parliament* (Report of Chair of CRC, 1995) (*Micah Report*), p 2.

10 Ibid, p 5.

11 Ibid, p 3.

12 See Permanent Parliamentary Referral Committee on Justice, *Report Relating to the Proposed Constitutional Laws on Provincial and Local-level Governments* (National Parliament, Port Moresby, June 1995), p 4.

Of these groups, the Islands Premiers Council promoted the greatest criticism of the reform proposals.[13] The attack on the CRC proposals was followed by strong threats of secession.

In the light of all this opposition, the government used its numerical strength to sweep the Bills into law on 27 June 1995. The passage of the Bills was quickly challenged by one of the displaced provincial premiers, Isidor Kaseng of Western Province. The case, *Kaseng v Namaliu* [1995] PNGLR 481, was presided over by a full bench of five judges of the Supreme Court. In a majority decision, the court dismissed the challenge by Kaseng, thereby affirming the constitutionality of *Constitutional Amendment No 16* 1995[14] and the OLPGLLG.

Kaseng v Namaliu challenged the two laws on three grounds. These were (at 484-485):

> "1. The gazetted proposed laws were circulated less than one month before the proposed laws were formally introduced into the Parliament; and
>
> 2. There was no proper opportunity to debate the merits of the proposed laws by the National Parliament.
>
> 3. In the alternative, the Organic Law was purportedly passed before the *Constitution* had been amended to enable or authorise such an Organic Law."

On the first ground, Kaseng relied on s 14 of the *Constitution*. This provision provides the procedure for altering the *Constitution* and Organic Laws. One of the principal requirements is that Members of Parliament must be informed of a proposed law one month before it is formally introduced in Parliament. In this case, the court found that the proposed Bills were circulated for only 21 days. The majority ruled that although s 14 was mandatory, without the relevant Standing Orders clarifying the manner of circulation, s 14 at the moment is directory. Therefore, the 21 days circulation was sufficient compliance.

Kapi DCJ, who gave a very strong and convincing dissenting judgment, found that (at 496-497):

> "there are relevant *Standing Orders* which specially deal with the manner in which a bill is circulated before it is introduced in the Parliament. The relevant *Standing Order* is s 200."

Hinchliff and Andrew JJ, disagreeing with the findings of Kapi DCJ, stated (at 510):

> "Section 200 refers to the circulation for the 'second reading of a Bill'. It is something very different to the circulation of a proposed law to alter the *Constitution* or a proposed Organic Law."

On the second ground, the majority held that since no single Member of Parliament complained about this issue, there was adequate opportunity for debate. Kapi DCJ dealt more with the substantive issue than the other judges, and stated the principles as follows (at 503):

> "It is apparent from all the facts I have referred to that the proposed laws were speedily introduced, without any opportunity to enable the Parliament to adequately and meaningfully debate the proposed laws on the merits.

13 Permanent Parliamentary Referral Committee on Justice, *Regional Submission: Provincial Government Reform and How it will Collectively Affect the Islands Region* (National Parliament, Port Moresby, May 1995).

14 This was the constitutional amendment that repealed and replaced Pt VIA of the *Constitution*.

> I accept that eight members of the Parliament debated the proposed laws. After this, Mr Andrew Baing moved a motion to close debate, and the motion was carried.
>
> However, having regard to the matters I have discussed, I cannot conclude that there was opportunity for adequate and meaningful debate on the merits of the proposed laws on 29 March 1995."

As to the third ground, Kapi DCJ and Los J disagreed with the majority view that the OLPGLLG was expressly authorised by the *Constitution*. According to the two judges, the enactment of the OLPGLLG simultaneously with *Constitutional Amendment No 16* did not guarantee the existence of the OLPGLLG, because *Constitutional Amendment No 16* had not yet become operative to authorise the enactment of the OLPGLLG.

The OLPGLLG and *Constitutional Amendment No 16* came into effect on 19 July 1995, two months before the Supreme Court handed down its decision on the case on 20 September 1995. An interim period of 12 months was given to enable the country to adjust to the new system. Some parts of the OLPGLLG became operational only after the 1997 national elections.

8.4 PROVINCIAL AND LOCAL-LEVEL STRUCTURES UNDER THE OLPGLLG

The OLPGLLG is a very complicated law, and some of its provisions are unclear. The Organic Law is also much longer than its predecessor, with 140 sections and six schedules.[15] The Permanent Parliamentary Referral Committee on Justice identified a number of defects in the law. Some of these include:[16]

- *Elective members of the provincial assemblies:* The committee argued strongly that there was a possible inconsistency between the OLPGLLG and s 187C(2) of the *Constitution*. The constitutional provision provided for elective members of provincial assemblies, but the OLPGLLG made provision for membership to the assembly by election to offices other than the provincial government.
- *Bougainville:* The committee was concerned that the application of the OLPGLLG to Bougainville after the 1997 national elections would jeopardise the open-ended peace process that was continuing between the government and the Bougainvilleans. This concern was accommodated by Parliament by amending s 4 of the OLPGLLG several times to enable Bougainville to remain outside the reformed system. This arrangement was abandoned in late 1997, when there was a fall-out between the government of Bill Skate and the Opposition, which resulted in the Opposition pulling out their numbers to prevent Bougainville remaining outside the system. Bougainville consequently fell under the auspices of the OLPGLLG in 1998.
- *Complexities and uncertainties:* Three of the issues raised under this heading were: (a) the size of the OLPGLLG, which made it complex to follow; (b) the requirement to physically serve all provincial and local laws on the Minister. The committee realised that to require 20 governors and about 260 council presidents to physically serve all enacted laws on the Minister from time to time was practically difficult; and (c) the NEC is empowered under the OLPGLLG to suspend 20 provincial governments and about 260 local-level

15 The former OPLG had 116 sections and only two schedules.

16 Permanent Parliamentary Referral Committee on Justice, op cit n 13, p 12.

governments. The committee felt that administratively this was a difficult task.

- *Drafting errors:* The committee found that there were just too many drafting errors in the law. It identified four major areas that needed fixing. Some of these defects were rectified by *Constitutional Amendment No 17* and a series of amendments to the OLPGLLG.
- *Financial difficulties:* The committee noted that the reformed system would require a massive transfer of labour and skills to the provinces and districts. It further noted that these skilled personnel, who were living comfortably in urban areas, had to be enticed especially to the rural areas. The committee concluded that funding to the provinces and districts would be enormous.
- *Ombudsman Commission:* The committee realised that the reformed system increased the workload of the Ombudsman Commission by about 200 per cent or more because, under the new system, all provincial and local-level members would be subject to the *Leadership Code*. The committee concluded that this added responsibility watered down the concept of leadership entrenched in the *Constitution.*

Many of these issues were ignored by the Parliament. The Parliament passed the Bills into laws as they were presented by the CRC. According to the CRC, the reformed system:

> "... does not replace the principle of decentralisation. We are also not changing it. ... We therefore are not only retaining the principle of decentralisation but are going to enhance it by rationalising the present institutional arrangements through which the principle can be implemented effectively."[17]

In practical terms, the impact of this policy differs significantly from the visions of the CRC.

The system of provincial governments and local-level governments is created by s 187A of the *Constitution* and s 5 of the OLPGLLG respectively. The provincial and local-level governments are empowered by s 6 of the OLPGLLG to acquire, hold and dispose of property, and may sue and be sued. Section 8 of the OLPGLLG guarantees recognition of their laws, records and proceedings throughout PNG. Provincial and local-level governments are also entitled, under s 9 of the Organic Law, to choose their seat of government, emblems, motto and seals. Where the Minister is of the opinion that some of these matters are not in the interest of the country, he or she may disallow them by exercising his or her powers under s 9(3) of the OLPGLLG.

Provincial structure

Provincial governments for each province are created under s 10(1) of the OLPGLLG. A provincial government consists of a provincial legislature (s 10(2)), the chairperson of the provincial assembly (s 14), the provincial governor (s 17), provincial executive council (s 23) and provincial assembly committees (s 16A). These different organs perform the various functions of the provincial government.

Membership of the provincial assembly is not by direct election. Six different categories of members are created under s 10(3). These are:

17 *Micah Report*, p 9.

(a) all Members of Parliament from the province;
(b) heads of all rural local-level governments;
(c) a representative of the urban local-level councils;
(d) a paramount chief where there is a chieftaincy system in the province;
(e) a woman representative; and
(f) three nominated members.

Apart from the provincial governor who is elected directly to the post in a national election, all the other members of the assembly are non-elected members. The membership to the provincial assembly entitles a member to vote on all matters relating to the province, and to be appointed to the provincial executive council. The *Organic Law on National and Local-level Elections* 1996 (OLNLLE) makes provision for such elections: ss 10, 11, 12, 14, 15, 16 and 16A.[18]

A Provincial Executive provides leadership: OLPGLLG, ss 107-108. Each province[19] has a Provincial Governor: ss 17-25. There are two other key officials.[20] They are the Provincial Administrator (ss 43, 72, 73 and 74), whose staff are appointed under ss 75-81 and 109, and the Provincial Treasurer who is appointed under s 112. In *Kumar v Wama* [1993] PNGLR 38, the court noted (at 40) that a Provincial Administrator is an agent of the national government. Accordingly, he or she has no legal authority to control and manage a company. The Provincial Administrator's role is to report to the NEC through the Minister on the operation of the province. The Provincial Treasurer has financial control and responsibility for provincial finances: ss 113 and 114.

Local-level structure

The local-level governments[21] mirror the provisions of the provincial governments, and include similar officers and arrangements. There is a local-level legislature. The OLPGLLG establishes the composition, qualifications and remunerations for members: ss 29, 31-35. Local-level elections are provided in ss 37-39 of the OLNLLGE. A Local-level Executive is established (s 36), as well as a District Administrator (ss 72-78 and 81) and a District Treasurer (s 112). To improve the management of local-level administration, a Joint District Planning and Budget Priorities Committee (s 33A) is established.

Legislative powers of provincial and local-level governments

The provincial and local-level governments have limited rule-making authority (law making power): OLPGLLG, ss 40, 41, 42, 140 and 138.

In *SCR No 7 of 1992; Re Forestry Act 1991* [1992] PNGLR 514, the legislative powers of provincial governments over forestry and similar matters were considered and held to be limited. This Supreme Court decision is also supported by s 141. Similarly, in *Wango v Andakundi* [1992] PNGLR 45, the court held (at 46) that the

18 It was held earlier, in *Electoral Commissioner of PNG v Maniho* [1987] PNGLR 449, that an election to a provincial assembly could be deferred under s 113 of former OLPG due to irrelevant factors, except where it would coincide with a national election.

19 See OLPGLLG, s 43 (principal administrative functions) and ss 46-49 (judicial matters).

20 *Getsi v PNG Harbours Board* [1993] PNGLR 408 establishes that employees of provincial governments are liable for their own costs in legal proceedings where the provincial government is not a party.

21 Note that town authorities validly established by relevant statutes have the power to impose licensing fees on traders operating within the town boundaries: *Mt Hagen Town Authority v Steamships* [1990] PNGLR 350.

powers to make laws on health were concurrent with national powers of law-making, but national law prevails because of the national interest. Finally, in *Kapua Wasant v Nangai* [1987] PNGLR 308, the court held that a delegated law-making power enjoyed by the provincial government is valid and enforceable, provided that it is exercised within the scope of the delegation. In this case, the power concerned liquor licensing and control.

Financial powers of provincial and local-level governments

Again, provincial and local-level governments have certain fiscal powers, which are limited. The general financial power is provided in s 82 of the OLPGLLG. Provincial and local-level governments have limited powers of taxation (ss 85-90) and limited powers to make grants (ss 91 and 92-97). In *Re Provincial Government Grants* [1990] PNGLR 532, the court held that provincial grants approved by Parliament in a National Budget cannot be reallocated by the executive without Parliament's approval. The effect of this decision is that amounts that have been appropriated must be paid without any reduction. Provincial and local-level governments may share in benefits from natural resources: s 98. Powers over investments and loans[22] are provided for in ss 100 and 101.

Inter-governmental relationships

Relationships between the different tiers of government are also provided for in the OLPGLLG. The process of inter-governmental consultation is provided for in s 139. In respect of personnel matters (s 109) there is a requirement for consultation. In *Kembol v The State* [1990] PNGLR 67, the court held that where assigned public servants are appointed, there is a need for consultation between the provincial and national governments before appointment: OLPG, s 50. In *Public Services Commission v PNG* [1994] PNGLR 603, the court held that consultation for appointment of a Provincial Secretary is mandatory.

The National Fiscal Commission reviews financial matters: s 117. Finally, there is mediation and arbitration (s 118) of inter-governmental disputes.

Suspension and re-establishment of provincial and local-level governments

Ultimate control over the provincial and local-level governments rests with the national government. In cases of difficulties, there can be a withdrawal of powers (OLPGLLG, ss 51-53) from provincial or local-level government. There is also provision for suspension (ss 54-68) of their powers.

In *PNG v Kapal* [1987] PNGLR 417 it was held that the power to partially suspend a provincial government is entirely within the discretion of the NEC. This power can only be fettered or interfered with by the court if it can be shown that the NEC exceeded or abused its powers. In *SCR No 3 of 1986; Reference by Simbu Provincial Executive* [1987] PNGLR 151 there was a provisional suspension by a simple majority vote on the grounds of corruption and mismanagement of the Simbu provincial government. In *Southern Highlands v PNG* [1993] PNGLR 402 the court held that a provisional suspension of a provincial government must be preceded

22 On accounting, see OLPGLLG, ss 102-105A.

by efforts to exhaust all avenues under the OLPG before approaching the court. In *Kavali v Wama* [1993] PNGLR 504 the court held that while a provincial government is under suspension, the NEC assumes all powers. Similarly, where a Provincial Administrator of a suspended provincial government is a delegate of a Minister, that Minister can direct public servants through the Provincial Secretary.[23]

Where the difficulties have been resolved, there is power to re-establish the powers of provincial or local-level governments that have been withdrawn or suspended: see OLPGLLG, ss 69-71.

23 See also *PNG v Gulf Provincial Government* [1994] PNGLR 34 at 36 and *Gulf Provincial Government v Minister for Village Services* [1994] PNGLR 435.

Chapter 9

CONSTITUTIONAL RIGHTS AND FREEDOMS

9.1 INTRODUCTION

The protection of the rights and freedoms of individuals is an important consideration in a constitutional system. These rights and freedoms may be protected either by the constitution[1] or an ordinary statute.[2] The *entrenchment* of rights in the constitution began in the United States with the first ten amendments to its *Constitution,* which are known as the *Bill of Rights*. The concept of entrenchment means that the legislature cannot easily alter these rights. In Papua New Guinea (PNG) stringent methods are set out by the *Constitution* to alter the rights which are guaranteed by the *Constitution*.

The concept of human rights "has developed over centuries in various countries of the world".[3] However, two distinguished scholars and two revolutions are identified as having promoted and encouraged the formalisation and globalisation of human rights. The first scholar was John Locke, who argued that the power of the sovereign was limited and the people had a right to resort to violence against the sovereign in circumstances where their liberty and freedoms were infringed. These sentiments were echoed by another scholar, Thomas Paine, whose views were influential in the American Revolution in 1775 and the French Revolution in 1789.[4] John Locke's work influenced the enactment of the *Bill of Rights* of 1689 in England. The enactment of the *Bill of Rights* was the first attempt to formalise the rights and freedoms of individuals as an Act. After the American and French Revolutions, other countries in Europe, such as Sweden in 1809 and Holland in 1815, began to entrench human rights in their constitutions.

The emergence of human rights at the global level was made apparent by the adoption of the *Universal Declaration on Human Rights* by the United Nations in 1948. In 1966 the *International Covenant on Civil and Political Rights* and the *International Covenant on Economic, Social and Cultural Rights* were adopted by the United Nations. These documents together represent an international *Bill of Rights*.[5]

By the time PNG emerged as an independent nation, the concept of human rights had taken root in many parts of the world and was particularly popular with the

1 This practice was initiated by the United States of America and has been followed in many countries, including India, PNG and many of the Pacific Island states.
2 The United Kingdom, Canada and Australia are good examples of this practice.
3 Constitutional Planning Committee, *Constitutional Planning Committee Final Report (Part 1)* (Government Printer, Port Moresby, 1974) (CPC, *Final Report*), Ch 5, p 5/1/1.
4 Hilaire, *Constitutional & Administrative Law* (Cavendish Publishing Ltd, London, 1997), pp 555-560.
5 Ibid, p 560.

newly emerging States. PNG's Pacific neighbours, such as Tonga, Western Samoa (now Samoa), Nauru and Fiji entrenched human rights in their *Constitutions*.[6] It was, therefore, no surprise when PNG decided to adopt a bill of rights and entrenched in its *Constitution*.

The nature and content of human rights vary in detail, but not in fundamentals, from one country to another. As one commentator pointed out, "attitudes to human rights differ from place to place; nations which have embodied human rights in their national constitutions have similarly displayed varying degrees of attitude to the provisions".[7] The nature of human rights discussed in this chapter is particular to PNG because it reflects the particular values, aspirations and circumstances of the country.

9.2 ORIGINS OF THE CONSTITUTIONAL PROVISION

Colonialism imported a particular form of legal system into PNG. Between the theft of land, the "punitive raids", the floggings, the taxation system, and its corollary the indentured labour system, human rights were accorded little formal or practical notice until the late colonial period. It was, therefore, not surprising that the issue of human rights was very much at the heart of the report of the Constitutional Planning Committee (CPC), which said:

> "We Papua New Guineans are all too familiar with authoritarian governments, having been ruled by them for almost ninety years. The last years of colonial rule have, of course, been enlightened by world standards, but in earlier times the basic rights and dignity of our people were frequently suppressed or ignored."[8]

The CPC was mindful of the *Public Order Ordinance* 1970, which empowered the colonial administration "to restrict processions and public meetings, and included a number of offences relating to demonstrations and other forms of disobedience".[9] The CPC was also aware that other former colonies, such as India, Pakistan, Nigeria and Malaysia, had entrenched basic rights and freedoms in their independence constitutions. Therefore, the CPC strongly recommended the inclusion of human rights and freedoms in the new constitution. The CPC also recommended that these rights and freedoms be enforceable. It suggested that the Supreme and the National Courts should be given the mandate to enforce the rights and freedoms.[10]

A year before the CPC was established, a Member of the House of Assembly, Rev Percy Chatterton, had introduced, and the Assembly passed, the *Human Rights Ordinance* 1971. The introduction of this Act was in direct response to the *Public Order Ordinance* 1970, which itself was introduced by the colonial administration "partly as a response to militant political activity in Bougainville and East New Britain, and partly as a 'trial run' for similar repressive legislation designed for use in Australia against opponents of the Vietnam war".[11] The *Human Rights Ordinance*

6 For a comparative analysis of these and other Pacific Island states' constitutions guaranteeing human rights, see O'Neill, "Human Rights in Pacific Island Constitutions" in Sack, *Pacific Constitutions* (Australian National University, Canberra, 1982), p 307.

7 Amankwah, "Human Rights in the Superior Courts" in James and Fraser, *Legal Issues in a Developing Society* (UPNG, Faculty of Law, Port Moresby, 1992), p 170.

8 CPC, *Final Report*, Ch 5, p 5/1/3.

9 Ibid.

10 Ibid, pp 5/1/8-5/1/9.

11 Goldring, *The Constitution of Papua New Guinea* (Law Book Co Ltd, Sydney, 1978), p 212.

was based on the human rights provisions of the *Constitution* of Nauru and Nigeria.

The *Human Rights Ordinance* contained 11 rights and freedoms. These were:

- Right to life;
- Right to personal liberty;
- Freedom from slavery and forced labour;
- Freedom from inhuman treatment;
- Right to protection of property;
- Right to protection from arbitrary search and entry on premises;
- Protection of law to ensure no imprisonment except on a proper charge and after a fair trial;
- Freedom of thought, conscience and religion;
- Freedom of speech and the right to publish;
- Freedom of peaceful assembly and association; and
- Freedom of choice of employment.

A person whose right was infringed could seek its enforcement in the Full Court of the Supreme Court under the *Ordinance*. The first case to come before the court regarding the *Ordinance* was the case of *Re Cornelius John Boxtel* [1973] PNGLR 283. The applicant, an expatriate, was arrested and charged first for rape and was committed to stand trial in 1972. Sometime later he was again arrested and charged for conspiracy. The prosecution decided to proceed with the case of conspiracy first and then deal with the rape case after the conclusion of the conspiracy case. The applicant sought a declaration in the Supreme Court that the delay in proceeding with the rape case was a violation of his right to a fair hearing within a reasonable time pursuant to s 16(2) of the *Human Rights Ordinance*. After reviewing the facts, the court agreed with the applicant that to delay the rape proceeding was a violation of his right under s 16(2).

In 1973 the same section of the *Ordinance* was invoked by some Papua New Guineans in *R v Abia Tambule* [1974] PNGLR 250. At the trial, the prosecution called all the relevant evidence against the defendants, who were charged with wilful murder. Before closing its case, the prosecution filed a *nolle prosequi*. The trial judge reserved a question to the Full Court of the Supreme Court for direction. The question was: "Should a *nolle prosequi* have been entered in respect of the three accused and the accused discharged or should a verdict of not guilty have been entered?" The defendants argued that the *nolle prosequi* denied them a right to a fair hearing as stipulated under s 16(2) of the *Human Rights Ordinance*. The court held that the filing of the *nolle prosequi* at the end of the prosecution case denied the defendants a fair hearing under s 16(2).

A third case involving the same legislation was *R v Edison Kopada Besia* [1975] PNGLR 74. The accused, a police sergeant, was charged for having unlawfully confined a woman in a police cell. The woman was suspected of possessing stolen goods, which were found in her house. The accused arrested the woman and locked her up at the Banz Police Station Cells. The police had hoped that by detaining the woman her husband would confess and she would be released. The woman remained in the cells for a week without being charged. After hearing evidence from the parties, the court held that the detention of the village woman was contrary to s 11 of the *Human Rights Ordinance*, which stated that "a person who is arrested or detained shall be informed promptly, in a language which he understands, of the reasons for his arrest or detention and of any charge against him".

These three cases highlighted two fundamental points. First, the judiciary was very prompt in dealing with abuses of human rights. Secondly, ordinary Papua New Guineans were quick to invoke their rights under the *Ordinance*.

The *Ordinance* had considerable impact on the CPC, which adopted the 11 rights and freedoms under the *Ordinance* and added five new ones to its list. The Constituent Assembly, the Government and the Opposition readily accepted the recommendations of the CPC that these rights and freedoms should be entrenched in the *Constitution*.

9.3 THE CONSTITUTIONAL ARRANGEMENT

The *Constitution* contains 16 rights and freedoms. The CPC recommended 16 rights and freedoms, including the 11 that were available at that time under the *Human Rights Ordinance*.[12] These rights and freedoms are:

- Right to freedom (s 32);
- Right to life (s 35);
- Freedom from inhuman treatment (s 36);
- Protection of the law (s 37);
- Liberty of the person (s 42);
- Freedom from forced labour (s 43);
- Freedom from arbitrary search and entry (s 44);
- Freedom of conscience, thought and religion (s 45);
- Freedom of expression (s 46);
- Freedom of assembly and association (s 47);
- Freedom of employment (s 48);
- Right to privacy (s 49);
- Right to vote and stand for public office (s 50);
- Right to Freedom of information (s 51);
- Right to Freedom of movement (s 52); and
- Equality of citizens (s 55).

In *SCR No 5 of 1985; Re Raz v Matane* [1985] PNGLR 329, the Supreme Court held that the words "right or freedom" mean the "rights" or "freedoms" guaranteed by the *Constitution*. Some of these rights and freedoms are available to every person, while all of them are available to the citizens of PNG, and some of these rights and freedoms are unalterable, while others can be altered in special circumstances. Because of the complexity of the constitutional structure on rights and freedoms, it is appropriate to deal with them under specific headings to assist in a better understanding of them.

Defining the rights

The constitutional provisions on basic rights begin with s 32 and end at s 56. Sections 32, 33 and 34 define and explain the provisions on rights contained in

12 See the analysis by Kwa, "Enforcement of Human Rights in Papua New Guinea: Tru o Giaman" in Kwa, Bhalla, Muroa, Linge, Tennent and Yapao (eds), *Development of Administrative Law in Papua New Guinea* (UPNG & UBSPD, School of Law and Business Studies, New Delhi, 2000), p 179.

ss 35-56. With the exception of s 32(2), these three sections do not themselves create rights.

Right to freedom: s 32

Section 32(1) defines the concept of freedom. It states that:

> "Freedom based on law consists in the least amount of restriction on the activities of individuals that is consistent with the maintenance and development of Papua New Guinea and the society in accordance with this Constitution and, in particular, with the National Goals and Directive Principles and the Basic Social Obligations."

This definition gives an understanding of all the freedoms provided elsewhere in the *Constitution*. The underpinning concept of a freedom is the lack of, or limited restriction of, individual activity. Where there is a limited restriction, the restriction must be based on initiatives which will enhance the development of PNG. In the words of Kapi DCJ in *The State v NTN Pty Ltd* [1992] PNGLR 1, "freedom (under s 32(1)) should be enjoyed with the least amount of restriction" (at 9). The same sentiment was expressed by the Supreme Court in *Re Internal Security Act* [1994] PNGLR 341 (at 347). In *University of PNG v Ume More* [1985] PNGLR 48, the National Court held that "by erecting barricades and forcibly disrupting classes and the lecturers' freedom to lecture and the students' freedom to attend lectures if they want to", there were violations of s 32. Bredmeyer J did not address s 32 specifically, but a range of rights and freedoms. He reasoned that, because some students and lecturers were prevented from exercising their freedom in attending and giving lectures, there was a violation of s 32.

Section 32(2) may envisage rights that are not expressly set out in the *Constitution*. These additional rights may include, for instance, the right not to participate in a police identification parade, as discussed in *The State v Kusap Kei Kuya* [1983] PNGLR 263 (at 269) (though note the limited extent of the right if police have no duty to inform a person of the right that could be used to impose such a duty). Section 32(2) may also provide a constitutional basis for a right to remain silent when interviewed by police investigating an offence. Whatever these rights are, they must, however, be exercised within the ambit of the law. As the Supreme Court explained in *Re Internal Security Act* [1994] PNGLR 341 (at 347):

> "Freedom vested by s 32(2) assumes rights of others to be in peace, not be injured, or killed. ... No individual is free to do whatever he likes, and the *Constitution* s 32(1) acknowledges that ...".

Other rights and freedoms: s 33

Section 33 provides for other rights to be created either under an Organic Law or an Act of Parliament. Thus, under s 33 it is possible to protect rights and freedoms by other laws, which can also reduce the scope for limits on rights under s 38. It might also provide for enforcement bodies, such as the proposed Human Rights Commission, which was to be established in 1996.[13]

13 The establishment of the Human Rights Commission was strongly promoted by the Department of Attorney-General after its inception was proposed by the government in 1995 and supported by the Commonwealth Secretariat. The proposal was not supported by the then Prime Minister Sir Julius Chan and, therefore, it was never formally established. See generally, Gene, "The Human Rights Commission" in Kwa et al (eds), op cit n 12, p 211.

Section 34 deals with the application of the rights provisions, clarifying that they normally apply to government bodies, companies and associations, and not just to individuals. In *The State v NTN Pty Ltd,* Kapi DCJ held that the respondent, which was a company, was entitled to enforce its rights under s 46 of the *Constitution* by virtue of s 34.

Definitions of rights

A closer look at the constitutional provisions on basic rights reveals that each of the rights provided for in ss 35-37 and ss 42-55 is defined in the section that provides for the right. In most cases, the rights are not clearly defined. There is normally simply a statement of broad principle, such as "that personal liberty, shall not be deprived". The courts are then required to determine what is meant by these broad statements.[14] In some other sections, there are more detailed definitions, as in s 46(2) (defining "freedom of expression and publication").

Three categories of rights

In general, rights under the *Constitution* are of three kinds:

(i) the "fundamental rights" under ss 35-37;

(ii) the "qualified rights of all persons" under ss 42-49; and

(iii) the "qualified rights of citizens" under ss 50-56.

Sections 35 to 37 provide for "fundamental rights". They are fundamental in the sense that they apply to all persons and that they are open to far less restriction and qualification than other rights and freedoms provided for under the *Constitution.* Not only is s 38 inapplicable to these rights, but they are not open to restriction during a state of emergency (s 233(3)) except that the rights under s 37 may be limited by emergency laws providing for internment.

9.4 FUNDAMENTAL RIGHTS

Fundamental rights apply to every person in PNG regardless of their race, ethnicity, colour, creed, religion or sex. These rights have been defined and enforced under various circumstances by the courts.

Right to life: s 35

Section 35 declares that every one has the right to life. The right to life can, however, be taken in certain exceptional circumstances which are allowed under the section itself. In *The State v Paege* [1994] PNGLR 65, the court held that the right to life under s 35 can be legally taken where the Parliament has imposed a death penalty for the offence of wilful murder under s 299 of the *Criminal Code* (as amended).

Freedom from inhuman treatment: s 36

Section 36 provides for freedom from inhuman treatment. Subsection (1) prohibits torture and cruelty to another person. Thus, it was held in *Re Heni Pauta and Kenneth Susuve* [1982] PNGLR 7 that prisoners who were subjected to serious

14 The court did this in relation to s 42 in *SCR No 5 of 1987; The State v Songke Mai and Gai Avi* [1988] PNGLR 56.

assaults by prison warders were entitled to the protection accorded by s 36(1). In *Tom Amaiu v Commissioner for Corrective Institutions* [1983] PNGLR 449, a case also involving a prisoner, the court held that although a prisoner is not entitled to the normal privileges of a free person, he or she has a right to be treated in a way which is not cruel, inhuman or oppressive. The protection under s 36 also extends to persons detained by police (see *David Wari Kofowei v Augustine Siviri* [1983] PNGLR 449).

Protection of the law: s 37

Protection of the law is provided to every person by s 37. Apart from being a general right available to every person, it also contains specific rights which are available only to a certain category of people, namely, those who are in custody or detained by police (s 37(1)). In *Premdas v Independent State of PNG* [1979] PNGLR 329, the Supreme Court held that the whole of s 37 originates from the *European Convention on Human Rights*. It is to this Convention to which the courts in PNG have turned for guidance.

Generally, a person whose right has been violated can seek protection under s 37. Thus, it was held in *University of PNG v Ume More* [1985] PNGLR 48 that an act which prevented the free exercise of the rights of a person under the *Constitution* was a violation of those rights and those affected by that act could seek the protection of the law under s 37.

Section 37(1) stipulates that every person has the full protection of the law. The National Court ruled in *Tom Amaiu v Commissioner for Corrective Institutions* that even prisoners who were detained in a maximum security prison and who were punished over and above normal punishment were entitled to the protection of this section. The court further held that where there was a violation of a constitutional right in the circumstances, the prisoner was entitled to compensation. In *The State v Mana Turi* [1986] PNGLR 221, it was held that the detention of the accused by the police for more than five days without being charged was a violation of his rights under ss 37(1) and 42(3)(b) of the *Constitution*.

Under s 37(2), with the exception of contempt of court,[15] a person cannot be convicted of an offence that is not defined by law. In the words of the court in *Urata v Chris* [1993] PNGLR 163, a person cannot be "imprisoned under an Act which did not exist". An attempt to go behind this provision and punish innocent persons can be opposed by the courts, as was the case in *SCR No 1 of 1981; Re Inter-Group Fighting Act* [1981] PNGLR 151. In an attempt to reduce tribal fighting in the Highlands, the Parliament amended this legislation to enable the police to detain and punish the leaders of the groups involved in tribal fights. This approach was taken because of the difficulty of identifying the perpetrators and instigators of a tribal fight. The Supreme Court ruled that the amendments were in violation of ss 37(3), 37(4), 37(5), 37(8) and 42 of the *Constitution* and were, therefore, invalid. Insofar as s 37(2) was concerned, the court ruled that the requirement that the accused should show cause why he should not be imprisoned by a notice issued by the magistrate was an offence not recognised by a law and, therefore, invalid.

In *Re Internal Security Act* [1994] PNGLR 341 (at 347, 349 and 352), the Supreme Court was asked to decide whether s 3 of the *Internal Security Act* was in breach of s 37(2). Section 3 of the Act, which is entitled "Prevention of Terrorism", defined certain activities which were aimed at preventing terrorism. The court ruled that

15 For examples of cases involving contempt, see *Re Passingan Taru* [1982] PNGLR 292 and *Ambre v PNG* [1995] PNGLR 453.

if a person knowingly engaged in those activities in the pursuit of terrorism, then his or her actions amounted to a breach of the Act and, therefore, s 3 did not violate s 37(2).

In a case involving sexual intercourse between a man and his cousin sister, the National Court had to grapple with the question of whether "sister" included "cousin sister" for the crime of incest under s 223(1)(b) of the *Criminal Code Act*. If the "cousin sister" was not covered by the term "sister" under the Act, then the sexual intercourse between the accused and his cousin sister was not an offence under s 223(1)(b) and, as such, by application of s 37(2) of the *Constitution*, the accused would be innocent. The court held in *The State v Burin* [1994] PNGLR 15 (at 17) that the term "sister" included cousin sister, and thus the accused was not protected under s 37(2).

A person who is charged with an offence must, unless the charge is withdrawn, be afforded a fair hearing within a reasonable time by an independent and impartial court. This right is spelt out in s 37(3). This right is available only to those persons who have been charged with a criminal offence. The three main elements of this provision are:

(i) a "fair hearing";
(ii) "a reasonable time"; and
(iii) an "independent and impartial court".

As to what is "a reasonable time", the courts have presented differing views on the appropriate length of time. In *The State v Peter Painke (No 1)* [1976] PNGLR 210, O'Leary AJ held that, where the accused was committed to stand trial for stealing and the trial had not proceeded after 11 months from the date of committal, it was unreasonable and, therefore, a violation of s 37(3). A similar ruling was made by Frost CJ, in *The State v Peter Painke (No 2)* [1977] PNGLR 141.[16] The principles in the above cases were considered and applied by Sawong AJ, in *The State v Watinga* [1994] PNGLR 255 (at 258). Doherty J held in *The State v Watul* [1992] PNGLR 475 that where a trial was part-heard and the prisoners escaped and one accused was recaptured, an adjournment of four months was a reasonable time. Obiter, her Honour decided that any delay after the four months was going to be a breach of s 37(3). On the other hand, Sevua J ruled in *The State v Tubol* [1994] PNGLR 378 that, where the accused were represented by counsel throughout the proceeding and they had failed to prepare their defence within the four months, there was *no breach* of their right under s 37(3). In *The State v Fancy* [1994] PNGLR 548, Los J, refused to grant an application for a mistrial in the middle of the trial. According to his Honour, for the proceeding to be abandoned would be a breach of the accused's right to a fair trial within a reasonable time as required by s 37(3).

These cases show that where the delay is caused by the authorities being empowered or required to accord the accused this special right, the court will not hesitate to rule in favour of the accused. The Supreme Court has ruled that the procedures of the National Court should not be used to cause unnecessary delay against an accused. Thus, in *The State v John Rupet Kaputin (No 1)* [1979] PNGLR 532, the Supreme Court held that where the National Court has not decided on the facts and issues in a matter and then makes a reservation for the Supreme Court, it is a violation of the right of the accused to a fair trial within a reasonable time under s 37(3). The same obligation, however, does not apply to the

16 The first case involved the offence of stealing. The second involved the offence of fraudulent false accounting. One of the arguments raised by the accused in each of these cases was the undue delay in prosecuting the case.

Ombudsman Commission provided the Commission has complied with all the necessary procedures under the *Organic Law on the Ombudsman Commission* and the *Organic Law on Duties and Responsibilities of Leadership*.[17]

Section 37(4) creates five rights which are available to a person charged with an offence. These rights are "guaranteed for every person in Papua New Guinea, whether they are citizens or non-citizens" per Kidu CJ, in *The State v Avia Aihi* [1982] PNGLR 92 (at 99). The rights are more readily available to those persons who "have been charged with an offence".

Of these five rights, the most fundamental and also the most controversial is "the right to be presumed innocent until proven guilty according to all law", which is set out in s 37(4)(a). This right is the "golden thread" that transcends the whole legal system of PNG. The right to be presumed innocent is referred to as the "golden thread" of the English criminal law. It derives its origins in *Woolmington v DPP* [1935] AC 462. In PNG the position of this common law rule has been elevated to be "a right" by the *Constitution*. The right provides that a person charged with an offence:

> "shall be presumed innocent until proved guilty according to law, but a law may place upon a person charged with an offence, the burden of proving particular facts which are, or would *[with the exercise of reasonable care]* be, peculiarly within his knowledge".[18]

A number of observations can be made here:

- A person must be proved guilty according to law. The burden to prove guilt is, therefore, on the prosecution.[19] Moreover, the law here is that which is provided for under s 9 of the *Constitution*. Thus, in *SCR No 2 of 1990* [1991] PNGLR 211, it was held that the underlying law recognised by the phrase "according to law" imports a range of criminal procedure under common law.
- A close examination of this provision reveals that the quoted paragraph has two parts. The first part requires that the accused must be presumed innocent until proven guilty according to law. The second part provides possible exceptions to the general rule. These exceptions mainly relate to defences raised by the accused[20] and where the statute expressly imposes a burden on the accused.[21]
- In 1991, this right was amended and the phrase "with the exercise of reasonable care" was deleted from the paragraph.
- Supreme Court judgments have had an impact on s 37(4)(a). These are: *Constitutional Reference No 3 of 1978; Re Inter-Group Fighting Act 1977* [1978] PNGLR 421; *SCR No 1 of 1980* [1981] PNGLR 28; *SCR No 2 of 1980; Re s 14(2) of the Summary Offences Act 1977* [1981] PNGLR 50 and *Court Reference No 1A of 1981; Re Motor Traffic Act* [1982] PNGLR 122.[22] In the first case, the Supreme Court was asked by the National Court in Mt Hagen to decide

17 *Balakau v Ombudsman Commission* [1995] PNGLR 70 at 72.

18 The history of this provision is set out in some detail by Saldanha J in *Supreme Constitutional Reference No 3 of 1978; Re Inter-Group Fighting Act 1977* [1978] PNGLR 421 at 428.

19 However, see the judgment of Greville Smith J in *SCR No 1 of 1980* [1981] PNGLR 28, where his Honour said that particular defences and excuses had to be proven by the accused.

20 For instance, the defence of insanity provided by s 28 of the *Criminal Code Act*.

21 See s 147 of the *Criminal Code Act* and s 2 of the *Summary Offences Act* (Ch 264). For an understanding of the phrase "lawful excuse", see *Kupu v Doria* [1988-1989] PNGLR 1. For a case dealing with a statutory defence, see *Steamships Trading Co Ltd v Leva* [1988-1989] PNGLR 248.

22 As to how these cases impact on the burden of proof, see the analysis by Kaburise, "Reversing the Burden of Proof: Constitutional Prescription and Judicial Exposition" 12 MLJ 1 at 1-23.

whether s 11(3) of the *Inter-Group Fighting Act* 1977 was invalid as it contravened s 37(4)(a) of the *Constitution.* Section 11(3) provided that a person charged with an offence against that section was guilty of that offence unless he proved that he did not take part in the tribal fight. The court ruled that s 11(3) shifted the burden of proof to the accused and was, therefore, in breach of s 37(4)(a) and, thus, invalid. In the second case, similar issues arose for the determination of the Supreme Court. The Supreme Court was asked to decide whether s 22A of the *Police Offences Act (Papua)* 1926-1977 (repealed), which provided that an accused charged with passing a cheque not paid on presentation is guilty, unless he proves that "he did not intent to defraud". The court ruled that the shifting of the burden to the accused by s 22A of the Act was valid because it was within the scope of the exceptions provided by the second limb of paragraph (a) of s 37(4). The third case also involved similar issues raised in the other two cases. Here the Supreme Court was asked to consider whether s 14(2) of the *Summary Offences Act* (Ch 264) was in violation of s 37(4)(a). Section 14(2) stated that a defendant charged with the offence of passing a valueless cheque had a defence if he proved that he had reasonable grounds to believe that the cheque would be paid in full on presentation. In this case, the Supreme Court went further than it did in the previous two cases and considered whether the section fell within the exceptions under s 37(4)(a). The court held that s 14(2) involved facts which were peculiarly within the knowledge of the accused and, therefore, s 14(2) was a law which was an exception to the general rule and, consequently, valid. In the last case, the Supreme Court was asked to decide on the constitutionality of certain amendments made by Parliament to the *Motor Traffic Act* 1950, the *District Courts Act* 1963 and the then *Local Courts Act* 1963. The underpinning of the amendments was to empower the police and the magistrates of the inferior courts to enter guilty verdicts on traffic offenders without first being heard. Following the similar principles laid down in the three previous decisions, the Supreme Court held that the amendments impugned s 37(4)(a).

The next right under s 37(4) of the *Constitution* is the right of the person charged with the offence to be "informed promptly in a language which he understands, and in detail, the nature of the offence with which he is charged". In *SCR No 1 of 1981; Re Inter-Group Fighting Act,* the court held by a majority that ss 16,17 and 20, which imposed a penalty before the accused was accorded the right stipulated by this provision, was repugnant to s 37(4)(b) and, therefore, invalid. The decision highlights that the judiciary will prevent the legislature from limiting or eroding the rights of an accused (provided for under s 37) in any attempt to curb crime and lawlessness in the country.

The other right under this provision that has been decided on by the courts is the right under s 37(4)(e) and (f). For the former the Supreme Court held in *In re Joseph Mavuk* [1980] PNGLR 507 that the right of an accused to legal representation was not absolute. It held that the exercise of that right was "subject to all proper exceptions". Thus, where a counsel had acted as the prosecution counsel in the matter and later became the defence counsel in the same matter, the Supreme Court ruled that the removal of counsel from the case was not an infringement of s 37(4)(e). In relation to the other right under consideration, the National Court ruled in *Madeline Kiso v Angela Manumanua* [1981] PNGLR 507, a case of adultery under the *Native Regulations (Papua),* that the right of an accused to give evidence under s 37(4)(f) could not be overridden by an ordinary statute or practice.

The next right is the right to be present in court when a trial is being conducted. This right is provided by s 37(5). This provision has two limbs. The first limb is the general rule that a trial shall not take place without the consent of the accused. The second limb provides the exceptions which, in the words of the Supreme Court in *Peter v South Pacific Brewery* [1976] PNGLR 537 is a "proviso". In this case the District Court at Port Moresby made a reference to the Supreme Court for its opinion on the question as to whether s 131 of the *District Courts Act* 1963, which permitted the court to hear and determine an information of a simple offence in the absence of the defendant, was consistent with the proviso to s 37(5). Section 131 empowered the District Court to proceed with a trial in the absence of the defendant and, upon conviction, could impose either a fine, imprisonment or both. The court considered the relevant rules of construction permitted by s 10 of the *Constitution* and concluded that, if it read down the section, then it would limit the operation of s 131 and save the section from being severed completely. It concluded, therefore, that the term "summary offences" did not include a penalty of imprisonment (imprisonment being applicable only after default) and, thus, saved s 131. A similar approach was taken by the Supreme Court in *SCR No 1A of 1981; Re Motor Traffic Act* [1982] PNGLR 122. In this case, however, the Supreme Court ruled that the amendments to the *Motor Traffic Act*, the *District Courts Act* and the *Local Courts Act* violated s 37(5) and were invalid. In *The State v Watul* [1992] PNGLR 475, the National Court proceeded with the trial of the accused in their absence and found them guilty. The court took this approach because the defendants escaped half-way through their trial and it was not possible to recapture them. The court was of the view that its action (continuation of trial) was not in violation of s 37(5). However, in *Re Ereman* [1993] PNGLR 120, the court held that, where the defendant was not served with the relevant documents to appear before the District Court, and the court proceeded to imprison him, the conviction was entered in breach of s 37(5).

Section 37(6) empowers the legislature to make a law imposing certain conditions which may be met by the defendant before his or her witnesses are summoned at public expense to testify on the defendant's behalf. This provision is not clear. It is possible that because the prosecution is allowed to spend public funds to bring in witnesses to testify for the state, a similar allowance should be accorded the defendant. The conditions that may be imposed on the defendant may include a refund to the state if he or she wins, or the defendant may be required to pay some money into court before the witnesses are summoned to testify on behalf of the defendant.

Section 37(7) provides that no person shall be convicted of an offence on account of an act that, at the time it took place, did not constitute an offence. In *Re Internal Security Act* [1994] PNGLR 341 (at 348), one of the questions that was put before the Supreme Court was whether Pt IV of the *Internal Security Act* was inconsistent with the provisions of s 37, including s 37(7). Part IV of the Act provides for offences and penalties for terrorism. The Supreme Court made no attempt to consider the application of this provision to the part of the Act in question. The justification for this approach was, as the Supreme Court put it, that the issue was covered adequately in the discussions relating to s 37(2) and (3).[23]

The *Constitution* also protects a person from being prosecuted again for an offence for which he has been convicted or acquitted. This is the express prohibition under s 37(8). The exposition of this rule was established in *The State v Nugints*

23 With respect, it is suggested that the court should have considered the provision on its own merits because of the specific nature of the right contained in s 37(7).

[1994] PNGLR 493. In this case the defendant was acquitted in the District Court on a charge of unlawful assault under the *Summary Offences Act.* The state then proceeded to indict him on a charge of grievous bodily harm pursuant to s 319 of the *Criminal Code.* The court followed the pre-independence case of *Masuve v Bryant* [1974] PNGLR 61 and ruled that a plea of *autrefois acquit* as a defence was established by the defendant. Based on this common law principle and s 37(8) of the *Constitution,* the court discharged the defendant on the charge of grievous bodily harm.

The protection under s 37(8) covers both individuals and corporate bodies. In *Keke v PNG Colour Laboratories Pty Ltd* [1992] PNGLR 265 the appellant, an employee of the respondent, appealed against the decision of the District Court dismissing an information laid by the appellant against the respondent for wrongful dismissal under the *Industrial Relations Act* (Ch 174). On appeal, Brown J held that, as the information was dismissed by the District Court, there could be no appeal against the finding of "not guilty". His Honour said that s 37(8) protected the company from any further prosecution in the matter (at 268).

According to s 37(9), a person who has been pardoned cannot be tried again for that offence. Further, s 37(10) stipulates that where a defendant agrees to be a witness in his own case he is a competent witness, but not a compellable witness.[24] This provision guarantees a defendant the right to silence at his trial. In the pre-independence case of *R v John Loe (No 1)* [1969-70] PNGLR 12, the court ruled that the right to silence originates from the common law maxim *nemo tenetur se ipsum accusare* (no-one is bound to incriminate himself). Section 37(10) is clearly based on this common law maxim. Thus, where a defendant exercises this right to remain silent at his or her trial, no inference of guilt can be drawn by the court: see *Paulus Pawa v The State* [1981] PNGLR 498.[25] This position has been reaffirmed by the Supreme Court in *Mara v The State* (1986) SC320 per Kidu CJ.

Section 37(11) provides that a determination of the existence or extent of a civil right or obligation can only be made by an independent and impartial court or authority prescribed by law, or upon an agreement by the parties, and proceedings for such a determination shall be fairly heard within a reasonable time. As to the definition of "civil rights", Prentice CJ held in *Premdas v Independent State of Papua New Guinea* that there was no definition of this term in Art 6(1) of the *European Convention on Human Rights.* His Honour, however, ruled that the grant of an entry permit did not amount to a "civil right" but a mere licence revocable at any time by the government.[26] In *Application of Biki* [1995] PNGLR 336, Doherty J held that the "concept of being fairly heard includes giving the person a chance to speak on his own behalf or have someone speak for him" (at 340). Further, in *Amadio Pty Ltd v Mt Kare Holdings Pty Ltd* [1992] PNGLR 218, Woods J held that although an application for leave was an ex parte principle, s 37(11) required the attendance of a defendant at the hearing of the application (at 220).

To avoid any suspicion and to ensure fairness, s 37(12) requires that all court proceedings, apart from the exceptions provided therein, must be heard in public. Section 37(13) provides that, notwithstanding s 37(12), a court or other authority has the power to bar a person or a class of persons from the proceedings before the court. In *The State v Rave* [1993] PNGLR 85, the court used its powers under this

24 This provision must be read together with ss 12 and 14 of the *Evidence Act* (Ch 48).
25 Consider the analysis by Chalmers, Weisbrot, Injia and Andrew, *Criminal Law and Practice of Papua New Guinea* (3rd ed, Lawbook Co, Sydney, 2001), pp 644-648.
26 This conclusion was also accepted by Raine DCJ and Saldanha J.

provision to exclude members of the public in order to enable the prosecutrix in a rape case, who was about 15 years old, to give her evidence confidently.

Section 37(14) requires that where an accused has not been tried four months after being committed, the Chief Justice must submit to the Minister a report setting out the reasons for the delay. This provision must be read in conjunction with s 37(3). The main distinction here is that under this provision the Chief Justice has a duty to report to the Minister for Justice about the delays. Section 37(14) must be read together with s 154 of the *Constitution*. Section 154 talks about the administration of justice and states that the national justice administration consists of the National Judicial System, which includes the Supreme and the National Courts, the Minister for Justice and the Law Officers of PNG. The reporting mechanism under s 37(14) is solely for the administration of justice and not the review of the exercise of judicial power. Seen in this context, there is an encroachment of the powers of one arm of government over the other.

A person who has been convicted of an offence has a right under s 37(15) to have his or her conviction and sentence reviewed by a higher court according to law. This right of review does not, however, extend to non-criminal cases: *SCR No 8 of 1992; Application by Mionzing* [1992] PNGLR 122 (at 126). The Supreme Court held in *Constitutional Reference No 2 of 1978; Re Corrective Institutions Act 1957* [1978] PNGLR 404, and again in *Re Internal Security Act* [1994] PNGLR 341 (at 348), that this right to review cannot be ousted by an ordinary statute. However, in *Avia Aihi v The State* [1981] PNGLR 81, the Supreme Court ruled that the phrase "according to law" connotes that the right to review is not unlimited. Following from this rationale, the Supreme Court held that the right to a review of sentence can be regulated by an Act which, in that particular instance, was the *Supreme Court Act* 1975.

Section 37(16) stipulates that no person shall be deprived of his right of appeal against his conviction and sentence. In *Avia Aihi v The State* [1981] PNGLR 81, the Supreme Court refused to be drawn into the discussion of the issue of whether s 37(15) and (16) were separate and distinct. However, the Supreme Court did hold in *Constitutional Reference No 2 of 1978; Re Corrective Institutions Act 1957* [1978] PNGLR 404 that "review" is equivalent to "appeal". Kidu CJ and Kearney DCJ agreed with the conclusion reached in the latter case. Accordingly, the right of appeal under this provision can also be regulated by a statute.

Section 37(17) prevents the abuse of detainees and s 37(18) permits the segregation of prisoners from unconvicted persons. Section 37(19) also permits the separation of minors from adult prisoners while in custody. And s 37(20) prevents the transfer of prisoners far away from their normal place of residence. In *Re Heni Pauta and Kenneth Susuve* [1982] PNGLR 7, the court found that the two prisoners were assaulted and abused and that their rights under s 37(17), (18) and (19) were violated by the warders at the Bomana Jail.

Freedom from slavery: s 253

The right to freedom from slavery, contained in s 253 of the *Constitution*, is a fundamental right as it is not subject to qualification.

9.5 QUALIFIED RIGHTS

Sections 42 to 49 provide rights of all persons which may be qualified by a law permitted under s 38 and ss 50-56 provide for rights of citizens only which may be qualified in the same manner. The most important rights under this category are those which are enumerated by s 42. Sections 40 and 41 do not provide for any particular rights. The former relates only to restrictions on rights during *states of emergency* and appears largely to repeat what is provided for in s 233(2).

Section 41 provides a general remedy against acts done under valid laws, but which are harsh or otherwise problematic. The extent of its application is uncertain, as shall be seen by reference to the cases.

Proscribed acts: s 41

Section 41 provides a general restriction on the application of acts which are harsh and oppressive in nature, not warranted, are disproportionate to the circumstances or are not reasonably justifiable in a democratic society. Three decisions of the Supreme Court shed light on the nature and characteristics of s 41. The first decision was in *Premdas v Independent State of PNG* [1979] PNGLR 329. In this case the Supreme Court was asked, among other questions, whether the revocation of the appellant's entry permit by the Minister for Foreign Affairs and the Ministerial Review Committee, established under the *Migration Act* 1963 unlawful acts within the meaning of s 41. The Supreme Court held that the exercise of the powers by the Minister and the Review Committee were valid and did not contravene s 41. The Supreme Court also laid down the rule that although the *Migration Act* does not give a right to appeal to the foreign national, the National Court has a right to inquire into an act based on s 41.

In the second case, *SCR No 1 of 1984; Re Minimum Penalties Legislation* [1984] PNGLR 314, the Supreme Court dealt indirectly with the issue of s 41. Two members of the court (Kapi DCJ and Bredmeyer J) discussed s 41. In this case, the court went beyond *Premdas* to consider whether s 41 was a constitutional right. Bredmeyer J said that s 41 conferred a "right" within the meaning of that word under s 57. Kapi DCJ, on the other hand, held the view that s 41 did not contain a "right" which could be enforceable under s 57. His Honour said that s 41 provided a remedy, which was distinct from a right encompassed by s 57. When the same issue arose in *SCR No 5 of 1985; Re Raz v Matane* [1985] PNGLR 329, Kidu CJ (at 331) agreed with Kapi DCJ's views in the above case.[27] Kapi DCJ reaffirmed his position in *SCR No 1 of 1984; Re Minimum Penalties Legislation* and rejected Bredmeyer J's views (at 336).

Section 41, therefore, only provides a remedy for persons aggrieved by actions which are prohibited under that section. This provision was considered at length by Brown J in *Curran v PNG* [1994] PNGLR 230. In this case the applicant, a lawyer, had his work permit revoked by the government and ordered to leave PNG. He applied to the National Court seeking declarations that the decision of the Minister for Foreign Affairs was harsh and oppressive as specified under s 41. Brown J reviewed the three principal cases above and agreed with the views of Kapi DCJ. His Honour, however, disagreed (at 235) with the approach taken by McDermott AJ in *Raz v Matane* [1986] PNGLR 38. In that case the court proceeded to consider a writ for certiorari and quashed the decision of the Minister and the Committee. The correct approach, according to Brown J, is not for the courts to review the manner in which the Minister or the Committee reached its decision,

27 When Joseph Lemuel Raz's case went back to the National Court in *Raz v Matane* [1986] PNGLR 38. McDermott AJ proceeded to hear the application for certiorari and quashed the decision of the Minister and the Ministerial Review Committee.

but to attack an act which is otherwise lawful. Brown J's view is the correct exposition of the law as established by the Supreme Court in *Premdas* and *Raz v Matane*.

The meaning and the application of the phrase "harsh and oppressive" have been considered by the judiciary. In *Jivetuo v The Independent State of Papua New Guinea* [1984] PNGLR 174, the National Court ruled that two weeks given to squatters to vacate state lands, without due regard for the length of occupation of the land by the settlers, was harsh and oppressive. This definition was accepted by Doherty J in *Bai v Morobe Provincial Government* [1992] PNGLR 150 (at 157). Also, in *National Airline Employees' Association v Air Niugini* [1992] PNGLR 291, it was held that one month's notice to vacate the premises was not a harsh and oppressive act. The issues on s 41 were not fully argued in this case. However, Brown J seemed to have accepted the brief submission from the defendant's counsel that the actions of the defendant to order its former employees to vacate its premises were valid. In *Gopalan v Uni Transport Pty Ltd* [1986] PNGLR 101, the applicant tried to extend the meaning of a "harsh and oppressive" act to include damages awarded against his employer, who was in receivership, and the damages being unpaid by the receiver. The court (Cory J) held that the receiver was empowered to make the payments according to the *Companies Act* (Ch 310) and, as such, the applicant had no remedy available under s 41. Similarly, in *Bank of Papua New Guinea v Basa* [1992] PNGLR 271, the defendant attempted to invoke s 41 to prevent the bank from possessing his property after he fell into arrears. The court ruled that as the relationship of the parties was governed by a valid contract, s 41 could not shield the defendant from the enforcement of the contract. Claims that a decision of the court would be harsh and oppressive to the losing party and would thus violate s 41, was held to be purely ancillary and misconceived by the Supreme Court in *Mudge v Secretary for Lands* [1985] PNGLR 387.[28] Further, in *Balakau v Ombudsman Commission* [1995] PNGLR 70, Mr Balakau argued that the investigative procedures used by the Ombudsman Commission, which resulted in his referral to the Public Prosecutor, was draconian or "KGB" style and, therefore, harsh and oppressive within the meaning of s 41. Sheehan J rejected this argument after finding that every opportunity was given to Mr Balakau as required under the *Organic Law on the Ombudsman Commission* and the *Organic Law on Duties and Responsibilities of Leadership*. He concluded that the Ombudsman Commission determines its own procedures and that there was no prejudice to Mr Balakau. A similar argument was raised by a former policeman in *Vema v Tokam* [1995] PNGLR 368. In this case, the applicant was dismissed from the Police Force by the Commissioner of Police after he was found guilty of having sexual intercourse with a woman whom he had picked up in a police car while he was on duty. The court held that the Commissioner's action was not harsh and oppressive within the meaning of s 41 because the applicant's own conduct was disgraceful. Los J, in *Nowra No 8 Pty Ltd v Swokin* [1993] PNGLR 498, held that the forfeiture of the state lease by the Minister against the appellant was harsh and oppressive because the penalty was disproportionate to the failure of the appellant and, therefore, the Minister's actions fell under s 41 and, consequently, were void.

In *Tarere v ANZ Bank* [1988] PNGLR 201, Hinchliffe J warned the judiciary to be mindful of the inappropriate use of this section by frequently declaring acts made under valid laws to be harsh and oppressive.

---

28 *Emas Estate v Mea* [1993] PNGLR 215 at 226 (Brown J).

Liberty of the persons: s 42

Section 42 begins by declaring a general right with exceptions and then sets out specific rights for persons who are arrested or detained for questioning.

Section 42(1) declares that no person shall be deprived of his liberty. This right can, however, be restricted in any one of eight situations. These restrictions encommpass execution of a court order, suspicion of commission of an offence, the prevention of the spread of a disease, removal of aliens, and persons of unsound mind.[29] In *Agua Bepi v Aiya Simon* [1986] PNGLR 233, the husband claimed for desertion, child maintenance and repayment of bride-price against his wife under the *Deserted Wives and Children Act* (Ch 277) and succeeded in the District Court. On default, the wife was sentenced to imprisonment and ordered to pay maintenance and repay the bride-price. On appeal, the National Court held that the *Deserted Wives and Children Act* could not be invoked by a husband against his wife and, consequently, the court orders against the appellant were wrong in law and her imprisonment was not protected under s 42(1)(c). The National Court also ruled in *The State v Tulong* [1995] PNGLR 329 that a person suspected of committing an offence under s 128 of the *Criminal Code* (conspiring to defeat justice) could not be detained without first being arrested on a warrant. The court held that because the accused was arrested and detained without a warrant of arrest, his detention was not covered by s 42(1)(d).

Section 42(2) provides three specific rights for a person who is arrested or detained. These rights are:

(i) A person who is arrested or detained shall be promptly informed in a language he understands of the reasons for his arrest or detention.

(ii) A person who is arrested or detained shall be permitted to communicate without delay and in private with a member of his family or a friend and with a lawyer of his choice.

(iii) A person arrested or detained shall be given adequate opportunity to give instructions to a lawyer of his choice.

These three rights are similar to those found under s 37(4). The distinction between these two provisions is that the protection under s 37(4) is accorded to a person who has been charged with a criminal offence. The rights under s 42(2) protect a person who has been arrested or detained.

The rights under s 37(4) seem to be more substantive than those under s 42(2). Taking this line of argument, the Supreme Court judgment in *Reference No 1 of 1977* [1977] PNGLR 362, becomes clearer. In this case the fundamental issue was whether evidence obtained in breach of s 42(2) rendered that evidence inadmissible. The Supreme Court ruled that the breach of a right under s 42(2) alone would not render evidence inadmissible. The court further held that, because the power of the National Court under s 57 is readily available, an aggrieved party can rely on that provision to request the court to use its discretion to exclude the evidence obtained in violation of s 42(2). In the words of Ellis J in *The State v Anis* [1990] PNGLR 239, the Supreme Court "established the 'discretionary rejection' as the appropriate test for excluding evidence obtained in breach of s 42(2)". In *SCR No 5 of 1987; The State v Songke Mai and Gai Avi* [1988] PNGLR 56, the court had to distinguish between the words "arrest" and "detained"

---

29 This last exception is provided for under s 42(1)(h), which was amended by *Constitutional Amendment No 11 of 1991*. The amendment expanded the scope of the restriction to include vagrants and minors.

under s 42(2). The court ruled that the word "arrest" means deprivation of personal liberty within the scope of the *Arrest Act* (Ch 339), while "detained" means the deprivation of personal liberty short of arrest. It was held in this case that the right to communicate immediately with counsel or a family member applies only to a person who has been arrested and not a person who has been merely detained. This decision and others were reviewed by Ellis J in *The State v Anis* [1990] PNGLR 239, where he concluded that the right to communicate with counsel or a family member must be adequately exercised by the defendant.[30] Thus, where a record of interview is being conducted and the defendant is asked whether he or she wants to see counsel or a family member and the answer is affirmative, the record of interview should be suspended. Failure to suspend the record of interview will render the evidence inadmissible.

In contrast, a breach of a right under s 37(4) will promptly render an evidence inadmissible: see *Davinga v The State* [1995] PNGLR 263 and *Bishop v Bishop Bros Engineering* [1988-89] PNGLR 533 (at 541). The "discretionary rejection" rule does not apply under this provision.

The other right of a person arrested or detained under s 42 is the right to be brought before a court of law without delay. This right is expressed by s 42(3) and entails a three-step process:

(i) a person is arrested or detained either on the orders of the court or on reasonable suspicion of committing or has committed an offence;

(ii) the person arrested or detained must be charged; and

(iii) the person who is charged must be brought before a court of law without delay.

The criteria has been held, in *The State v Win Kwainfelin* [1986] PNGLR 106, to include the right of the accused to be interviewed within a reasonable time after being arrested and charged. In the above case the court found that the three steps were followed by the police and that they interviewed the accused after 28 days in custody. The court applied the *Judges Rules* in conjunction with s 42(3) and held that the record of interview obtained 28 days after the accused was arrested, detained, charged and brought before the court was unconstitutional and thus inadmissible. Similar decisions were reached by the National Court in *The State v Turik* [1986] PNGLR 138 and *The State v Mana Turi* [1986] PNGLR 221.[31] In the latter case, the court correctly held that s 42 should be considered in light of the other rights provisions, especially s 37, and where the court finds a breach, it should exclude the evidence.

The *only exception* to the strict requirements of s 42(3) is set out under s 42(4). This provision provides that a person can be detained longer than is necessary if there are difficulties relating to transportation. This provision may have been inserted recognising the insufficient, or even lack of, infrastructure development in the country at that time. The framers of the *Constitution* were aware that it would be

---

30 His Honour made a thorough review of the previous decisions of the courts on the issue of the "record of interview", which was, in this case, conducted in breach of s 42(2). It would be helpful for a reader who is dealing with this issue to read this case. See *The State v Kwambol* (unreported, N 91, 1977); *The State v Joseph Maino* [1977] PNGLR 216; *Schliebs v Singh* [1981] PNGLR 364; *The State v Silih Sawi* [1983] PNGLR 234; *The State v Karara Peter* (unreported, N 488, 1983); *The State v Konts Kot* (unreported, N 623, 1987); *The State v Paro Wampa* [1987] PNGLR 120; *The State v John Koga Ivoro* (unreported, N 772, 1989).

31 The three cases cited here also establish that the *Judges Rules* form part of the law of PNG, as they are part of the underlying law. However, McDermott AJ correctly points out in *The State v Mana Turi* [1986] PNGLR 221 that the *Judges Rules* should not be the paramount consideration in these types of cases, as ss 37 and 42 of the *Constitution* now take precedence over the *Judges Rules*.

quite difficult to bring an accused person immediately before the court if, say, the accused person was from a very remote part of the country.

Interestingly, section 42(5) imposes a duty on the National Court to inquire into allegations of unlawful detention of accused persons. This provision empowers the National Court to release a detainee if it finds that the detainee is being held unlawfully. Thus, in *Maris v Nalik Village Court* [1994] PNGLR 314, it was held by Doherty J that, where a person was held in prison in breach of the *Village Courts Act* 1989, the National Court had the power under s 42(5) to discharge him. In addition, if the detainee is awaiting trial and the length of time is long, the judge can order the release of the detainee either unconditionally or conditionally. This right does not extend to foreigners who have been detained for breaching the *Migration Act* 1963. This was the explicit ruling in *Re Jacob Hendrich Prai* [1979] PNGLR 42 and *Perryman v The Minister for Foreign Affairs and Trade* [1982] PNGLR 339.

Section 42(6) vests the right of an accused to bail at all times. This provision must be read in conjunction with the *Bail Act* (Ch 340), especially s 9 of the Act. The combined effect of s 42(6) and s 9 of the Act is that bail is to be granted generally. The Supreme Court ruled in *Re Fred Keating* [1983] PNGLR 133 that the grant or refusal of bail pursuant to s 9 of the Act is *discretionary* in all cases other than to those who have been arrested, detained and charged for treason or wilful murder. Section 9(1) of the *Bail Act*, however, enumerates a number of factors that can be used by the courts to refuse bail.[32] These factors range from serious assaults, threats with violence, use of dangerous weapons and protection of the accused to possible interference with witnesses. In *Re Keating*, Kidu CJ considered ss 42(6) and 9(1) and concluded that there are two categories of bail applications – Category A and Category B. According to his Honour, Category A applicants are those who have been charged with wilful murder and treason and Category B applicants are those who are charged with other offences. His Honour (at 135) said that Category A applications can only be dealt with by the National and Supreme Courts, while Category B applications can be dealt with either by the Police, Local Courts or the District Courts.[33]

The Supreme Court also ruled that the matters enumerated under s 9(1) are not exhaustive. Other relevant and substantive factors may be taken into account by the court in deciding whether or not to refuse bail. *Re Keating* is the leading authority on bail. It has been affirmed and applied in the various cases dealing with bail.[34]

Freedom from forced labour: s 43

Section 43 protects persons from forced labour. Subsection (2) specifies certain forms of labour which are exempted from the prohibition. These include labour which is required, under law,[35] in disciplined forces and in military service. This section, which must be read with s 253 of the *Constitution*, outlaws slavery in PNG.

32 For those who are interested in reading other cases on this area of the law, see *Re Herman Kagl Diawo* [1980] PNGLR 148, *Ipara Natesa Atingi v Temi Joshiah* [1982] PNGLR 286; *The State v Paul* [1986] PNGLR 97.

33 The Chief Justice also referred to the repealed Local Courts.

34 See also the Supreme Court decision in *The State v Tohian* [1990] PNGLR 173. Generally, s 42 has been specifically raised and applied in a number of cases for the benefit of the defendant. Some of these cases include *The State v Joseph Maino* [1977] PNGLR 216; *The State v Wik Kor* [1983] PNGLR 24 and *Re Internal Security Act* [1994] PNGLR 341.

35 Examples of such labour are the imposition of hard labour by the court, or communal labour required under local-level government law.

The freedom provided by this provision is a *qualified right* and therefore, can be restricted by another law. This was expressed by the Supreme Court in *Application by Imoning Et Al; Finschhafen Open Electorate* [1992] PNGLR 119 (at 121). In *SCR No 1 of 1992* [1992] PNGLR 73, the Supreme Court held that a law that restricts this freedom and other qualified rights must be considered under s 38 of the *Constitution*. A law that restricts the freedom under s 43 and does not meet the special procedural requirements of s 38 will be declared null and void.

Freedom from arbitrary search and entry: s 44

Freedom from arbitrary search and entry is provided for in s 44 of the *Constitution*. The expression of this prohibition is in the positive sense. The provision states that this freedom can be regulated by a law, but such a law to restrict or regulate this freedom must set out in precise terms the nature of the search and entry. In *Application by Chai Chen Sheng* [1993] PNGLR 105, the court ruled that where a government official goes beyond what is specified in the law, the evidence that is obtained outside of the parameters of that law will be contrary to s 44 and inadmissible.

The specific law that restricts the freedom under s 44 is the *Search Act*. There are, however, other laws which empower appropriate officials to enter and search specific properties which are relevant to their work.[36]

The *Search Act* spells out the criteria for obtaining the necessary approvals from the District Court to enter and search premises or a person. It was held in *John Alex v Martin Golu* [1983] PNGLR 117 that where evidence is obtained by police in breach of s 44 and the *Search Act*, that evidence will be inadmissible. In this case the police raided the defendant's premises and obtained a blue bag containing cannabis. The defendant was charged for being in possession of a dangerous drug under the *Dangerous Drugs Act* (Ch 226). At the trial in the District Court it was revealed that the police obtained a blue bag from the defendant's premises without any search warrant under the *Search Act*. The magistrate considered the matter and accepted the blue bag as evidence. The defendant applied to the National Court for enforcement of his right under s 57 of the *Constitution*. In considering the application, Kapi DCJ, held that although s 44 may be unfair to the police in their investigations of crime, if any evidence was obtained in breach of s 44 or the *Search Act*, that evidence must be inadmissible.

The same views were expressed by Pratt J in *The State v Evertius and Kundi* [1985] PNGLR 109. The two defendants were charged with the offence of attempted robbery. While in police custody they were interrogated and their evidence was reduced to writing in the record of interview. They then applied to the court to reject Evertius' record of interview on the basis that they were placed in custody after the police entered Evertius' premises without a valid search warrant. Pratt J, following the principles set out in *John Alex v Martin Golu*, rejected the record of interview. In *Application by Chai Chen Sheng*, the National Court was asked by the captains of two foreign vessels, charged with illegal fishing, to reject evidence obtained from their ships in breach of s 44. The relevant evidence was contained in documents obtained by officers from the Fisheries Department. The Department relied on s 9 of the *Fisheries Act*, which essentially states that an officer can board or enter a boat and search for fish and fishing equipment if that officer has reason to believe that the boat is in breach of the Act. Doherty J, after reviewing the relevant authorities, concluded that s 9 of the Act authorised the

36 For example, the former *Fisheries Act* (Ch 214) and the *Customs Act*.

Fisheries officer to enter or board a boat and search *only for fish and fishing equipment*. The right to enter and search *did not extend to obtaining documents* from the boat (at 110).

An application to enforce the right under s 44 will be enforced by the courts. Where the defendant seeks compensation for breach of s 44, the court will place monetary value on the breach, as shown in *Koimo v PNG* [1995] PNGLR 535 (at 539); *Kuriti v PNG* [1994] PNGLR 262; *Salamon v PNG* [1994] PNGLR 265 and *Apa v PNG* [1995] PNGLR 43. All these cases involve illegal raids on villages and destruction of properties by police in the Highlands of PNG.

Freedom of conscience, thought and religion: s 45

Freedom of conscience, thought and religion is provided for in s 45. This freedom has received less prominence since independence, the reason being that this freedom has been exercised freely with little or no restriction.[37] The main recurring issue relating to this freedom is the freedom of religion. This issue continues to be raised by Papua New Guineans who are predominantly Christians and who question the existence of other religions in the country. Many Papua New Guineans doubt their *Constitution*, which allows the practice of other religions in the country.[38]

It is suggested that freedom of religion is an ongoing issue because of the misunderstanding by the people of the nexus between s 45 and the Preamble to the *Constitution* which purports to declare that "Papua New Guinea is a Christian country". Amet CJ puts this in another way:

> "Many Christians today focus much energy and attention on the conflicts, dissections and emotional reactions between members of different denominations of the Christian faith and between different religions including Christianity. And unfortunately this causes much imbalance in our perspective."[39]

The Chief Justice points out that the nexus between the Preamble and s 45 of the *Constitution* is that:

> "The Constitution recognises a universal fact that there are other religions in the world other than Christianity. We are part of the world community of nations and given the fact that we have chosen to adopt democratic form of constitutional government, we must also respect the rights of other people in their beliefs."[40]

Freedom of expression: s 46

Freedom of expression is spelt out by s 46 of the *Constitution*. Section 46(1) states that every person has the right to the freedom of expression and publication. This right extends not only to living persons, but also to corporations.[41] According to s 46(2), freedom of expression and publication includes:

---

37 In *Re Internal Security Act* [1994] PNGLR 341, the Supreme Court downplayed the opportunity to make a firm determination on this section. Kapi DCJ did attempt to make reference to it at 354, but fell short of making any substantive comments on it.

38 Amet, "A Legal Perspective on Religious Freedom in PNG" in Arets (ed), *Religious Freedom in Papua New Guinea* (PNG Council of Churches, Port Moresby, 1994), p 67.

39 Ibid, p 68.

40 Ibid, p 67.

41 *The State v NTN Pty Ltd* [1992] PNGLR 1 at 5.

- freedom to hold opinions, to receive ideas and information and to communicate ideas and information, whether to the public generally to a person or class of persons; and
- freedom of the press and other mass communication media.

The exceptions to the exercise of this freedom are provided by s 46(1). In the words of Barnett J in *The State v NTN Pty Ltd* [1992] PNGLR 1, "[s]ection 46 creates a qualified right which can be regulated or restricted by a law of the type referred to in s 46(1)(a), (b) and (c)" (at 13). The exceptions include the restrictions on public office-holders and non-citizens. These two categories of people are restricted from expressing their personal views publicly. In the first category, the case in point is the infamous "Rooney Affair",[42] which resulted in the jailing of Ms Rooney, who was the Minister for Justice in 1979. In *Public Prosecutor v Nahau Rooney (No 2)* [1979] PNGLR 448, the Supreme Court established that Ms Rooney, as Justice Minister, circulated a series of letters showing her disapproval of the manner in which the judiciary was handling the *Premdas Case*.[43] The correspondence was subsequently published in a daily newspaper. The Supreme Court held that s 46 could not protect Ms Rooney and found her guilty on charges of contempt of court and sentenced her to eight months imprisonment.

The principal case on s 46 is *The State v NTN Pty Ltd* [1992] PNGLR 1. This case involved the issue of a licence by the state to the respondent for the use of electromagnetic spectrum (airwaves) under the *Radiocommunications Act* (Ch 152). The licence was issued to the respondent in 1985 after both parties agreed to the establishment of a commercial television station in PNG. There was a change of government in 1986 and the new government enacted the *Radiocommunications (Television) Regulation* 1986, which effectively prohibited television broadcasting until 31 January 1988. This new law outlawed the activities of the respondent. The respondent then sought declarations from the National Court to declare the *Radiocommunications (Television) Regulations Act* 1986 null and void. On the day on which the National Court declared that the Act was *ultra vires* the parent legislation, the Parliament passed the *Television (Prohibition and Control) Act* 1986, which prohibited television broadcasts until 31 January 1988. The respondent then sought declarations in the Supreme Court that the *Television (Prohibition and Control) Act* 1986 was inconsistent with the terms of ss 46 and 38 of the *Constitution*.

The Supreme Court had to consider the validity of the Act. Barnett J said that "[a]s far as the *Television (Prohibition and Control) Act* 1986 is concerned, to be valid in the circumstances it was enacted it must comply with s 38 of the *Constitution*" (at 13). Kapi DCJ and Barnett J[44] held that the *Television (Prohibition and Control) Act* 1986 was a law that was *not* reasonably justifiable in a democratic society.[45] The court agreed on three major points:

(i) the right to the freedom under s 46 can be restricted or regulated by a law;
(ii) "regulate or restricted" can mean temporary prohibition; and
(iii) the law that restricts s 46 must specify which of the purposes under s 38(1)(a) it seeks to achieve.

42 See the background of the case in *Premdas v Independent State of PNG* [1979] PNGLR 329 and *Re Rooney (No 1)* [1979] PNGLR 403.
43 *Premdas v Independent State of PNG* [1979] PNGLR 329.
44 Kidu CJ, Amet J and Woods J unanimously agreed.
45 See Chalmers, "Human Rights and What is Reasonably Justifiable in A Democratic Society" (1975) 3 MLJ 92.

On these three counts, the court ruled that the *Television (Prohibition and Control) Act* 1986 failed on the third point and thus was invalid and of no effect.

There are other laws in place which regulate this freedom. Examples include the *Censorship Act*, the *Defamation Act* and the *Organic Law on National and Local-level Elections* 1996. Various provisions of these laws impact on the right to freedom of expression. For instance, under s 102 of the former *Organic Law on National Elections*, it was an offence for a candidate to unduly influence voters. Thus, in *In re Menyama Open Parliamentary Election* [1977] PNGLR 298, the court held that where the candidate spoke at a party, and the words contained threats, amounted to undue influence and, therefore, his election as a Member of Parliament was void.

The relationship between the *Defamation Act* and s 46 has been considered by the courts in a number of cases. In *Cory v Blyth (No 1)* [1976] PNGLR 274, the plaintiff sued the defendant for slander. The defendant raised the defence that he had the right to the freedom of expression provided by s 46 and, therefore, his statements against the plaintiff were protected. The court held that the defendant could not hide behind s 46 and issue defamatory statements against the plaintiff. Where the publication of material which is defamatory in nature, but is the truth, is important for public consumption, an application to restrain its publication will not succeed because of the freedom expressed under s 46.[46]

Where an act or omission will infringe the right to freedom of expression, such as where staff and students are prevented from going to lectures by striking students, the court will seek to enforce that right under s 46, as was the case in *University of PNG v Ume More* [1985] PNGLR 48. The courts will not, however, enforce the right to freedom of expression if that freedom is used as a vehicle to destabilise the country: *Re Internal Security Act* [1994] PNGLR 341 (at 348).

Freedom of assembly and association: s 47

Papua New Guineans are free to assemble and join any association without restriction under the *Constitution*. Section 47 guarantees this freedom. Like its counterparts, this freedom can also be restricted or regulated by a law. The restrictions that may be imposed under this provision are those which apply to non-citizens, public officials and associations.

Some of the laws that have restricted the right to the freedom of assembly and association are the:

- *Internal Security Act* 1993;
- *Industrial Organisations Act* (Ch 173);
- *Associations Incorporation Act* (Ch 142);
- *Companies Act* 1996;
- *Lawyers Act* 1986; and
- *District Courts Act* (Ch 40).

The Supreme Court has ruled in *Re Internal Security Act* [1994] PNGLR 341 (at 348) that this freedom can be restricted under the *Internal Security Act* if the assembly and association of citizens will be a threat to the security of the nation. The Supreme Court has also ruled in *Application by Karingu* [1988-89] PNGLR 276 that for a person to practise as a lawyer, he or she must comply with the requirements of the *Lawyers Act* 1986. The *Lawyers Act* required that a person must be a member

46 *Hetura Paz Development Co Pty Ltd v Niugini Nius Pty Ltd* [1982] PNGLR 250.

of the Papua New Guinea Law Society before he or she is able to practise law. In this case, the Supreme Court held that when the word "shall" under the Act was substituted with the word "may", the Act was not in violation of s 47 as membership to the Law Society would be optional and not compulsory.

Being a member of an association does not entail the forfeiture of individual rights contained in the *Constitution*. In *National Airline Employees' Association v Air Niugini (No 2)* [1992] PNGLR 291, Brown J made it clear that, although the association could make an application to enforce the rights of its members, individual members still had the option to pursue the matter on their own behalf. His Honour advised that it was more appropriate if an individual member applied to enforce his or her rights because then the orders sought, if granted, would be more relevant and appropriate to the individual than if he or she was in an association (at 292).

Freedom of employment: s 48

The right to freedom of employment is guaranteed by s 48. The right to employment does not mean that every Papua New Guinean *must be employed* in the literal sense. The main tenet of this provision is "required qualification". The *Constitution* is silent on this issue. In *Application by Karingu* [1988-89] PNGLR 276, Kapi DCJ suggested that "required qualification" relates to "qualities and the conditions which a person must meet in order to practise a vocation or profession". In other words, this tenet refers to requirements, such as educational qualification, skills and training, membership and, to some extent, age and, in extreme cases, sex (at 289).

This provision first came before the court in *Application by Karingu*. In this case, Karingu, who was a practising lawyer, refused to pay the relevant fees to the PNG Law Society created under the *Lawyers Act* 1986. The Act stipulated that for a lawyer to practise law in PNG he or she had to be registered with the PNG Law Society. In his submissions Karingu argued that s 9 of the *Lawyers Act*, which provided for the mechanism, was contrary to s 48 and was, therefore, null and void. The Supreme Court, by a majority of 4:1, rejected the proposition that the Act infringed the right of the applicant to employment. The court ruled that s 48 does not relate to practice of employment but *to choice* of employment. The right to employment can be restricted but it cannot be prohibited. Thus, where the *Public Services (Management) Act* 1986[47] stipulated that a public servant over the age of 60 years cannot be re-employed into the public service, such a provision was not in conflict with s 48. This was clarified by the Supreme Court in *NEC v PEA* [1993] PNGLR 264 (at 270).

Right to privacy: s 49

The right to privacy must be read together with the right to the freedom from arbitrary search and entry. The Supreme Court has maintained that the right to privacy is a special right of a person and it will not hesitate to come to the aid of any person whose right to privacy has been violated through unlawful means. It has ruled that the records of patients are private and should not be disclosed to other people: *SCR No 2 of 1984; Re Medical Privilege* [1985] PNGLR 247. The court has also ruled that taking the photo of a voter for election purposes is a violation of his or her right to privacy: *SCR No 5 of 1992* [1992] PNGLR 114 (at 115).

---

47 This legislation has now been repealed and replaced by the *Public Services (Management) Act* 1995.

The right to privacy cannot be restricted by an Emergency Regulation during a state of emergency: *Re Internal Security Act* [1994] PNGLR 341 (at 354). An Emergency Act can, however, restrict this right. In *Koimo v PNG* [1995] PNGLR 535 (at 539), the court ruled that even during a police raid, the right to privacy must be respected by the police. The raid does not give police a licence to violate the rights of citizens and non-citizens.

9.6 QUALIFIED RIGHTS OF CITIZENS

The rights under ss 50-56 are qualified rights of citizens. Only a citizen is entitled to exercise these rights and also seek their enforcement where there is a breach.

Right to vote and stand for public office: s 50

This right must be read together with the *Organic Law on the National and Local-level Government Elections* (OLNLLGE) 1996,[48] the *Organic Law on the Integrity of Political Parties* (OLIPP) and ss 101 and 103 of the *Constitution*. The former Organic Law regulates the manner in which elections are conducted, results of elections and the procedure for disputing the elections. The latter Organic Law regulates the actions of elected members and also, to some extent, how a person can became an elected Member of Parliament (that is, through the political party system). The right to vote and stand for public office applies to all elective public offices.[49]

The right to stand for and hold public office is a *qualified right* and therefore it can be restricted by Parliament through legislation. Parliament has invoked this power on several occasions. In 1981 the Parliament, in anticipation of the 1982 National Elections, amended the *Organic Law on National Elections* (OLNE) by increasing the nomination fee from K100 to K1,000. The Ombudsman Commission challenged the increase in *Re Organic on National Elections* [1982] PNGLR 289, arguing successfully that the increase in the fees would deter many Papua New Guineans from standing for public office and, consequently, their rights under s 50 would be violated. The Supreme Court agreed with the Ombudsman Commission and struck down the amendments. In 1991, the Parliament again increased the nomination fee from K100 to K1,000. Again the Ombudsman Commission approached the Supreme Court in *SCR No 1 of 1992* [1992] PNGLR 73 (at 76) and raised the same arguments which had been raised a decade earlier. This time the Supreme Court ruled that the increase in nomination fee from K100 to K1,000 was not an infringement of s 50.

The amendment which was passed in 1991 also required that every voter should be identified by an identification card. A person without an identification card would not be eligible to vote. The Ombudsman Commission also challenged this amendment in *SCR No 5 of 1992* [1992] PNGLR 114. The Ombudsman Commission argued that to compel the voter to have his or her photo taken for voting purposes was a violation of his or her right to privacy and also that the procedure for identification for voting purposes was a prohibition of the right to vote and, therefore, was inconsistent with s 50. In this case the Supreme Court agreed with the Ombudsman Commission. The Supreme Court also held that the requirement of identification for voting purposes was a violation of s 50(1)(d) because it did not give the electors a reasonable opportunity to vote in the elections.

---

48 This Organic Law repealed the *Organic Law on National Elections* in 1996.
49 The elections also include provincial elections: see *Yarekei v Electoral Commission* [1992] PNGLR 223.

This right usually becomes topical either before, during or after an election. In cases before an election, this provision has been raised by candidates to prevent their opponents from contesting an election. This approach was taken in *Kevin Masive v Iambakey Okuk* [1985] PNGLR 105. On appeal, in *SCR No 2 of 1985; Kevin Masive v Iambakey Okuk* [1985] PNGLR 263, the Supreme Court laid down the rule that the person who opposes the nomination of a candidate must himself or herself be qualified to stand for election in that electorate. In *Dihm v Returning Officer* [1992] PNGLR 377, the court held that where an eligible candidate was prevented from standing for elections in his electorate due to the negligence of the electoral officials, the elections for his or her electorate could be delayed after all the formalities had been complied with by the aggrieved candidate.

The death of a candidate has also been raised as a ground to prevent the elections from proceeding: *Application by Imoning Et Al; Finschhafen Open Electorate* [1992] PNGLR 119 (at 120). However, in *SCR No 8 of 1992; Application by Mionzing* [1992] PNGLR 122, the Supreme Court ruled that an injunction given in the above circumstances would not stand if the voters had not yet cast their vote. The right to vote had not yet been exercised and thus there would be no breach of s 50 if the election proceeded. The voters could still exercise their right by voting for another person.

Right to freedom of information: s 51

The right to freedom of information is a right that is only available to citizens. Foreigners cannot claim this right. The provision itself is quite restrictive. It has been argued that this provision must be read together with s 46, which provides for freedom of speech. When ss 46 and 51 are read together, it becomes apparent that without information, or inappropriate information or misinformation, a person cannot fully exercise his or her right to freedom of speech if they cannot access relevant information.[50] In *Turama Forest Industries Pty Ltd v Soi & Associates* (unreported, 1996), the court took a simple approach to ss 46 and 51 and ruled that:

> "The evidence clearly shows that the landowners have not been a party to the negotiations between the developer and the State, and therefore, they cannot have access to the document as it was a private contract of a commercial nature and as such was confidential."

This case involved the issue of whether the landowners, through their lawyers, could access the project agreement executed between the state and the foreign logging company for the development of forestry resources within their area. The ruling was a blow to the landowners as they could not ascertain the nature of the agreement, and thus could not establish the type of development that was to take place in their area.

The manner in which information can be accessed is to be provided by legislation. Since 1995, the government has not been able to implement this provision. In 1993 the government introduced the *National Policy on Information and Communication of Papua New Guinea*.[51] This policy embodies a broad range of issues

50 Kwa, "The Imbalance of Information Power between the State and the Resource Owners in the Development of Natural Resources in Papua New Guinea with particular reference to Forestry and Mineral Resources Development Projects" (Paper presented at the 22nd Waigani Seminar, Port Moresby, 27-29 August 1997).

51 Department of Information and Communication, *National Policy on Information and Communication of Papua New Guinea* (Government Printing Office, Port Moresby, 1993).

which are pertinent to PNG. In introducing the policy, the then Minister for Communication, Mr Martin Thompson (MP), said:

> "Information and communication is part and parcel of this whole process of development and needs its own infrastructure. It is the thread which binds a nation and its people together."[52]

Unfortunately, this important thread that binds the nation and people together has not been advanced further, either through law or administrative arrangements. In an attempt to bring the issue back to the forefront and to address the issues which emerged from the *Turama Forest Industries v Soi & Associates* case, in 2000 Transparency International (PNG) Inc (a non-governmental organisation), embarked on an awareness campaign to gauge the support of the community in implementing s 51. The aim of the exercise was to encourage the community to formulate an appropriate legislation to submit to the Parliament for enactment.

Freedom of movement: s 52

Section 52 is guarantees every citizen the right to move freely around the country. This right is also available to people who are members of an organisation. Thus, it has been held in *University of PNG v Ume More* [1985] PNGLR 48 that where striking students prevent other students and staff from attending lectures through blockades, the striking students are interfering with the rights to freedom of movement of the students and staff.

Under s 52, the right to freedom of movement can be restricted in cases of war or emergencies and curfews. These situations and other foreseeable cases are covered by an array of legislation which is aimed at restricting the freedom of movement of people. These include the *Emergency (General Powers) Act* 1994, the *Curfew Act* 1987; the *Peace and Good Order Act* 1991 and the *Internal Security Act* 1993. In a state of emergency, certain powers can be invoked by the Controller of the State of Emergency under the *Emergency (General Powers) Act* to control the people in the locality of the emergency. During a curfew the police can issue certain orders under the auspices of the *Curfew Act* to restrict and control the movement of people in the area declared as the curfew area. The *Peace and Good Order Act* repealed the pre-independence *Public Order Act* and is aimed at preserving peace and good order within the community by controlling public meetings and creating offences for unlawfully being on another person's land.[53]

The *Internal Security Act* is a preventive law which anticipates emerging crises that may threaten the security of PNG. The Act's primary objective is to counter terrorism and internal strife. It gives the government wide-ranging powers to curtail certain rights of citizens, including the right to freedom of movement. The legislation was challenged by the Ombudsman Commission in *Re Internal Security Act* [1994] PNGLR 341 as being unconstitutional. One of the issues raised in that case was that the Act was inconsistent with s 52. The Supreme Court rejected this argument and instead ruled that there was no inconsistency between the law and s 52.

---

52 Kwa, op cit n 50.

53 Fraser, "Twenty Years of the Constitution: Part X of the Constitution - Emergency Powers" (Paper presented at the Twenty Years of the Constitution Conference, Port Moresby, 28-30 March 1996).

Protection from unjust deprivation of property: s 53

The issue of property, especially land, was a very contentious issue before and after independence. The CPC was concerned to protect citizens' rights to property. After considering all the issues, the CPC made its intention known:

> "... we have decided to recommend that the constitutional protection of property interests should be limited to our own citizens. The interests of foreign citizens can be protected in a number of ways by the Government of the day".[54]

Similar views were also expressed by the Commission of Inquiry into Land Matters.[55] Both committees were aware that foreigners were using their economic power to gain access to land which belonged to the people. The need to accord just compensation to foreigners for the expropriation of their property has been settled by *Minister for Lands, Surveys and Environment v Frame* [1980] PNGLR 433.[56]

To maintain a right under s 53, the aggrieved person must show that he or she does, in fact, have title over actual property, not just an assertion of title: *Donigi v Base Resources Ltd* [1992] PNGLR 110. The extent to which s 53 can be relied on to maintain a claim for breach of a right was considered in *PNG Ready Mix Concrete Pty Ltd v Independent State of Papua New Guinea* [1981] PNGLR 396 and approved by the Supreme Court in *SCR No 3 of 1990; Application by Lapan Assembly* (1990) SC384.

In cases where a resident destroys his or own property on land belonging to another person, it does not amount to deprivation under s 53: *Mark v Iki* [1995] PNGLR 116 (at 121). However, where the property of another person is obtained by an agent of the state unlawfully, it is a violation of s 53: *Application of Chai Chen Sheng* [1993] PNGLR 105 (at 106).

Equality of citizens: s 55

This is perhaps one of the most profound declarations by the *Constitution*, given the fact that PNG is predominantly a male-dominated society. This provision declares in unequivocal terms that every citizen, whether male or female, is equal.[57] This provision must be considered together with Goal 2 of the *National Goals and Directive Principles*, which encourages and promotes equality to government goods and services, participation in all forms of government activity and respect for each other. The relationship between Goal 2 and s 55 was accepted and applied by the National Court in *In the Matter of an Application under s 57 of the Constitution: An Application by ICRAF Inc; In Re Miriam Willingal* (1996) N1506.

Government services, such as education and health, must be equally accessed by citizens without differentiation of colour, sex or creed. This was clearly the declaration of the National Court in *Kembol v Wabag Community School* [1995] PNGLR 407. The applicant, who was rejected by the defendant community school because the applicant came from another type of school, sought declarations that

54 CPC, *Final Report*, p 5/1/15.

55 Commission of Inquiry into Land Matters, *Report 1973* (Government Printer, Port Moresby, 1973).

56 This was an appeal from the National Court decision in *Frame v Minister for Lands, Surveys and Environment* [1979] PNGLR 626.

57 See generally *SCR No 5 of 1992* [1992] PNGLR 114; *SCR No 1 of 1992* [1992] PNGLR 73 at 80; *Re Raramu v Yowe Village Court* [1994] PNGLR 486.

the refusal of the school to accept the applicant was a violation of s 55. The court accepted the applicant's arguments and ruled that the school should accept the applicant.

The courts have also expanded the scope of s 55 to cover marital relations and penalties for sexual offences. Thus, in *The State v Robinson* [1992] PNGLR 205 (at 208), the court ruled that even in marital relations both partners are to be treated as equal. The National Court also held in *In the Matter of an Application under s 57 of the Constitution: An Application by ICRAF Inc; In Re Miriam Willingal* (1996) N1506 that where, under custom, a young girl is given away as part of a compensation package against her will, is a violation s 55, and therefore that custom is invalid.

In *The State v Kuengu* [1993] PNGLR 124, the National Court held (at 125) that although the act of sodomy was between males, applying s 55, the principles of rape could be applied against the defendant.

The main difficulty with this provision is its incompatibility with custom in many parts of the country where custom plays a vital role in the sustenance of communities. In communities where custom is strong and there is very little accessibility to the outside world, or where there has been a deterioration in government services, the prevalence of abuse against women and children by males is high. This practical reality is, however, not only confined to rural communities. In towns and cities inequality is quite visible, especially among the affluent Papua New Guineans and their grassroots brothers and sisters.[58]

9.7 QUALIFICATIONS TO RIGHTS

It is the extent of qualifications permitted by the *Constitution* (together with the effectiveness of the actual recognition and enforcement of rights) which in general determines the scope of particular rights. Rights under the *Constitution* may be qualified in three main ways:

- (i) by virtue of exceptions and qualifications contained in the sections of the *Constitution* which create individual rights, most of which can only be given effect by a law, even if this is not explicitly stated;[59]
- (ii) by general qualifications which meet the criteria laid down in s 38 of the *Constitution*; and
- (iii) by an emergency law passed during a state of emergency.

While "fundamental rights" can only be qualified by the first category, most others are open to all three kinds of qualification.

It is not usual to have the first two approaches to qualification used in the same constitution. Reasons for inclusion of each of the first two kinds of qualification can be found in the CPC Report.[60] In that Report the CPC rejected the alternative bare statements of principles which could be qualified by laws open to review by the courts (the usual approach being provision for laws which are "reasonably necessary in a democratic society"). In the debate in the National Constituent Assembly, Mr Ebia Olewale also noted that detailed qualifications would help the

---

58 For instance, it will be easier for a lawyer, wearing his or her black and white attire, to gain access to a government building to see a friend, than it will be for a scruffy old man who is a local-level government member who has just arrived from the village and approaches the government agency for assistance for his people in the same office. The old man will have to go through a number of stringent checks, and will be given a hard time by the secretary.

59 As an example, see *Re s 42, SCR No 5 of 1987; The State v Songke Mai and Gai Avi* [1988] PNGLR 56 at 61, where Kidu CJ discussed the application of s 42.

60 The reasons for including qualifications within provisions creating particular rights can be found in CPC, *Final Report*, Ch 5, p 5/1/7, paras 31-36.

courts and ensure that they would not become law-makers, as under the United States *Constitution*.[61] The danger of rights being thereby frozen so as not to reflect changing values was to be dealt with by the provisions of s 33. Section 33 provides room for the creation of further rights and freedoms that may become available to the people. These new rights and freedoms can be created under an Act of the Parliament or an Organic Law. The reasons for including a variation of the more common qualifying formula can be found in the CPC Final Report.[62] However, there is no discussion in the Report of the possible implications of having both kinds of qualifications.

The general qualifications permitted under s 38 apply only to some of the rights (not even to all of the qualified rights – see, for example, ss 42 and 50). It must be read in conjunction with s 39.

Where s 38 does not apply, its requirements are of central importance. It provides important procedural steps which must be met by a law qualifying rights in accordance with s 38.[63] As to cases defining the requirements, see *SCR No 1 of 1986 Re Vagrancy Act* [1988] PNGLR 1; *The State v NTN Pty Ltd* [1992] PNGLR 1 and *SCR No 5 of 1992* [1992] PNGLR 114. Section 39 provides the definition of a key phrase used in s 38. The key phrase, "reasonably justifiable a democratic society having a proper regard for the rights and dignity of mankind" is clarified under s 39.[64]

9.8 ENFORCEMENT OF RIGHTS

Sections 57 and 58 of the *Constitution* provide for the enforcement of rights and compensation for breach of those rights. A range of people can initiate enforcement actions, and potential remedial action has few limits. Thus, in *In the Matter of an Application under s 57 of the Constitution: An Application by ICRAF Inc; In Re Miriam Willingal* (1996) N1506, where a young girl was given away as part of a compensation package to another tribe, a non-government organisation (ICRAF) was given standing to sue on behalf of the young woman to enforce her rights under ss 32 and 55.

The power to enforce rights is vested in the National Court. Generally the National Court has been very vigilant in fulfilling its constitutional mandate in enforcing the rights of citizens and foreigners. Many of the cases under this heading have already been considered above.[65] Where the applicants have been able to prove violation of their rights, the courts have readily invoked their power under s 58 and awarded compensation to the victims. Examples of these cases include: *The State v Wik Kor* [1983] PNGLR 24; *Wambun v The State* [1994] PNGLR 488 (at 490); *Apa v PNG* [1995] PNGLR 43 (at 49); *Koimo v PNG* [1995] PNGLR 535 (at 539). In other cases, the injuring parties have been ordered by the court to rectify the anomalies. Examples include: *John Alex v Martin Golu* [1983] PNGLR 117; *Dihm v*

---

61 National Constituent Assembly Debates, *Hansard* 1974, p 178.

62 CPC, *Final Report*, p 5/1/6.

63 See *Cory v Blyth (No 1)* [1976] PNGLR 274; *Re Jacob Hendrich Prai* [1979] PNGLR 42; *SCR No 8 of 1992; Application by Mionzing* [1992] PNGLR 122 at 130; *Re Internal Security Act* [1994] PNGLR 341 at 352; *Kaseng v Namaliu* [1995] PNGLR 481 at 496; *Koimo v PNG* [1995] PNGLR 535 at 545.

64 See *The State v NTN Pty Ltd* [1992] PNGLR 1 at 18; *SCR No 8 of 1992; Application by Mionzing* [1992] PNGLR 122 at 130; *Haivetta v Wingti (No 3)* [1994] PNGLR 197 at 221. For a discussion on s 40, see *Re Internal Security Act* [1994] PNGLR 341 at 352 and 358. See also Chalmers, op cit n 45.

65 Other cases include *The State v John Rupet Kaputin (No 1)* [1979] PNGLR 532; *Henao Batari v Employers Federation of Papua New Guinea* [1979] PNGLR 92; *Komidese v Commissioner for Correctional Services* [1985] PNGLR 212; *Lowa v Akipe* [1992] PNGLR 399 at 419; *Wambun v The State* [1994] PNGLR 488 at 490; *Re Heni Pauta and Kenneth Susuve* [1982] PNGLR 7; *Keke v PNG Color Laboratories Pty Ltd* [1992] PNGLR 265 at 269.

Returning Officer [1992] PNGLR 377; *In Re Organic Law on National Elections* [1982] PNGLR 289 and *SCR No 8 of 1992; Application by Mionzing* [1992] PNGLR 122.

9.9 RIGHTS IN A STATE OF EMERGENCY

The provisions as to states of emergency set out in ss 226-246 of the *Constitution* provide for one of the major ways in which rights can be altered. Once an emergency is declared, Acts of Parliament called *Emergency Laws*, and laws passed by the NEC if Parliament is not sitting (*Emergency Regulations*), can alter or restrict various rights. An *Emergency Law* can restrict more rights than an *Emergency Regulation.*[66] In general, these laws cannot restrict the fundamental rights (ss 35-37) except that an Act of Parliament providing for internment under ss 244-245 can limit the right to protection of the law under s 37. The limits permitted under s 233 are subject to the general requirements of ss 43(2) and 40. This means the courts have to assess two things:

(i) Is the restriction necessary to deal with the emergency and matters arising from it?

(ii) Is the restriction necessary to deal with the emergency than is reasonably justifiable?

Where the answers are in the affirmative, the restriction will prevail.

9.10 SOCIAL AND ECONOMIC RIGHTS

The rights in ss 35-56 of the *Constitution* are largely parallel to those provided for in the Universal Declaration of Human Rights and the International Covenant on Civil and Political Rights. Rights of a kind envisaged by the International Covenant on Social and Economic Rights have to a large extent been left unenforceable in the shape of the National Goals and Directive Principles.[67] The provision of s 63 on enforcement of the Basic Social Obligations follows closely the rights provisions in their place in the constitutional framework, reflecting the concern of the CPC that the rights of citizens be balanced by their duties.[68]

The reason that the social and economic rights provisions are summarised in the Preamble and appear in the debates of the National Constituent Assembly is because the rights as set out in the body of the *Constitution* contained too much detail for the ordinary person to understand.

9.11 CONCLUSION

The notion of individual human rights has to some degree emerged out of European culture and history. The European notion of rights is seen by some as alien to many cultures. However, there is relatively little controversy about the general concept of there being basic rights which are protected. The main debate has been about the content of the rights. Some would argue the emphasis should be more on the rights of groups and communities, rather than on the rights of individuals.

In a similar vein it has often been argued that the "developed" western countries over-emphasise the civil and political rights of individuals. In the period of the

---

66 *Constitution*, s 233(3) and (4).
67 CPC, *Final Report*, Ch 5, pp 5/1/1-5/1/4.
68 The Basic Social Obligations are set out in the Preamble to the *Constitution*.

1960s to the 1980s it was often argued that the real need of less developed countries was for the state to organise the economic and social life of a country, in large part to redress social and economic injustices. Those advancing such views tended to emphasise the social and economic rights. It was to a large extent the debate between socialist and western liberal states which resulted in the 1966 UN Covenants being separate documents. Only the covenant on civil and political rights was to be immediately enforceable, while that on economic and social rights set broad goals only. There is an important parallel here between the enforceable human rights provisions of a constitution such as PNG's and the essentially unenforceable state social and economic goals which are set out in the Preamble.

Chapter 10

CONSTITUTIONAL OFFICES

10.1 INTRODUCTION

Throughout the world there is a growing trend in the increasing power of the people to control government. Experience has shown that those in power tend to abuse it, "whether through use of public office, to accumulate personal wealth or through victimisation of opponents"[1] or through other means. For this reason, the accountability of government is usually a constitutional issue.

In Papua New Guinea (PNG) the Constitutional Planning Committee (CPC) considered the accountability of government in two senses. In the first sense, the CPC thought that accountability of government could be achieved through the fundamental concept that serves as the cornerstone for most democratic constitutions, namely the *separation of powers* and the *entrenchment of human rights*. The philosophy of the concept of separation of powers is that by dividing power between several different bodies, each will check the excesses of the others.[2] The concept is set out clearly in s 99 of the *Constitution*. It is now accepted that even though these bodies are required to function separately, they are nonetheless dependent on each other.[3]

In the second sense, the CPC envisaged that the accountability of government could be further strengthened by the creation of *independent institutions* that would operate outside the normal structures of government. These independent institutions would act as the "watch dogs" over the activities of government.

The CPC was more familiar with the concept of accountability in the first, rather than the second, sense. This attitude is clearly reflected in the prominence it gave to the separation of powers doctrine and human rights in its report. The position of independent institutions, also known as *constitutional offices*, was included in the second last chapter of the CPC's report. The manner in which the report describes the composition, roles and functions of these offices suggests that the CPC was not fully aware of the nature of these offices.

The CPC's lack of appreciation of the nature of constitutional offices continues to beset the people and leaders even today. This may be attributed to the fact that, apart from the Ombudsman Commission, most constitutional offices and the office-holders have a low profile. Their work is less familiar to the public than the work of the Parliament, the executive and the judiciary. For instance, in an outburst in Parliament on 11 March 1993, David Unagi,[4] a former national parliamentarian, said that:

---

1 Regan, *Accountability of Government – Protection of the Independence of Constitutional Office Holders, the Ombudsman Commission and the Leadership Code in the Papua New Guinea Constitution* (Unpublished paper written for the Fiji Constitutional Commission, 1996), p 1.

2 Alder, *Constitutional and Administrative Law* (Macmillan, London, 1993). See also Vile, *Constitutionalism and the Separation of Powers* (Clarendon Press, Oxford, 1967).

3 *Christopher Haiveta v Paias Wingti* (1994) N1118.

4 Mr Unagi was the former Member of Parliament for Port Moresby North East Electorate and the founding leader of the Peoples United Party and the former Lord Mayor of Port Moresby City.

> "The Bi-partisan Committee must review the amendment to the *Constitution* and make sure a parliamentary committee, consisting of both sides of Parliament is set up to be supervisors of all constitutional office-holders in this country. Right now, do these officers report to themselves?"

The position of constitutional offices in the *Constitution* is quite unique. They are neither state organisations nor above the *Constitution*. They are also independent of the government and not subject to control or direction by any person or authority. The main controversy has been about misgivings of some elements within the country about the "independence" of the constitutional offices. The Chan Government considered the issue very seriously in 1995, when the Constitutional Review Commission was asked to review the operations of constitutional offices and recommend proposals to ensure the accountability of these offices.

This chapter identifies the constitutional offices as created by the *Constitution*, their powers, functions and accountability.

10.2 CONSTITUTIONAL OFFICES AS DEFINED BY THE CONSTITUTION

In its efforts to formulate a constitution for an independent PNG, the CPC considered the creation of independent institutions to watch over the activities of government. The CPC was mindful that politicians and bureaucrats, who are supposed to serve the people, may tend to corruption or abuse of power. Politicians may also mismanage public resources and abuse the rights of the people.[5] Politicians and bureaucrats should, therefore, be held accountable. As Regan put it amicably:

> "[A]ccountability of politicians and bureaucrats is sought by various constitutional norms such as codes of conduct for leaders, ombudsman institutions, investigative parliamentary committees and so on".[6]

The CPC believed that one of the most effective ways of ensuring government accountability was to create constitutional offices whose principal function is to supervise the activities of the government. These offices were also to provide checks and balances on each other. Thus, the CPC recommended the creation of these offices in the second last chapter (Chapter 14: "General – Narrative") of its report.[7]

Chapter 14 of the CPC's report does not create "constitutional offices". It only talks about "constitutional office-holders". The CPC explained that "the Committee has recommended earlier in this report the establishment of a number of offices which we believe should be free from outside direction and control".[8] A review of the CPC's report reveals that it recommended the creation of 19 constitutional offices.

"Constitutional offices"[9] have been defined as "any office or institution established or provided for by this *Constitution*, other than the office of the Head of State or of a Minister, or the National Executive Council".[10] This definition is

5 Corruption and abuse of power is universal. See Clarke, *Corruption, Causes, Consequences and Control* (Frances Pinter, London, 1983). This publication contains studies on corruption in the United Kingdom, the Netherlands, Italy, Latin America and Africa.

6 Regan, *Limiting State Action: Comparative Perspective on Constitutionalism, Participation and Civil Society in Papua New Guinea* (Paper presented at the 21st Waigani Seminar, 28 August – 1 September 1995).

7 However, an important distinction that needs to be made is that this segment of Chapter 14 establishes and defines "constitutional office-holders" and not "constitutional offices".

8 Constitutional Planning Committee, *Constitutional Planning Committee Final Report (Part 1)* (Government Printer, Port Moresby, 1974) (CPC, *Final Report*), p 14/2.

9 See Regan, "Protecting the Independence of Constitutional Office-Holders" in Regan, Jessep and Kwa, *Twenty Years of the Papua New Guinea Constitution* (Lawbook Co, Sydney, 2001).

exclusionary, meaning that an office or institution not established or provided for by the *Constitution* is not a constitutional office. This point is important, because a fundamental error was made some years ago by the Ombudsman Commission when it included three institutions which are not created or provided for by the *Constitution* and omitted a number of constitutional offices from its constitutional offices list in its 1990 report.[11] The *Constitution* has established and provided for 21 constitutional offices,[12] presented here in tabular form.

Constitutional offices	Constitutional provisions
1. Auditor General	ss 213-214
2. Citizenship Advisory Committee	ss 75-76
3. Electoral Boundaries Commission	s 125
4. Electoral Commission	s 126
5. General Constitutional Commission	s 260
6. Judicial and Legal Services Commission	s 183
7. Law Reform Commission	Sch 2.13-2.14
8. Magisterial Services	s 173
9. National Court	ss 163-166
10. National Parliament	ss 100-104 and 109-116
11. Ombudsman Commission	ss 217-220
12. Parliamentary Services	s 132
13. Public Accounts Committee	ss 215-216
14. Public Prosecutor	ss 176-177
15. Public Solicitor	ss 176-177
16. Public Services Commission	ss 190-193[i]
17. Salaries and Remuneration Commission	s 216A
18. Supreme Court	ss 160-162
19. Police Force	ss 196-197
20. Defence Force	ss 201-202
21. National Economic and Fiscal Commission	s 187

i. These provisions have been amended by *Constitutional Amendment No 8*, 1986.

It would follow that those who occupy these offices are deemed to be constitutional office-holders. However, the *Constitution* complicates the difference between the office and the holder under s 221, by defining "constitutional office" as:

10 *Constitution*, s 221.

11 The Commission acknowledged this error in a recent discussion with the commissioners held on 8 January 1996.

12 Two constitutional institutions were created after independence. These are the Salaries and Remunerations Committee and the National Economic and Fiscal Commission.

> "any office or institution established or provided for by this *Constitution*, other than an office of the Head of State or of a Minister, or the National Executive Council".

It then defines "constitutional office-holder" as:

- "A judge; or
- The Public Prosecutor or the Public Solicitor; or
- The Chief Magistrate; or
- A Member of the Ombudsman Commission; or
- A Member of the Electoral Commission; or
- The Clerk of the Parliament; or
- A Member of the Public Service Commission; or
- The Auditor-General; or
- The holder of any other office declared by an Organic Law or an Act of the Parliament to be a constitutional office for the purpose of this part."

This definition raises a number of fundamental issues. Some of these are:

1. Are all "constitutional office" holders "constitutional office-holders"?
2. Who is a "constitutional office-holder"?
3. Which Organic Law defines a "constitutional office-holder"?
4. Which Act of Parliament defines a "constitutional office-holder"?

Questions 1 and 2 are similar and can therefore be dealt with separately from questions 3 and 4. A close examination of s 221 shows that not all persons who occupy constitutional offices are "constitutional office-holders". If the proposition that the definition of "constitutional office-holders" is exclusionary is accepted, then, apart from the list of officers spelt out under the same provision and those who have been defined as "constitutional office-holders" under an Organic Law or an Act of Parliament, persons occupying all other constitutional offices are not "constitutional office-holders". This distinction is crucial for the purposes of the *Organic Law on the Duties and Responsibilities of Leadership* and the *Organic Law on the Guarantee of the Rights and Independence of Constitutional Office-holders*. These two Organic Laws are the core laws that vest a number of powers, privileges and obligations on the holders of certain constitutional offices. According to s 221, the "constitutional office-holders" are those listed below.

Constitutional officers	**Constitutional provisions**
Auditor General	ss 213-214
Chief Magistrate	s 175
Clerk of Parliament	s 132
Judges	ss 164, 169-171 and 179-180
Members of Electoral Commission	s 125
Members of Ombudsman Commission	s 217
Members of Public Services Commission	ss 190-193[i]
Public Prosecutor	ss 177-178
Public Solicitor	ss 177-178

i. Two constitutional institutions were created after independence. These are the Salaries and Remunerations Committee and the National Economic and Fiscal Commission.

It is therefore imperative that, apart from these offices, no other institution can claim to be a constitutional office unless the *Constitution* was amended expressly.

10.3 THE POWERS AND FUNCTIONS OF THE CONSTITUTIONAL OFFICES

The powers and functions of these offices are set out below in a summary form. The offices are listed alphabetically.

Office	Power	Functions
1. **Auditor-General**	*Constitution*, ss 213-214	1. Inspect, audit and report on the public account of PNG: s 214(1) 2. Report on the control of, and on transactions with or concerning, the public moneys and property of PNG: s 214(1)
2. **Citizenship Advisory Committee**	*Citizenship Act*, Ch 12	See s 75 *Constitution* and *Constitutional Amendment No 5*. 1. Determine the number of open electorates and provincial electorates and their boundaries: s 125 2. Submit reports with its recommendation to the Parliament through the Minister: OLNE, s 39
3. **Electoral Boundaries Commission**	*Constitution*, s 125	Set and review electoral boundaries
4. **Electoral Commission**	*Constitution*, s 126	1. Organise and conduct elections to Parliament: s 126(1) 2. Conduct all elections at provincial and local-level: OLNE, s 15
5. **General Constitutional Commission**	See *Constitutional Commission Act*, Ch 21A	Inquire into the working of the *Constitution* and the Organic Laws: s 260(4)

Office	Power	Functions
6. **Judicial and Legal Service Commission**	See *National Judicial Service Act* 1987 (Staff)	1. Appointment of: (i) judges other than the Chief Justice (s 170(2)); (ii) Magistrates of Inferior Courts (s 172(3)); (iii) Chief Magistrate (s 175(2)); (iv) Public Prosecutor and Public Solicitor (s 16(2)); (v) Tribunal to investigate the removal of office of judges (other than the Chief Justice), Public Prosecutor, Public Solicitor or the Chief Magistrate (s 180(2)); and (vi) Members to independent tribunals (s 25(2)) and extensions of terms of office of acting judges (s 170(3)). 2. Supervise the Magisterial Services through the Chief Magistrate: s 173(3) 3. Remove from office judges, Public Prosecutor, Public Solicitor and Chief Magistrate: s 180(2) 4. Conduct a continuing review of the practice and procedure of all courts other than the Supreme Court and the National court: OLJLSC, s 8(a) 5. Make recommendations to the Law Reform Commission on any legislative changes: OLILSC, s 8(a) 6. Ensure adequate funding of the courts: OLILSC, s 8(b) 7. Ensure that adequate and proper statistics relating to the exercise of the jurisdiction of all courts are compiled and kept: OLJLSC, s 8(c)

Office	Power	Functions
7. **Law Reform Commission**	*Law Reform Commission Act* 1975	Investigate and report to the Parliament and the NEC on the development of law and the appropriateness of the rules and principles of the Underlying Law: *Constitution*, Sch 2.14 and *Underlying Law Act*, s 13
8. **Magisterial Service**	*Magisterial Services Act*, s 43 (Amendment of 1990)	Administer the magistracy
9. **National Court**	*National Court Act* (Ch 38) (Amendment 1987)	1. Enforce the *Constitution*: s 22 2. Enforce rights and freedoms: s 57 3. Review any exercise of judicial authority: s 155(3)(a)
10. **National Parliament**	Power to make laws for the peace and good government of PNG: *Constitution*, ss 100(1) and 109(1)	1. Review, order and deliberate on reports presented to Parliament 2. Approve, reduce or reallocate the budget: s 210, as amended by *Constitutional Amendment No 10*, 1988. 3. Declare war: s 227 4. Declare state of emergency: ss 228-239 See *Parliamentary Powers and Privileges Act* (Ch 24)
11. **Ombudsman Commission**	*Constitution*, ss 217-220	1. Investigate on its own initiative or on complaint by a person affected: (i) any state service or provincial service (s 219(1)(a)(i)); (ii) any other governmental body, an officer or employee of governmental body (s 219(1)(a)(ii)); (iii) any local government body or any office or employee of any such body (s 219(1)(a)(iii));

Office	Power	Functions
		(iv) any member of the personal staff of the Governor-General (s 219(1)(a)(v)); or (v) any other body or person set up by statute (s 219(1)(a)(vi)). 2. Investigate defects in any law or administrative practice: s 219(1)(b) 3. Investigate, on its own initiative or on complaint by a person affected, any case of alleged or suspected discriminatory practice: s 219(1)(c). 4. Enforce the *Leadership Code*: s 219(1)(d)
12. **Parliamentary Services**	See *Parliamentary Services Act* (Ch 26)	Provide services to the Parliament
13. **Public Accounts Committee**	*Constitution*, s 216	Examine and report to Parliament on the public accounts of PNG and on transactions with or concerning the moneys and property of PNG: s 216
14. **Public Prosecutor**	See *Public Prosecutor (Office of Functions) Act* (Ch 338)	1. Control the exercise and performance of the prosecution function before the Supreme Court and the National Court: s 177(1)(a) 2. Bring or decline to bring proceedings under the *Leadership Code*: s 177(1)(b)
15. **Public Solicitor**	*Constitution*, s 177	1. Provide legal aid for persons in need of help by the Public Solicitor: s 177(2) 2. Provide advice and assistance to persons in need of help by the Public Solicitor: s 177(2) 3.Provide legal assistance to accused persons: s 177(2)(a) 4. Provide legal assistance to any person as directed by the Supreme Court or the National Court: s 177(2)(b)

Office	Power	Functions
16. Public Services Commission	*Constitution*, ss 190-194	1. Review personnel matters with the National Public Service: *Constitutional Amendment No 8*, 1986, s 2 2. Continuously review the state government bodies: *Constitutional Amendment No 8*, 1986, s 2 3. Prepare annual reports and forward them to the Speaker, who shall present them to Parliament: *Constitutional Amendment No 8*, 1986, s 2
17. Salaries and Remuneration Commission	*Constitution*, s 131	Recommend to Parliament: (i) salaries, allowances and benefits for all or any Members of Parliament (*Constitutional Amendment No 9*, 1988, s 3(b)); (ii) salaries, allowances and benefits for all or any of the members of the Provincial Assemblies (*Constitutional Amendment No 9*, 1988, s 3(b)); (iii) salaries, allowances and benefits for all the judges (*Constitutional Amendment No 9*, 1988, s 3(c)); and (iv) salaries and benefits for all constitutional office-holders (*Constitutional Amendment No 9*, 1988, s 3(d)).
18. Supreme Court	*Constitution*, ss 160-162; *Supreme Court Act* (Ch 37) (and the 1987 Amendment)	1. Constitutional interpretation: ss 18 and 19 2. Enforcement of rights and freedoms: s 57 3. Review all judicial acts

The constitutional provisions

Some of the powers, functions and organisational structures are also set out in detail by specific enactments. These pieces of subordinate legislation are to be read together with the constitutional provisions establishing and providing for the constitutional offices. There are also three specific constitutional provisions relating to constitutional offices.[13] Section 222 is a skeletal provision, as it does not express any substantive matter. Section 224 allows for the enactment of specific Organic Laws and ordinary Acts that will provide "for the powers and procedures of constitutional offices, and generally for facilitating the performance of their functions, duties and responsibilities". A number of Organic Laws and Acts of Parliament were therefore enacted to implement this provision.[14] The third section is s 225, which poses a rather interesting scenario. This provision imposes a duty on the government to ensure that the offices are *properly funded* and adequately staffed to effectively carry out their functions. A few years ago, the former Chief Justice, the late Sir Buri Kidu, threatened to invoke this section to force the government to provide more funds to the judiciary to help it effectively carry out its constitutional duties. To avoid an embarrassing situation, the Parliament amended ss 209-212 of the *Constitution*, which deal with the budgetary process, to allow the Parliament to increase the budget allocation for the judiciary should the Finance Department cut back on the budget estimates of the judiciary. By this device, the judiciary is now guaranteed adequate funding under the *Constitution*, while other organisations have missed out in the arrangement.

The question is whether this provision should be expanded to include all the constitutional offices so that they are also guaranteed adequate funding under the *Constitution*.

Powers and responsibilities

An assessment of the powers and responsibilities of these offices reveals a number of factors. The problem of duplicity is apparent. It is obvious that some of these offices perform the same function. The only difference is the composition of these offices. For instance, the offices of the Auditor-General and the Public Accounts Committee, and the Electoral Commission and the Electoral Boundaries Commission overlap. The offices of the Auditor-General and the Electoral Commission are made up of public servants, while their counterparts are partly or wholly made up of politicians. The offices of the Judicial and Legal Services Commission and the Magisterial Service also have the same problem of duplication. Their overlap relates to classification of the personnel. The Magisterial Service looks after the welfare of the Magistrates, while the Judicial and Legal Services Commission looks after the interests of the judges and personnel of the National and Supreme Courts. The underpinning of these two offices is that they provide judicial services to the people.

There is a continuing issue of whether these functions should be amalgamated or their powers and responsibilities redefined. This is, in part, an issue of whether these offices effectively carry out their responsibilities. An initial discussion with some of the constitutional office-holders has revealed some common problems with the offices. The two persistent problems that have hampered the effective operation of the offices are lack of funds and acute shortage of skilled personnel.

Section 225 of the Constitution

The government has a duty under this section to:

---

13 *Constitution*, ss 222, 224 and 225.

14 Some of these are listed in the table above.

> "ensure, as far as it is within their respective legal powers, that all arrangements are made, staff and facilities provided and steps taken to enable and facilitate, as far as may reasonably be, the proper and convenient performance of the functions of all constitutional institutions and of the offices of all constitutional office-holders".

Can a constitutional office-holder sue the government under s 225 to ensure that the government complies with its duty under this provision? Certain of these constitutional office-holders are prepared to invoke this section, but have reserved this right because they understand the current financial problems in the country. The Supreme Court would have to decide on the effect of the provisions in this section.

Selection and dismissal of constitutional office-holders

The selection and dismissal procedures for constitutional office-holders to the offices are provided in s 223 and amplified in the *Organic Law on Certain Constitutional Office-holders* and the *Organic Law on the Duties and Responsibilities of Leadership.* The latter statute also applies to other leaders.

10.4 ACCOUNTABILITY OF CONSTITUTIONAL OFFICES

There are procedures to ensure that these offices are accountable.[15] Again, these are set out in tabular form.

Constitutional office	Accountability	Constitutional provisions
1. **Auditor-General**	(a) In the performance of its functions, it is not subject to the control and direction from any person or authority (b) Parliament	s 213(3) s 214(1)
2. **Citizenship Advisory Committee**	Minister for Foreign Affairs and Trade	s 76
3. **Electoral Boundaries Commission**	(a) In the performance of its functions, it is not subject to control and direction from any person or authority (b) Parliament	s 125(4) s 125(3)
4. **Electoral Commission**	Not subject to control and direction by any person or authority in the performance of its functions	s 126(6)

15 See Regan, op cit n 9.

Constitutional office	Accountability	Constitutional provisions
5. **General Constitutional Commission**		s 260(5)
6. **Judicial and Legal Services Commission**	Not subject to control and direction from any person or authority	s 183 (4)
7. **Law Reform Commission**	(a) Not subject to direction or control by any person or authority when dealing only with personnel matters (b) NEC (c) Parliament	s 192 (as amended) s 191(3)(a) (as amended) s 191(4) (as amended)
8. **Salaries and Remunerations Commission**	Parliament	s 216A(3) (as amended)
9. **Supreme Court**	(a) In the exercise of its judicial powers and functions it is not subject to direction by any person or authority (b) Parliament through legislation	s 157 s 157

Looking at the table, it is clear that most of the constitutional offices are held accountable to the Parliament, which is accountable to the people. A crucial distinction must be mentioned. The Parliament as a body is accountable to the people, usually at elections, while Members of Parliament as individuals are accountable, especially to the Ombudsman Commission, through the compilation of reports, and the Finance Department on acquittals of development funds allocated to each member.

The Citizenship Advisory Committee is in a precarious position. The committee is established by the *Constitution* and yet is controlled by the Minister for Foreign Affairs. How this situation came about is unclear. The CPC regarded this matter with great concern. In its report, the CPC strongly stressed that "neither personal whim or arbitrariness should be allowed to enter into the determination of as serious a matter as an application for citizenship".[16] The CPC therefore recommended the establishment of the committee, which should comprise "people of undoubted integrity and high standing within the community at large". They also recommended that the committee should be governed by the same rules and principles as applicable to other constitutional offices. Even before independence, the issue of citizenship was a very contentious issue.[17] The question is whether or not to resurrect the views of the CPC, in other words, to ensure that the committee is not directed and controlled by a single person.

Most of these offices are held accountable directly to the Parliament, or through the NEC to Parliament, by the reporting procedure. They are required under the *Constitution* and their respective subordinate legislation to report to the

16 CPC, *Final Report*, p 4/9.
17 Goldring, "Nationality and Citizenship in Papua New Guinea" (1972) 3 MLJ 75-76.

Parliament, or to the NEC to report to Parliament, annually. In this way, the Parliament checks on their activities and ensures that they are fulfilling their constitutional duties.

The Parliament is not the only institution to which these offices are accountable. These offices keep a check on each other. Professor Goldring correctly points out that the constitutional framework provides strict legal rules that ensure accountability of these offices.[18]

A series of questions can be posed: Is the reporting method appropriate? Should these offices report to Parliament, for example, every six months or every three months? What kind of accountability are we talking about – is it political accountability or administrative accountability? Does the reporting method reflect the quality and quantity of services provided to the people? What is the significance of the concept of "independence" today? Some of these issues have been carefully analysed by the General Constitutional Committee.

10.5 CONCLUSION

This chapter presented only a summary view of the constitutional offices. There is a need for detailed empirical research to be conducted on the matter of the constitutional offices.

Two crucial issues are worthy of such detailed empirical research:

(i) whether there is a need for a change or changes to all or any of the offices established under the *Constitution*; and

(ii) what changes are required to better co-ordinate the powers, responsibilities, and accountability of such offices.

18 Goldring, "The Executive Government: Power, Politics and Responsibility" in De Vere, Colquhoun-Kerr and Kaburise, *Essays on the Constitution of Papua New Guinea* (Government Printer, Port Moresby, 1985), p 69.

Chapter 11

ENFORCEMENT OF THE CONSTITUTION

11.1 INTRODUCTION

Consideration of the enforcement of a constitution requires an examination of the ways in which institutions are empowered to ensure that the constitution, as the fundamental higher law, is to be observed by the state, its instrumentalities and the people. The enforcement provisions of a constitution are vital for the effective implementation of the constitution.

A constitution may be good on paper, but without machinery for its enforcement it loses its significance as a special law. On the other hand, a constitution may contain impressive provisions on enforcement, but with little or no institutional framework and the necessary tools for its enforcement, it has very little meaning as a special law. Enforcement provisions in a constitution are therefore crucial. They ensure that a constitution is not subject to abuse. In many democratic countries, enforcement provisions prevent the rise and entrenchment of despotic governments.

Before considering the enforcement of constitutions, it is worth mentioning what is meant by "enforcement" in relation to statutes. The word "enforce" has a number of different meanings, but the relevant sense is to compel the observance of a law. Thus, a law that can be enforced means that obedience to it *can be compelled if necessary*. Enforcement of a statute can be achieved in a variety of ways. For instance, the police enforce the law when they apprehend a person suspected of committing an offence under the statute, and a magistrate enforces the law when imposing punishment on a convicted offender.[1]

It is not uncommon for statutes to make explicit provisions concerning their enforcement, in which case, depending on the context, enforcement of laws can mean quite different things.[2] The concept of constitutional enforcement was described by McWhinney as "institutional control of constitutionality" which, according to him, was:

> "an ultimate constitutional power of the courts to pass on executive and legislative actions and to rule on their compatibility or otherwise with the constitutional charter's express terms".[3]

---

1 Numerous cases in PNG illustrate this point. For an overseas case in point, see *Yelland v Powell Duffryn Associated Collieries Ltd* [1941] 1 All ER 278 at 284-285.

2 For example, in *R v Bates* [1982] NSWLR 894 it was held that a statute on regulation of motor traffic which gave the police sole responsibility for its enforcement did not necessarily also give police sole responsibility for initiating prosecutions for breaches of the statute. Further, the court stated that enforcement simply meant compelling or observing something, which did not extend to the initiation of court proceedings.

3 McWhinney, *Constitution-making: Principles, Process, Practice* (University of Toronto Press, Toronto, 1981), p 111.

Enforcement of statutes can be achieved in a variety of ways depending on the law being considered. It does not only involve criminal sanctions, but also civil awards of damages, injunctions, declarations and so on made by the courts. The courts, therefore, play an important role in the enforcement of a constitution and statutes. Apart from the courts, there may be administrative and other kinds of tribunals that have a role in enforcement. Bodies such as ombudsmen and other specialised investigative authorities may also have a role.

There are often provisions in a statute or a constitution that are not, strictly speaking, enforceable. Examples are provisions of a descriptive or empowering nature, or provisions which impose duties but which are interpreted to be merely "directory" in nature, rather than "mandatory" as was distinguished in *Kaseng v Namaliu* [1995] PNGLR 481.

The issue arises whether the concepts and methods of enforcement used in relation to normal statutes are relevant to written constitutions. All laws and other actions of government inconsistent with a constitution are normally stated by the constitution to be invalid and of no effect. If a constitution is to have the full effect that was intended by its makers, it needs to be enforceable. On the other hand, obedience to much of a constitution will not need to be compelled by sanctions. The concept of *constitutionalism* as a force in a state involves the acceptance by government of constitutional limits on its power.

In many countries (including Papua New Guinea) there is seldom a need to resort to sanctions as a means of enforcing a constitution against the major institutions of government. Even where breach of a constitution is alleged, it will often be the case that the only remedy sought is a declaration that the provision in question has been breached. Once such a declaration is made, it will normally be accepted and acted upon by government. This was clearly the case in *Haivetta v Wingti (No 3)* [1994] PNGLR 197. Another case in point is the recent Supreme Court judgment in *SCR No 3 of 1999* (unreported, SC, 1999). In this case, the Ombudsman Commission sought a declaration (among others) from the Supreme Court that the adjournment of Parliament by more than seven months was unconstitutional as it violated s 124 of the *Constitution*. The Supreme Court held that the Parliament was in breach of s 124 of the *Constitution*, but fell short of imposing any sanctions on the Parliament.

Finally, it must be emphasised that laws are not necessarily obeyed solely because of the threat of criminal sanctions. There may be a variety of factors, such as political, economic, cultural, etc. They all contribute to obedience to laws that may have little to do with sanctions and other enforcement mechanisms.

11.2 ENFORCEMENT OF THE CONSTITUTION

The *Constitution* of PNG declares that it is the supreme law, and that it should be obeyed. Section 10 makes it clear that the Organic Laws are to be read and interpreted subject to the *Constitution*, and that provisions of the Organic Laws are invalid to the extent that they exceed their constitutional authority. Section 11 declares that the *Constitution* and the Organic Laws together are the "Supreme Law", and that all "acts" inconsistent with them are "to the extent of the inconsistency invalid and ineffective". The "acts" in question include "legislative, executive or judicial" acts. If the *Constitution* is to be effective, those sections must be given their full effect.

The *Constitution* recognises this fact, and makes provision for enforcement. Under ss 18 and 19 it gives the Supreme Court the jurisdiction to interpret and apply the constitutional laws, thereby intending it to ensure that the constitutional laws prevail in the case of inconsistency with acts of government. Further, the *Constitution* uses the words "enforcement" and "enforceable" in relation to a number of sets of provisions of the constitutional laws. First, the heading to s 22 is "Enforcement of the Constitution" and provides:

> "The provisions of this *Constitution* that recognise rights of individuals (including corporations and associations) as well as those that confer powers or impose duties on public authorities, shall not be left without effect because of the lack of supporting, machinery or procedural laws, but the lack shall, as far as practicable, be supplied by the National Court in the light of the National Goals and Directive Principles, and by way of analogy from other laws, general principles of justice and generally-accepted doctrine."

Secondly, s 23, which provides sanctions for breach of some provisions of the constitutional laws, states that it applies to provisions where no other constitutional law or Act of the Parliament "provides for the *enforcement* of that provision". The clear implication is that not only is provision for enforcement of constitutional laws made elsewhere, but also that the s 23 sanctions are directed towards enforcement. It provides:

> "(1) Where any provision of a Constitutional Law prohibits or restricts an act, or imposes a duty, then unless a Constitutional Law or an Act of the Parliament provides for the enforcement of that provision the National Court may:
>
> (a) impose a sentence of imprisonment for a period not exceeding 10 years or a fine not exceeding K10 000.00; or
>
> (b) in the absence of any other equally effective remedy under the laws of Papua New Guinea, order the making of compensation by a person (including a governmental body) who is in default;
>
> or both, for a breach of the prohibition, restriction or duty, and may make such further order in the circumstances as it thinks proper.
>
> (2) Where a provision of a Constitutional Law prohibits or restricts an act or imposes a duty, the National Court may, if it thinks it proper to do so, make any order that it thinks proper for preventing or remedying a breach of the prohibition, restriction or duty, and Subsection (1) applies to a failure to comply with the order as if it were a breach or a provision of this *Constitution*.
>
> (3) Where the National Court considers it proper to do so, it may include in an order under Subsection (2) an anticipatory order under Subsection (1)."

Thirdly, in relation to the various rights and freedoms of persons provided in the *Constitution*, the heading to Pt III, Div 3, Subdiv D is "Enforcement".[4] The heading

4 According to Sch 1.3(2) of the *Constitution*, such a heading is part of the *Constitution*. This principle is consistent with the provisions of s 26 of the *Interpretation Act* (Ch 2), but contrary to the normal principles of statutory interpretation used in many common law countries. See Pearce and Geddes, *Statutory Interpretation in Australia* (4th ed, Butterworths, Sydney, 1996).

of s 57 is "Enforcement of Guaranteed Rights and Freedoms", and s 57 states that the rights and freedoms are to be "enforceable" in accordance with that section.

In addition, provisions made non-justiciable, or which are declared to apply only "in principle", are, in the main, unenforceable.[5] Provisions of the constitutional laws that provide for acts to be done in the "deliberate judgment" of a particular person or authority are also partially shielded from judicial enforcement. This is set out in s 62 of the *Constitution*.

Finally, it can be argued that provisions of constitutional laws imposing duties that can be interpreted as being merely "directory" rather than "mandatory" are not intended to be enforceable. This issue is discussed separately below.

11.3 POWER OF THE SUPREME COURT TO ENFORCE THE CONSTITUTION

Sections 18 and 19 of the *Constitution* empower the Supreme Court to enforce the *Constitution*. In exercising its jurisdiction under ss 18 and 19, which relate to interpretation and application of the constitutional laws, the Supreme Court has a major role in enforcing those laws. In exercising this jurisdiction, the Supreme Court has shown a readiness to make a wide range of orders that result in enforcement of the constitutional laws.[6] It has ruled numerous laws[7] and acts of executive government[8] to be invalid and ineffective. It has never, however, explored in any detail the source of its powers to make such orders.

Section 19(1) states that the power to give opinions on constitutional issues *includes* a power to give an opinion on the validity of a law or a proposed law, while s 19(2) states that an opinion under s 19 has the "same binding effect as any other decision of the Supreme Court". In other words, the constitutional interpretation jurisdiction under s 19 includes power to make binding decisions that laws or proposed laws are invalid by virtue of inconsistency with provisions of the constitutional laws. It is suggested that the main reasons for specifying such a power under s 19, when no equivalent provision is made in s 18, was to make it quite clear that the power to give opinions in relation to constitutional issues referred by the authorities listed in s 19(3) was more than merely advisory. Decisions in such matters were to be of binding effect. There would seem little doubt that similar powers exist in relation to constitutional interpretation and application proceedings under s 18.

As s 19(1) states that the power to give opinions on validity of laws is merely *included* in the powers of the court acting under s 19, it is clear that the court is intended to have somewhat wider powers than that. So what is the source and the extent of the powers of the Supreme Court under ss 18 and 19?

5 For a discussion of the reasons for inclusion of such provisions in Pacific Island constitutions, see Lynch, "Styles in the Drafting of Some Pacific Constitutions" in Ghai (ed), *Law, Politics and Government in the Pacific Island States* (Institute of Pacific Studies, USP, Suva, 1988), pp 206-224, particularly pp 210-211 and 220-224. See also the recent decision of the Supreme Court in *SCR No 3 of 1999* (1999) SC 628, where the Supreme Court held that "in principle" can be tantamount to enforceability.

6 The boldness of the Supreme Court in this regard is most recognisable in the cases of *Haivetta v Wingti (No 3)* [1994] PNGLR 197 and *SCR No 3 of 1999* (1999) SC 628.

7 See, eg, *SCR No 2 of 1984; Re New Ireland Constitution* [1984] PNGLR 81; *SCR No 2 of 1982; Re Organic Law* [1982] PNGLR 214; *SCR No 1 of 1992; Re Organic Law* [1992] PNGLR 73; *Re Internal Security Act* [1994] PNGLR 341.

8 For instance, see *Public Prosecutor v Rooney (No 2)* [1979] PNGLR 448; *Kila Wari v Ramoi and Dibela* [1986] PNGLR 112; *SCR No 1 of 1982; Re Bouraga* [1982] PNGLR 178; *The State v NTN Pty Ltd* [1992] PNGLR 1.

As noted, s 11(1) of the *Constitution* provides that "all acts (whether legislative, executive or judicial)" inconsistent with the constitutional laws "are, to the extent of that inconsistency, invalid and ineffective". By vesting the Supreme Court with a power to interpret and apply the constitutional laws, the *Constitution* must be empowering the Supreme Court to determine questions as to whether inconsistency exists and the consequences if it does – inclusive of determining invalidity of the act being considered. Having given the Supreme Court jurisdiction to deal with matters centring on such issues, the *Constitution* also gives it the powers it needs to make orders consequential upon its rulings. As a court of unlimited jurisdiction (s 99(2)(c)), the Supreme Court can make whatever "orders as are necessary to do justice in the circumstances of a particular case": s 155(4).

11.4 SANCTIONS UNDER THE CONSTITUTION

Section 22 of the *Constitution* is headed "Enforcement of the Constitution". In fact, it concerns a very narrow aspect of enforcement. It relates solely to the *Constitution*, and not to the Organic Laws. Its application is limited to *filling gaps* in "supporting machinery or procedural laws" where such gaps would render ineffective provisions of the *Constitution* that recognise rights of individuals, or confer powers or impose duties on public authorities. This section relates to enforcement only in the sense that such provisions of the *Constitution* would probably be unenforceable if the gaps in the "supporting" laws could not be filled by the National Court, as permitted by the section.

As with other laws, the ultimate means of ensuring provisions of the constitutional laws are in fact obeyed may sometimes have to be the availability of sanctions. The main relevant provision here is s 23 of the *Constitution*.

Overview

Section 23 is a complex provision. It provides sanctions in respect of breaches of provisions of constitutional laws that prohibit an act, restrict an act, or impose a duty. Sanctions under the section are available only if there is no other provision for enforcement made under a constitutional law or an Act of the Parliament. The sanctions are available only to the National Court and are potentially severe.[9]

The sanctions under s 23 are not merely directed towards punishment for breaches of prohibitions, restrictions and duties, but also to preventing such breaches occurring, and remedying such damage as actual breaches may cause. Section 23(2) empowers the National Court to "make any orders that it thinks proper for preventing or remedying a breach of prohibition, restriction or duty". It can also punish for failure to comply with an order directed towards preventing or remedying such a breach. To further strengthen its role under s 23(2) (of preventing and remedying breaches), s 23(3) gives the National Court power to make anticipatory orders.[10]

---

9 The sanctions include sentences of imprisonment for up to ten years, fines of up to K10,000, payment of compensation "by a person (including a governmental body) who is in default", or any other sanction that the National Court may order as it thinks proper in the circumstances: s 23(1).

10 Among the important issues arising from this section are: (1) What are the provisions of the constitutional laws which prohibit or restrict acts or impose duties, the breach of which *may* be the subject of sanctions under s 23?; (2) What provisions of constitutional laws or Acts of Parliament provide for alternative means of enforcement of provisions of constitutional laws, thereby excluding the operation of s 23?; and (3) Is s 23 intended to provide sanctions against the main institutions of government (eg, the Parliament and the National Executive Council)?

What conduct invites sanctions?

There are two clear examples of provisions that prohibit acts that are covered by the first issue. These are s 27(2) (prohibition on "leaders" using public office for personal gain) and s 253 (prohibition on slavery). There are numerous provisions that restrict acts, such as s 73 (regaining citizenship) and the provisions limiting the use of motions of no-confidence in the Prime Minister or the Ministry. Examples of the many provisions that impose duties include s 42(2) (which establishes duties to be carried out by police officers and others who exercise powers to arrest or detain persons) and the various provisions requiring constitutional office-holders to make annual reports to the Parliament.[11]

There are other provisions of the *Constitution* that operate only indirectly to prohibit or restrict acts or impose duties, which may nevertheless be the subject of s 23. For instance, in *SCR No 5 of 1985; Re Raz v Matane* [1985] PNGLR 329, the Supreme Court was asked to consider whether or not s 41 of the *Constitution* was a "right" which would be enforced by the National Court under s 23. The Supreme Court by a majority ruled that s 41 provided a "special right" and was, therefore, enforceable under s 23.

Exceptions to s 23 – provisions otherwise enforceable

Section 23 envisages that if particular provisions of constitutional laws are the subject of separate enforcement arrangements under either constitutional laws or Acts of Parliament, then the sanctions under s 23 will not apply. Some of the provisions of the *Constitution* which have made distinct arrangements for enforcement include:

- the human rights provisions,[12] where ss 57 and 58 provide a scheme of enforcement;
- the provisions on the *Leadership Code* in ss 26-31 of the *Constitution* and the *Organic Law on the Duties and Responsibilities of Leadership*, which are enforceable by the Ombudsman Commission under complex arrangements provided under s 28 of the *Constitution* and the same Organic Law;
- the provisions on parliamentary privilege, which are enforceable under the *Parliamentary Powers and Privileges Act* (Ch 24), an Act of the Parliament authorised by s 115(9); and
- many provisions of the *Organic Law on National and Local-level Government Elections* 1996, which are enforceable through its provisions in respect of criminal offences (ss 179-205) and the handling of disputed elections and returns by the National Court (ss 206-233).

The rulings in *SCR No 5 of 1985; Re Raz v Matane* and *Curran v The State* [1994] PNGLR 230 indicate that s 41 of the *Constitution* is enforceable under s 155(4) as well as s 23(2). If s 155(4) is available to provide a remedy to enforce a provision of a constitutional law, does it operate to exclude s 23 (by virtue of the limitation within s 23(1))? The Supreme Court did not consider this issue in either *Matane* or *Curran*. It can be argued that s 155(4) does not exclude s 23, for the exclusion in s 23(1) relates to provisions of constitutional laws or Acts of the Parliament directed specifically to enforcement of provisions of constitutional laws. By contrast, s 155(4) is a general grant of power to make whatever order is needed in

---

11 For example, see s 220 of the *Constitution*.

12 See Chapter 9 of this book and Brunton, "Human Rights 1996" in Regan, Jessep and Kwa, *Twenty Years of the Constitution* (Lawbook Co, Sydney, 2001).

any case in which the Supreme Court or the National Court already has jurisdiction. As s 155(4) is not directed primarily to enforcement of the constitutional laws, its availability to authorise orders that may result in enforcement of the constitutional laws in particular cases may not be a bar to s 23 sanctions applying. On this analysis, the approach of the courts in *Matane* and *Curran* is correct.

The question of whether the enforcement provisions in respect of human rights exclude the sanctions under s 23 is not a simple one. The issue was the subject of discussion in *Reference No 1 of 1977* [1977] PNGLR 362 at 368 (Frost CJ), 378 (Prentice DCJ), 381 (Williams J) and at 384 (Pritchard J). The issue here is that to the extent that any of the human rights provisions impose duties or prohibit or restrict particular acts, then arguably sanctions under s 23 may be available in addition to the remedies available in actions to enforce rights under s 57. For example, while s 42(2) of the *Constitution* provides special rights to a person whose basic right to liberty is lawfully restricted by being arrested, it also imposes duties on police officers or others who arrest or detain persons. Persons arrested or detained must be informed of their rights under the section, and afforded the right to communicate without delay with a lawyer and a family member or friend etc. In *The State v Wampa* [1987] PNGLR 120 at 121, Kapi DCJ took the view that if such duties are breached, the police officer involved may be liable to both sanctions under s 23 and compensation claims under s 58. The basic point is that s 42(2) rights of the person arrested could be enforced by a range of remedies available under s 57 (including exclusion of evidence obtained following a breach of the rights), while the person breaching the duty under s 42(2) could be the subject of the whole range of sanctions under s 23 – including imprisonment or fine.[13]

Availability of sanctions against government institutions

In the words of s 23 there is nothing to suggest that the section should not apply to government institutions. However, in *SCR No 4 of 1980; Re Petition by MT Somare* [1981] PNGLR 265 at 267, Kidu CJ suggested that s 23 was not intended to be used to punish or penalise the Parliament. In the same matter, Miles J said of s 23:

> "The section is directed towards the imposition of sanctions upon a person (including a governmental body) in breach of the prohibition, restriction or duty, and the National Parliament cannot be described as a person or a governmental body. Nor is it appropriate to talk of the National Parliament being subject to sanctions."[14]

With respect to the learned members of the Supreme Court, there is in fact no indication in s 23 that the range of bodies committing breaches, prohibitions, restrictions and duties covered by the section should be limited in any way. The only indication of the range of persons or bodies against which sanctions might be directed is in s 23(1)(b), which talks of compensation orders being made against a "person" in default, and defines "person" to include "a governmental body". Schedule 1.2 of the *Constitution* defines "governmental body" very widely to mean "the National Government", provincial governments, arms, departments, agencies or instrumentalities of the National Government or a provincial government, and statutory bodies.

13 There is an overlap between ss 23 and 58 in that compensation may be payable under both provisions.
14 *SCR No 4 of 1980; Re Petition by MT Somare* [1981] PNGLR 265 at 299.

Dicta in another Supreme Court decision suggested a wide potential application of s 23. In *Electoral Commissioner of PNG v Maniho* [1987] PNGLR 449, where the Electoral Commissioner had sought to justify delaying provincial government elections in terms of lack of resources needed to conduct the elections, the Supreme Court noted that under s 225 of the *Constitution*, it was the duty of "the National Government and of all other governmental bodies, and of all public office-holders and institutions" to ensure that all constitutional office-holders, such as the Electoral Commission, were provided with the staff and facilities needed to carry out their functions. More importantly, for present purposes, if the duty under s 225 were to be breached "by the Government or any of its bodies failing properly to fund constitutional institutions so as to enable them to perform functions entrusted to them by the *Constitution*", the National Court could be "petitioned to enforce the provisions [of s 225] by invocation of s 23 of the *Constitution*".

This issue was settled in *SCRA No 3 of 1999* (1999) SC 628. On the issue of whether the Parliament can be penalised under s 23, the Supreme Court held that the Parliament was not exempted under s 23. Kapi DCJ, giving the leading judgment (five members of the bench agreeing with him), held that:

> "The sanctions set out (in s 23) are very severe and the National Court is given very wide powers to give such other orders that it considers appropriate. Let there be no mistake that this provision is applicable to government bodies which includes the National Government. The National Government is made up of three principal arms; the National Parliament, National Executive and the National Judicial System. Where the Parliament may be found to have breached the duty, the National Court can make orders for the Parliament to remedy the breach."[15]

As it is clear that all the principal arms of the National Government fall within the definition of "governmental body", they are all liable to orders for compensation under s 23(1)(b). There is no reason why they should not also be liable to all other sanctions under s 23. On this approach, if any government institution, such as the Parliament or the National Executive Council, was to refuse to obey a declaration in relation to constitutional issues, or was to be otherwise in breach of a provision of a constitutional law that "prohibits or restricts an act, or imposes a duty", sanctions could be imposed. In this context, it should be noted that the range of sanctions available under s 23 is wide. It does not only require the imposition of fines, imprisonment or compensation, but extends to whatever orders the National Court thinks appropriate in the circumstances.

In *SCRA No 3 of 1999*, the Supreme Court did not shy away from the possible tension it would create between itself and the Parliament. It was forthright in its decision that if pursued further the Parliament could easily be penalised by the National Court for breaching s 124 of the *Constitution*.

In almost all the cases where the Supreme Court has intervened in the actions of the Parliament and the executive, the Parliament and the executive have acted on the rulings of the Supreme Court under ss 18 and 19, or to declarations in other proceedings. There is the further consideration of the potential for tension between the judiciary and the other arms of government should sanctions be ordered.

Finally, the question arises as to the consequences of the imposition of sanctions that are ignored by a major institution, such as the National Executive or the

---

15 *SCRA No 3 of 1999* (1999) SC 628 at 19-20.

Parliament, and which cannot be enforced effectively. In general, the courts would want to avoid the possibility of a confrontation of that kind, and so would need to exercise considerable care in imposing sanctions on government.

Proceedings under s 23

Proceedings under s 23 are to be initiated as a civil matter. Therefore, the normal practice and procedure of the civil law apply. In *Ume More v University of PNG* [1985] PNGLR 401, the Supreme Court firmly held that the "relevant practice and procedure of the civil law is applicable to proceedings to enforce the *Constitution* (s 22), to enforce sanctions (s 23) and to enforce guaranteed rights and freedoms under s 57".

11.5 ENFORCEMENT BY BODIES OTHER THAN THE COURTS

The *Constitution* provides for a number of authorities with important roles in keeping government institutions accountable. Of course, an important aspect of accountability includes enduring adherence to constitutional principles. Bodies such as the Ombudsman Commission, the Auditor-General, the Public Prosecutor and the Public Solicitor can be regarded as having important roles in relation to enforcement of the *Constitution*.[16]

The most obvious role in this regard is that of the Ombudsman Commission in relation to the enforcement of the *Leadership Code* under s 218(d) of the *Constitution*. This is very much a formal enforcement role, as it involves investigations of alleged misconduct and the recommendation of prosecutions that can have significant consequences, including loss of office, for persons found guilty of misconduct in office. However, the Ombudsman Commission has other, though less formal, enforcement roles. In particular, ss 25(4) and 63(4) of the *Constitution* give it a role in ensuring the enforcement of the National Goals and Directive Principles and the Basic Social Obligations. Those provisions are reinforced by s 219(1)(a) and 219(3) of the *Constitution*, in relation to the functions of the Ombudsman Commission. In particular, while s 219(3) prevents the commission from making inquiries into the justifiability of policies of the National Government and Ministers, it permits the commission to make such inquiries to the extent that such policies may be contrary to the National Goals and Directive Principles and Basic Social Obligations. The Ombudsman Commission has limited powers upon completion of an inquiry in that it can do little more than make a report to the relevant authorities as specified under s 219(6). However, such reports can have a major impact on the subjects of the reports, especially where prosecutions or other actions of a disciplinary nature are recommended in the reports.

The comment of the draftsperson of PNG's *Constitution* should be noted:

> "It should also be remembered that Auditors-General ... and ... Public Accounts Committees may have strong, though indirect, powers equivalent to enforcement which may also, because these are administrative rather than judicial authorities, go beyond purely financial matters."[17]

---

16 The roles that these institutions and other constitutional offices play in the constitutional framework are discussed in detail in Chapter 10 of this book.

17 Lynch, op cit n 5, p 211.

11.6 "MANDATORY" VS "DIRECTORY" PROVISIONS

Statutory provisions often impose a duty without specifying the consequence that follows if the duty is not carried out. Quite often the duty will be imposed using imperative language such as "shall" or "must".

It is helpful to distinguish a bare duty to do something from a duty to do something in a particular manner, or subject to certain conditions. As to a bare duty to do a particular thing, a statute might say that a person in a particular public office, or a particular institution, shall or must make annual reports to the Parliament. As to examples of the duty to do a thing in a particular manner, or subject to conditions, a statute may state that walls of a building shall or must be constructed of bricks or stone, or that when applying for registration of a particular kind of commercial dealing by a government office, the original stamped documents connected with the dealing shall or must be filed or produced. Where there is no indication in the statute of the consequences of failure to carry out the duty, or to carry it out in the manner specified, how should a court requested to deal with that failure decide the consequences? Does failure to carry out the bare duty attract sanctions (for example, in a statute which has a general penalty clause imposing sanctions for failure to comply with its provisions) or invalidate the thing done if it has not been done in the precise way the statute specifies?

The use of imperative language, such as "shall" or "must", will not necessarily help a court. Courts have found that in many instances where such language is used, it would nevertheless be unjust to impose a penalty or invalidate what was done. This point is illustrated in the case of *Application of Karingu* [1988-1989] PNGLR 276, where the Supreme Court had to read down s 9 of the *Lawyers Act* 1986 against s 47 of the *Constitution,* and held that the term "shall" in the Act meant "may". By substituting the term "may" for "shall", the Supreme Court was able to validate the relevant provisions of the Act.

The courts have to determine what the Parliament intended should follow from the breach. In so doing, the courts have developed the distinction between mandatory and directory duties – sometimes referred to as mandatory or directory provisions of a statute. In place of the word "mandatory" duty, the terms "absolute", "obligatory", "imperative" and "strict" are sometimes used, while in place of "directory", the terms "declaratory" or "permissive" are sometimes used.

The question is whether the same distinction, so often made in the interpretation of normal statutes, can be made in relation to a written constitution. If the distinction does apply, then it is potentially of great importance. It may well be a complete answer to proceedings in respect of a breach of a provision of a constitutional law to show that the provision is merely declaratory or directory in effect.

Although the majority decisions in the two main relevant Supreme Court decisions[18] have favoured applying the mandatory/directory distinction to the constitutional laws, strong dissenting opinions have suggested the opposite view should apply.

In *SCR No 1 of 1986; Re Vagrancy Act* [1988] PNGLR 1, one of the issues concerned the requirement in s 38(2)(c) of the *Constitution,* which states that a law regulating or restricting rights of persons in accordance with s 38 must not only be made by

18 *SCR No 1 of 1986; Re Vagrancy Act* [1988] PNGLR 1; *Kaseng v Namaliu* [1995] PNGLR 481.

an absolute majority, but must also be certified by the Speaker of the Parliament as having been made by an absolute majority. Barnett J, with whom Kidu CJ and Amet and Cory JJ concurred, held that the certification requirement was not mandatory. Therefore, the failure of the Speaker to certify an Act as required by s 38(2)(c) did not invalidate the Act. The argument was that the essential requirement of s 38 was that a law made in accordance with s 38 had to be made by an absolute majority of the members of the Parliament. The requirement for a certificate was merely to assist proving the majority, and in the absence of a certificate, compliance or non-compliance with the requirement could be established in other ways.

The dissenting opinion of Woods J (at 10-11) emphasised the nature of the constitutional provision being considered. He noted that the provisions of s 38(2)(c) had been inserted by the founding fathers to ensure that the members of the Parliament thought carefully about proposals to limit rights. The special certification requirement contained in s 38(2)(c) was additional to the certification required in respect of all statutes under s 110 of the *Constitution*. He said that the requirement was a constitutional provision, and, as such, it should be interpreted strictly.

While Woods J did not consider the general issue of whether the mandatory/directory distinction was applicable to constitutional laws, his analysis does not leave much room for such a distinction.

In *Kaseng v Namaliu* [1995] PNGLR 481, a central issue was whether certain requirements of s 14 of the *Constitution* were mandatory or directory. These were the requirements that proposed amendments to constitutional laws be circulated to members of the Parliament a month in advance of introduction into the Parliament, and that there be opportunities for debate on the merits of the proposed amendments. The leading majority judgments, those of Amet CJ and Hinchliffe and Andrew JJ, held that the requirements as to circulation were mandatory. However, as the manner of circulation of proposed amendments had not been specified in the Standing Orders, the circulation requirement was "only directory at the moment": Hinchliffe and Andrew JJ (at 510). As for the opportunity for debate, the majority ruled that there had been such an opportunity.

Kapi DCJ, in a strong dissenting judgment, was of the view that all the requirements were mandatory. He expressed doubt that the principles on the mandatory/directory distinction drawn from interpretation of ordinary statutes were helpful. He said (at 493):

> "We are dealing with the provisions of the *Constitution* which is different in nature and character [from ordinary statutes] and therefore, must be guided by principles peculiar to its character."

As to the provision on circulation of proposed amendments, he held that s 14 contained separate requirements; one as to the period before the proposed law was introduced, and the other as to the manner of circulation. Even if procedures as to the manner of circulation were lacking, the time requirement still had to be met. He was of the view, however, that there were procedures as to circulation in the Standing Orders. While Kapi DCJ is less convincing in his arguments that there was no opportunity for debate, his arguments as to advance circulation are compelling. Additional arguments can be marshalled to support his specific conclusions on that issue, namely:

- s 13 of the *Constitution* states that the *Constitution* can only be amended by a law that is "made and certified in accordance with s 14"; and
- in requiring various procedural steps to be taken, s 14 states that each thing "must" be done, an imperative word, stronger in meaning than either "may" or "shall" (at 489-506).

More generally, it is far from clear that the mandatory/directory distinction should be made in relation to PNG's *Constitution*, which itself not only defines provisions that are not enforceable (those that are non-justiciable or apply only in principle), but also contains a sanctions provision of general application in relation to breaches of duties imposed by constitutional laws that are not otherwise enforceable.

Index

[References are to page numbers]

www.ingramcontent.com/pod-product-compliance
Lightning Source LLC
LaVergne TN
LVHW080044210926
848481LV00011B/3273
9789980939500